C000045969

A BOOK OF
EXMOOR

F.J. SNELL, M.A.

First published by Methuen & Co 1903
Second edition 1923
Third facsimile edition 2002

ISBN 1 84114 168 2

British Library Cataloguing-in-Publication Data
A CIP record for this title is available from the British Library

HALSGROVE
Halsgrove House
Lower Moor Way
Tiverton, Devon EX16 6SS
T: 01884 243242
F: 01884 243325
sales@halsgrove.com
www.halsgrove.com

Printed and bound in Great Britain by
Bookcraft Ltd, Midsomer Norton

CONTENTS

CONTENTS

PART IV

FOLKLORE

PART V

WORTHIES

PREFACE

THIS work is an attempt to supply what has long been needed—namely, a general account of Exmoor, with illustrations of its natural features, etc. Nothing precisely answering to this description has yet been offered to the public. Mr. J. Warden Page's *Exploration of Exmoor and the Hill Country of West Somerset*, as a guide-book, is of the first order of merit, and the publications of the Homeland Association are also decidedly useful. The writer has consulted them all with the utmost advantage, and as the present work is constructed on other lines, with other ends in view, he ventures to recommend their perusal to those of his readers who desire to master the locality. Apart from these excellent guide-books there have been produced from time to time more or less expensive monographs on particular subjects, such as Mr. E. J. Rawle's *Annals of the Royal Forest of Exmoor*, Mr. Charles E. H. Chadwyck-Healey's *History of Part of West Somerset* (both of which consist largely of transcripts from documents preserved at the Record Office), and, more recently, Mr. Philip Evered's charming work *With the Devon and Somerset Staghounds*. When this work was first contemplated Mr. C. P. Collyns' *Chase of the Wild Red Deer* had long been out of print, and can now only be obtained in the Hon. L. Bathurst's extremely handsome, but somewhat costly, edition. The Hon. John Fortescue's work on the same subject, though originally projected as a record of the hunting associations of his own family, is sufficiently comprehensive from a stag-hunter's point of view, but is confined to that standpoint. Richard Jefferies' *Red Deer* is a valuable study, and, like all his writings, full of charm, but, while not absolutely restricted to the habits of stags and hinds and their progeny, is desultory in its treatment of their human environment.

The present writer, who has known and loved Exmoor from boyhood, and during the last few seasons has been in close touch with the better educated and more intelligent class of pilgrims to the land of *Lorna Doone*, has been able to form what he believes to be an accurate idea of the requirements of the situation, and has collected at considerable pains abundance of information on topics which lie entirely outside the scope of ordinary guide-books—the breed of Exmoor sheep, for instance. On this subject he has derived some interesting particulars from Mr. J. Coleman's *Sheep, Cattle, and Pigs of Great Britain*, but he has extended his researches to other sources specified in the text.

On the whole, it may be said that his aims have been principally two in number. The first has been to render accessible to the public a world of facts hitherto locked up in costly volumes, or ·in volumes, like Mr. Hancock's *History of Selworthy*, the late Mr. Hook's *History of Porlock Church*, or Mr. Thornton's *Reminiscences of an old West-country Clergyman*, which have been issued for private circulation or in extremely small editions; or, as in the case of Miss Alice King's contributions to local folklore, dis-

tributed among a medley of ephemeral periodicals—to
be almost forgotten. The writer, for his own amusement, has been addicted for many years to jotting down
scraps of information, and, by utilising these memoranda
as well as by making inquiries amongst his many
Exmoor friends and acquaintances, has exerted himself
to add to the sum of knowledge. His second aim has
been to provide a series of pictures, which, though
commonly relevant to the text, are, in some few instances, rather complementary. He has to express his
warm thanks to Mr. F. Carruthers Gould for the free
use of his inimitable sketches, peppered, so to speak,
through the sections on hunting.

                                              F. J. S.

TIVERTON, N. DEVON,
          April, 1903

Part I

THE STORY OF THE FOREST

B

A BOOK OF EXMOOR

CHAPTER I

BRITON, SAXON, AND DANE

FOR many ages—from Saxon times to the year
1818—Exmoor ranked as a royal forest, and it is
mainly the history of the moor regarded in that light
that we propose to trace in this section. Its treeless
condition nowadays is suggestive of anything rather
than a forest, and most people find it hard to fancy that
at any epoch the bare uplands, so cold in winter and
swept by such pitiless gales, can have been topped with
luxuriant woods. Experiments made with that toughest
of trees, the black fir, have been entirely unsuccessful,
and this circumstance, when known, confirms the sceptics
in their scepticism. The question also may be asked,
What has become of the timber? According to an
Exford tradition, it was felled to supply the mines there.*
Leaving the tradition to take care of itself, we will state

---

* In the abstract this tradition is very far from being improbable. In
Drayton's *Polyolbion* the Sussex forests complain of their altered lot and
reduced area consequent on the iron mines—

> "These iron times breed none that mind posterity."

Those who wish for information on the use of wood in mines may be
referred to an excellent article in G. Roberts' *Social History of the Southern
Counties*, pp. 346-348.

certain reasons for the belief that Exmoor was once—it is impossible to say when—a wooded region.

We had been told that Mr. A. Kingdon, of Driver's Farm, was the possessor of some interesting curios, which his own hand had carved out of bog-oak found on the farm ; and, partly for that reason, we made a point of calling at his hospitable abode, where the articles were shown to us. Mr. Kingdon then conducted us to the spot where the oak was dug out. It was in one of the gutters leading down from the Chains, which was at first quite narrow, but is now rapidly assuming the character of a small gorge. Our guide kept putting down his hand and pulling up "mor" after "mor"—the West Country word for "root." There could be no doubt of it—here were the remains of a former wood, possibly of an ancient forest in the common acceptation of the term.

Another point for consideration is the peaty nature of the soil. Peat is formed by vegetable deposits, mosses and other marsh plants, often in association with the stumps of trees; and it is in the highest degree probable that the depth of earth for which Exmoor is noted—it is seven or eight inches before you get to the hard rock —is due in some measure to the enrichment of the soil by decayed timber, "moots" and "mors." Mr. Kingdon, influenced perhaps by the blackness of the wood, thought that the forest might have been burnt down. Quite possibly. The destruction of forests on a large scale has been a frequent historical event, especially under the Romans, who, on military grounds, reduced the practice to a system. Hatfield Moor in Yorkshire, now consisting of 12,000 acres of peat, is said to have been a forest of firs, until "Ostorius, having slain many Britons, drove the remnant into the forest," which the victors destroyed.

Rivalry between Briton and Roman on Exmoor may be taken, if not as proved, as probable. At a point below Simonsbath, near which the Sheardon water enters the river Barle, may be seen, rising in the midst of the valley, three circular hillocks, the loftiest of which is known as Cae, or Cow, Castle. This is beyond question an old British fort, about one thousand four hundred feet in circumference. The rampart is ten feet at its highest, and except where the ground slopes away, is defined by a fosse. To the west, just outside the boundary of Exmoor proper, is Showlsborough Castle, which Mr. Page considers indubitably Roman. About four hundred and eighty feet from north to south, and four hundred and twenty-nine feet from east to west, it is quadrangular in form, and round it on three sides runs a double vallum or rampart. The outer mound is about three feet high, and the inner from four to seven feet. Between them lies a shallow fosse, some thirty feet wide. The only entrance to the castle is on the west; and in the north-east angle is a mound about eighty feet in circumference. This mound, which has been opened, may have been the praetorium, or headquarters; but, if so, its position is irregular. It is said that two Roman swords, one having a golden hilt, have been dug up in the vicinity, while other articles of interest have been found at various intervals by turf-cutters. Tradition associates Showlsborough Castle with King Alfred, who is stated to have held it against the Danes.

Roman coins have been picked up at Brendon and at Exe-head, one of the most desolate spots in all Exmoor; and we were told at Simonsbath of a tradition that the Romans worked a white iron mine at Barkham, on the road to Southmolton. On the other hand, there is a complete lack of trustworthy historical evidence indicating that the Romans penetrated to the west of the Quantocks.

Hearne does, indeed, suggest that a legion under

Ostorius advanced westwards after subduing the Cangi, but the only reason for locating the Cangi near the Quantocks appears to be the name Cannington, and that, it is needless to point out, is not conclusive. It is quite possible that the works at Showlsborough Castle and in Dunster Park—the latter goes by the name of Cæsar's Camp—may have been constructed by Britons, who had learnt the art of war from the all-conquering legions.

It is natural to find some connection between these half-British, half-Roman fortifications and the menhir on Winsford Hill, for though the inscription is in Latin (of a sort),* the name Curatacus—the reading, however, is very uncertain—is British. Caractacus, it will be remembered, was the name of the heroic King of the Silures, a South-Welsh tribe, who fought long and well against the Romans, but at last fell into their hands and was exhibited by the Emperor Claudius in 51 A.D. Mr. Page suggests that the Exmoor chief may have been related to the famous soldier. In 1900, however, Mr. W. H. P. Gresswell, in a paper on the "Quantocks and their Place Names," advanced what we believe to be an entirely new theory. He suggests that the true version may be "Carantaci," the name of a churchman contemporary with King Arthur. Carhampton is supposed to have been called after this saint, who was the son of Keredic (or Caradoc), Prince of the Province of Cardigan. Crossing the Bristol Channel, he settled at Carhampton, built an oratory there, and spent his time in praise and prayer. Leland says that in his time a chapel of the saint, formerly the parish church, was still standing. If we associate Carantacus with the Winsford stone and the Winsford stone with the forts, we may imagine these to have been built by half or wholly Romanised Britons, who, in the

* Said to be CVRATACI(N)EPVS.

fastnesses of Exmoor and Brendon, fought their last gallant fight against the heathen hordes of English wolves. All over Exmoor and the neighbourhood are cairns or barrows, and the contemplation of the spectacle drew from the historian Freeman the eloquent words: " Here upon this desolate spot, which perhaps never experienced the labours of the industrious husbandman, but has remained for a long succession of many thousand years, the eye of reflection sees stand uninterrupted a number of simple sepulchres of departed souls; whether of warriors, priests, or kings, it matters not; their names have long been buried with their persons in the dust of oblivion, and their memorials have perished with their mouldering urns. A morsel of earth now damps in silence the éclat of noisy warriors, and the green turf serves as a sufficient shroud for kings."

We spoke of St. Carantacus as a contemporary of King Arthur. A more famous saint, who lived in close intercourse with that monarch, was Dubricius, the patron saint of Porlock Church. Bishop of Llandaff, and Metropolitan of Caerleon, he died in 522. About 517 Arthur was crowned by Dubricius (Welsh *Dyfrig*) at Caerleon, and it was Dubricius, too, who solemnised the marriage between the great king and Guinivere. Many will remember Tennyson's lines :—

> " Then Arthur charged his warrior, whom he loved
> And honour'd most, Sir Lancelot, to ride forth
> And bring the Queen ; and watched him from the gates :
> And Lancelot passed away among the flowers
> (For then was latter April), and returned
> Among the flowers in May, with Guinivere.
> To whom arrived, by Dubric the high saint,
> Chief of the church in Britain, and before
> The stateliest of her altar-shrines, the King
> That morn was married, while in stainless white
> The fair beginners of a nobler time,
> And glorying in their vows and him, his knights
> Stood round him, and rejoicing in his joy.

And holy Dubric spread his hands, and spake
'Reign ye, and live, and love, and make the world
Other, and may thy Queen be one with thee,
And all this Order of thy Table Round
Fulfil the boundless purpose of their King!'
So Dubric said . . ."

According to the Book of Llandaff, where the statement is several times repeated, Dubricius lived to the good old age of a hundred and fifty years, and died, not in 522, but in 612.

"To cross seas and traverse broad countries is rather a delight than a trouble to British priests," says Gildas, writing about 560 A.D.; and the borders of Exmoor received more than one missionary from Wales. The true name of Culbone is Kitnor; it is called Culbone after the patron saint of its tiny church, St. Columban. Watchet Church, again, is dedicated to St. Decuman, variously stated to have crossed the Bristol Channel on a faggot, a hurdle, and a cloak. He had a faithful attendant in a cow, who accompanied him of her own accord in his wanderings, and fed him with her milk. St. Decuman lived as a hermit on the hill where the church now stands, and there was martyred. The martyrdom, however, was in a sense incomplete, since the saint is alleged to have taken up his head, struck off by the executioner, borne it to a spring, and washed off the blood. According to one version, St. Decuman swam the channel with his head under his arm!

To what extent was Exmoor Saxonised? The general policy of the invaders was slaughter, extermination. "French," says John Richard Green (who, by the way, once projected a History of Somerset), "is the tongue, not of the Frank, but of the Gaul whom he overcame; and the fair hair of the Lombard is now all but unknown in Lombardy. But the English conquest was a sheer dispossession of the people whom the English conquered. In all the world-wide struggle

between Rome and the German invaders no land was
so stubbornly fought for or so hardly won. The conquest of Britain was indeed only partly wrought out
after two centuries of bitter warfare. But it was just
through the long and merciless nature of the struggle
that of all the German conquests this proved the most
thorough and complete. At its close Britain had become England, the land, that is, not of Britons, but
of Englishmen. It is possible that a few of the van-
quished people may have lingered as slaves round the
homes of their English conquerors, and a few of their
words (if these were not brought in at a later time)
mingled oddly with the English tongue. But doubtful
exceptions such as these leave the main facts untouched."

In the region known as "West Wales," which em-
braced Cornwall, Devon, and a good part of Somerset,
including Exmoor, the West-Saxon conquest was delayed, and probably never so complete as that of their
brethren in other parts of the kingdom. And the result
appears to have been that a much larger proportion
of the older inhabitants survived. "From the Axe
to the Tamar," says Freeman, "and still more from
the Parret to the Tamar, the people are still very largely
of Welsh descent, though they have spoken English for
many ages."

As regards language, though the Exmoor folk talk
English, and their English, as will hereafter appear,
is broad Saxon, there is at least one old British word
which is constantly heard on their lips—the word
"combe." This is nothing but the Keltic *cwm*, meaning
"valley." To the ear of the stranger it mingles oddly
with the English tongue. We find it in many place-
names, notably in "Cutcombe," the first syllable of
which is really *coed*, so that the whole signifies a
"wooded valley." "Timberscombe," the name of an
adjoining village, may be considered a translation of

"Cutcombe." Unlike *coed*, which is not, we believe, found elsewhere, *cwm* had evidently been adopted into the Saxon vocabulary, for it continually crops up in conjunction with pure English words. Thus we have "Thorncombe" (from *thorn*, a thorn); "Nettlecombe" (from *netele*, a nettle); "Ashcombe" (from *aesc*, an ash); and Withycombe (with which compare "Withy-pool"), derived from *withig*, a willow.

This last example reminds us of Selworthy, which takes its name from *salig* (a sallow), and that again of "Allerford" (Ford by the Alders), which comes from the Old English *alr*, *aler*, or *olr*. "Worthy" is a variant of "worth," which in Old English meant a farm or estate. When combined with another word, it is almost always contracted in the local dialect into "ery." Thus "Badgeworthy" is pronounced "Badgery"; "Pink-worthy," "Pinkery"; and "Holworthy," "Hollery." This circumstance has led us to question the orthodox derivation of Dunkery—viz. *dun creagh*, or *cerrig*, the rough hill.* According to this theory, the name is an inversion of "Croydon." If, on the other hand, "ery" represents "worthy," the full name-word would be "Dunk-worthy." The meaning of "worthy" we know; as for "dunk," is it quite incredible that it is a stunted form of "donkey"? On the Blackdowns there is a village called "Dunkeswell," which may very probably be "Donkey's Well"; and all over Exmoor are names attesting a lively interest in natural history—*e.g.* "Mouse-hanger" (the Wood of the Mouse), near Winsford; "Goosemoor," near Cutcombe and Stoke Pero; "Fox-twitchen," near Withypool; "Raven's Nest," near

---

* Another matter in which we are inclined to be sceptical is the etymology of "Luccombe," the first part of which is supposed to be *loc*, and the meaning of the whole "an inclosed valley." Our theory is that the true derivation is "low combe," just as "Hiccombe," in the parish of King's Brompton, is a corruption of "high combe." Jefferies correctly defines "coombe," as it is usually spelt singly, as "a fold in the hills."

ALLERFORD

Simonsbath; "Hawkridge," "Hawkcombe Head," "Cow Castle," and others. "Pink" in "Pinkworthy" obviously refers to the colour. That West Somerset people were sensitive to colour is proved further by "Red Stone," a well-known landmark, near Exford, "Yellowcombe," near Winsford, and "Green Barrow," near Withypool. An impartial survey of Exmoor place-names would lead to the conclusion that the English, rather than the British, element preponderates.

After the Saxons the Danes. Have the latter left any traces of their presence? Well, the word "Dane" is of frequent occurrence in local names; the only point is whether it is not an independent term. Thus an affluent of the Barle, which joins it at Castle Bridge, near Dulverton, is called the "Danesbrook." At Selworthy, again, "Danes Lane" leads down from the cliffs and the moor to East Lynch, the cross-way above East Lynch is called "Danes Cross," and the fields about the cross-way "Danes Fields." There seems to be a notion in the parish that "Danes," in this connection, is merely a local pronunciation of "Deans." Even were this so, however, the word might still be reminiscent of the sea-rovers, for, with the perversity of which we shall hear more by-and-by, that is precisely how Somerset people of the old school pronounce "Danes." Alluding to the Quantocks, where so many Exmoor names turn up again, Mr. Greswell observes: "I cannot find that the Danes, *or Denes, as the old men call them*, have left many place-names behind them. They might have left their name to Danesborough, but there are so many possible derivations for this word, *e.g.* Dinas, Dane, or Dawns, *i.e.* beacon borough. Perhaps the Quantocks, or Cantactune, as King Alfred's domain, was not hospitable enough to them to allow of their staying long." As we shall see, however, the Danes paid several

visits to the seaboard of Exmoor, and they may have
taken up temporary quarters in the " Valley of Rocks "
at Lynton, of which John Ridd remarks: " Our home-
folk always call it the ' Danes,' or the ' Denes '; which
is no more, they tell me, than a hollow place, even
as 'den' is "—another possible derivation.   On the other
hand, " den," in one instance, may stand for " Dane."
We refer to the western patronymic "Densham," *i.e.*
" the home of the Danes," just as we have " Jutsham,"
" the home of the Jutes."   Traditions about the Danes,
at any rate, have not yet perished.   It is said that
elders never flourish save where Danes have died, and
that Danish blood is dark in colour, as is seen when
the ripe berries are pressed, and they bleed.   According
to the Anglo-Saxon Chronicle the defeat of the Danes
by the Ealdormen Eanwulf and Osric and Ealstan,
Bishop of Sherborne, in 845 A.D., took place at the
mouth of Pedridan, or Parret, but tradition asserts that
it occurred in the parish of Stogursey, somewhat nearer
Exmoor.

Another overthrow of the Danes befell when Alfred
the Great, whose career is so intimately associated with
Somerset, was King of the English.   In the year 878,
under their chief Hubba, the heathens appeared in the
West, and for a time carried all before them.

"That same year," says Asser, "a brother of Halfden and
Inguar, with three-and-twenty ships bearing the legion of
Demetia, where he had wintered, after he had made great
slaughter of the Christians of those parts, set sail for Devon,
and there, with twelve hundred men, rashly doing, he was
in the end defeated and slain by the King's officers before the
Castle Cynwit.   For within the enclosure of this same castle
many of the King's officers, with their men, had taken refuge
together.   Now when the pagans saw that the castle was
destitute of provisions, and without means of defence of any
kind, save that it had walls after our fashion, they did not
attempt to carry it by assault ; but, as the nature of the ground

rendered it very safe except towards the east, they began to lay siege to it, thinking that those men, driven by hunger and thirst, would soon be compelled to surrender, for there was no water nigh to the castle. The Christians waited not to be reduced to such extremities, but inspired by heaven, and deeming it far preferable to earn either death or victory, suddenly rushed down on the pagans, and assailing their enemies like wild boars, put the greater part of them to the sword, together with their king."

The only clue—a very uncertain one—to the scene of this leaguer and sortie is the name "Cynwit." Roger de Hoveden asserts that Hubba was buried at "Cynwich," which some have identified with Combwich on the Parret. Near Combwich is a tumulus, which may have been Hubba's tomb, and Upper Cock Farm, in the same neighbourhood, may have been originally *Hubba Coc*, or "Hubba's Heap." Others hold that a tumulus near the sea at Stogursey is Hubba's grave. The late Bishop Clifford was of opinion that the fight took place in the hollow below Cannington Park quarries, whilst Mr. Sloper was convinced that Countisbury, where a rampart yet remains, is more likely to have been the site, because the Chronicle places Cynwit in Devon. This argument, however, is not conclusive, since geographical limits were then less sharply defined. Hume locates the battle at the estuary of the Taw, where there is said to be a rock called Hubbastone. Wherever the encounter took place, the Danes seem to have lost their banner. "And the same winter," says the Anglo-Saxon Chronicle, "the brother of Hinguar and Halfdene came with twenty-three ships to Devonshire, in Wessex ; and he was there slain, and with him eight hundred and forty men of his army, and there was taken the war-flag which they called the Raven."

Writing of this invasion, *sub* "Porlock," old Gerard says quaintly : "The badness of the harbour (and sure it is bad enough) was not sufficient to keep off the

Danes, who in yᵉ yeare of Grace 886, having harryed most of yᵉ Western Ports of this Kingdome, came hither, I dare say before they were welcome, who firing yᵉ Towne and lading themselves with the Pillage, returned to the shipps."

Under 918 the Chronicle records another invasion—that of the Lidwiccas. "'In this year a great fleet came over hither from the south, from the Lidwiccas, and with it two earls, Ohtor and Rhoald, and they went west about till they arrived within the mouth of the Severn, and they spoiled the North Welsh everywhere by the sea-coast where they passed." After describing their defeat by the men of Hereford, and their promise to depart King Edward's dominions, the Chronicle continues : " And the King had so ordered it that his forces sat down against them on the south side of the Severn mouth, from the Welsh coast westward to the mouth of the Avon eastward, so that on that side they durst not anywhere attempt the land. Then, nevertheless, they stole away by night, on some two occasions ; once to the east of Watchet, and another time to Porlock. But they were beaten on each occasion, so that few of them got away save those alone who there swam out to the ships."

The Lidwiccas appear to have come from Brittany, and, not improbably, formed part of a colony planted there by Rollo. Northmen by descent, they were by constitution fond of the sea, and resumed, if they ever left off, their ancient habits of massacre and piracy. On the second occasion, the English leader is said to have been Ælle, governor of Bristol, in his time a noted pirate-queller.

Ælle is the subject of one of the unhappy Chatterton's remarkable imitations of the antique. The poem is given in Evans' *Old Ballads*, together with the following introduction :—

"[About the year 920 Ælle was governor of the Castle of Bristol and gained many signal victories over the Danes, particularly at Watchet. The following song was made to the memory of this chief by Thomas Rowlle, a Carmelite friar and father confessor to William Canynge, founder of St. Mary Redcliffe Church. It was written in the year 1468, and the original is now in the hands of Mr. Barret, surgeon, in Bristol.]

"O THOU (or whate remaynes of thee),
    Ælle, the darlynge of futuritye !
  Lette thys mie songe bolde as thie courage bee,
    As everlastynge to posteritye !
  Whanne Dacyas sonnes, with hair of blood-red hue,
Like kynge-coppes brastynge with the mornynge dewe,

  "Arraung'd in drear arraye
    Upon the lethal daye,
Spredde farre and wyde on Watchet's shore ;
    Thenne didst thou brondeous stonde,
    And with thie burlye honde,
Bespryngedde all the mees wythe gore ;

  "Drawn by thyne aulace fell,
    Down to the depthes of hell
Thousands of Dacyans went ;
    Brystowans, menne of might,
    Ydared the blodie fyghte
And acted deedes full quent.

  "O thou ! where 'ere (thie bones att rest)
    Thie spryte to haunte delyghteth best,
Whether in the blod-embrued playne ;
    Or where thou keen'st from farre
    The blatant cryes of warre,
Or seest some mountayne made of heapes of slayne,

  "Or seest the hatchedde stede
    Yprauncynge o'er the mede
And neigh to be amongest the poyntedde speres ;
    Or, in black armour, stalk'st arounde
    Embattelede Brystowe, once thie grounde,
And glow'st ardurous onne the castle steers,

  "Or fierie round the mynsterne glare—
    Let Brystowe still be made thie care :
Guard it from fomenne and consumynge fire.
    Like Avon's streame encyrque it rounde ;
    Ne lette a flamme enharme the grounde
Tyll ynne one flame all the whole worlde expyre."
C

Regarding this invasion, Camden states that "in a field called Knap Dane, in the parish of Nettlecombe, were found a vast number of human bones, supposed of the Danes, who landed at Watchet A.D. 918." There certainly is a field of that name at Nettlecombe, and adjoining it are others, called respectively Brick Dane and Furze Dane. One old man told Mr. Warden Page that a sword had been found at Knap Dane, but he could give no further account of it. Objection has been taken to Camden's suggestion, on the ground that the Danes are recorded to have landed east of Watchet, and to have been merely "beaten"—a term, it is thought, which does not imply a regular engagement. However, the process may have cost lives, as at "Cynwit." In the middle of Knap Dane is a mound in the shape of a rough square, clearly artificial, and about four feet above the general surface. Perhaps, however, the battle may have occurred in A.D. 988, when "Watchet was ravaged, and Goda, the Devonshire thane, slain, and with him much slaughter made."

In 997 there was another visitation of the Danes. They landed at Watchet, and "wrought much evil by burning and manslaying." What attracted these corsairs to Watchet is believed to have been the fact that one of King Ethelred's mints was established there ; and it is some confirmation of this theory that, after the sack of Watchet, they sailed to South Devon, and, proceeding up the Tamar and Tavy, spoiled Lydford, where the King had another mint.

A mile from the sea, and close to the little town of Williton, are several fields, known collectively as "Battle-gore." According to immemorial tradition, this was the scene of one of the battles between the Danes and the men of Wessex. Probably, however, this is a Keltic rather than a Danish battle-ground, the barrows being of a strictly British type. The chief point in favour of

AT PORLOCK WEIR

the tradition is that the fields are south-east of Watchet,
while Knap Dane is south ; but the circumstance of the
Danes landing east of Watchet in 918, in their first
incursion, has been unduly emphasised.

We come now to the very last occasion on which the
Danes can be regarded as invading West Somerset.
This time—it was in 1052—the enemy were led by no
warrior of their own ; their chief was, in fact, the ill-fated
Harold, whose defeat at Senlac laid England open to the
Normans. Harold was lord of the manor of Dulverton,
and his sister Eadgyth—"Edith the Fair"—was lady of
Selworthy, on the opposite side of the moor. The lord
of Porlock, on the other hand, was Aelfgar, son of
Leofric, the great Earl of Mercia, and hereditary rival
of Harold, who was the son, of course, of Earl Godwin.
On Godwin's disgrace, Eadgyth, the wife of King
Eadward, shared the misfortunes of her family, and was
deprived of all her property, including the manor of
Selworthy.

Here, perhaps, we have the explanation of Harold's
invasion of West Somerset, where his family was unpopular. Proceeding first to Ireland, where there were
a number of Danish settlements, he succeeded in enlist-
ing a band of adventurers, and, with nine strong ships,
set sail for the Bristol Channel. He landed somewhere
between Porlock and Porlock Weir. Incidentally we
may observe that, in a field called "Hellbyes," not many
years ago, fragments of swords and warlike implements
were disinterred. They may have been relics of Harold's
expedition. Be that as it may, the invasion met with
stout resistance. Beacons flamed from Dunkery to
Plymouth, and the whole country was in arms against
the raiders. Harold's men, however, had much the best
of the affair. Thirty thanes and a host of lesser people
were slain, and he "took of cattle, and of men, and of
property as it suited him."

A mile and a half south-west of Porlock Church is an oval encampment, the entrance to which is on the south side, whilst the upper trenches are very deep. This fort may have been prepared against some earlier attack of the Danes, but the late Prebendary Hook believed that it was improvised on the occasion of Harold's attempt. Collinson asserts that Porlock was fired, and that only a few years before he undertook his *History of Somerset* (about 1750) men of the place used to point out buildings burnt, as they supposed, at the great foray. Writing of this Porlock story, Freeman protests against the way in which it has been slurred over by Thierry and St. John. He then passes his own judgment on the incident. " This part of Harold's conduct cannot be defended, and ought not to be concealed. It is enough that he wiped out the stain by his refusal, on a later occasion, to ravage one inch of the kingdom which had been given him to guard." In 1067, after Harold and his brother had fallen at Senlac, their mother, Gytha, embarked at Watchet for the Steep Holm, a barren rock in the Bristol Channel, where she, with other noble ladies, "abode some time." Afterwards they retired to St. Omer.

A curious trace of Anglo-Saxon supremacy is the name of a cairn at the extreme north-east of the parish of Exmoor, viz. Alderman's Barrow, known in mediæval times as Osmund's Barrow. The origin of the name is apparently shrouded in mystery.

On the accession of William the Conqueror, the Norman family of Mohun acquired great possessions in the neighbourhood, William de Mohun receiving Dunster Castle and much land as a reward for bringing fifty-seven valiant knights to the standard of his prince. One of the most distinguished of the race was John de Mohun, who lived in the reign of Edward III., and fought in the French wars of the period. He was also one of the first knights of the Most Noble Order of the Garter. He married Joan, daughter of his guardian, Bartholomew de Burghersh, and concerning her a variant of the Godiva legend is reported. The story of Godiva's ride at Coventry is entirely apocryphal, being only one of many similar stories current in India and elsewhere. Probably the story of Joan is equally fictitious, since it is founded merely on tradition. However, the tale is that, on receiving a petition from the inhabitants of Dunster for certain lands adjacent to the town, whereon to depasture their cattle freely and in common, John de Mohun granted his lady, who had interceded on the townspeople's behalf, as much land as she could go round barefoot in one day, which land she might afterwards bestow on her dependants.

CHAPTER II

FOREST LAW AND FOREST LIFE

UP to the period of the Conquest, and probably for a long time after that event, the history of Exmoor proper must be considered merged in that of the surrounding country, from which perhaps there was nothing to distinguish it either in law or natural features. Before husbandry was introduced and land was parcelled out, everything was forest. In the days of King John the whole of Devonshire was accounted forest, which was, in fact, the normal condition of the kingdom. As acre after acre was inclosed, the wild beasts, driven from their accustomed haunts, betook themselves to the wilder regions, where they existed in great numbers. Hunting was the favourite pastime of kings, and those vigorous monarchs were not willing that animals adapted for the chase should be exterminated in the interests of tillage. Accordingly they formed for themselves large reservations, in which hart and hind might roam and multiply. Those tracts which had never been brought under cultivation were known as "ancient forests," in contradistinction to districts like the New Forest, previously corn-land and tillage. The making of the New Forest has always been reckoned one of the most despotic acts of the Conqueror, who showed by this action that he thought more of stags than of his fellow-creatures and, as was said of him, "loved the tall deer as if he were their father." Of the "ancient forests" no less than five were in the county of Somerset—namely, Selwood, Neroche, Mendip, North Petherton, and Exmoor. Exmoor was at once the largest and wildest.

A remarkable fact about Exmoor is that, practically, it is all grass. Patches of heather may be found here and there, but the prevailing tint is a sort of grey green, and the general aspect of the moor is bleak and bare, especially in winter. On the surrounding commons— Anstey Burrows, Withypool Common, Lynton Common, Brendon Common, Winsford Hill—heather grows in abundance, and the absence of it sufficiently indicates where the common ends and the forest begins. This is notably the case at Picked Stones Farm, where the difference is at once apparent. The natives are firmly convinced that the existence of heather points to cultivation at some period, probably in feudal times. Even now, they say, if a plot of ground is cultivated and then allowed to relapse, heather commences to grow on it. The same effect follows if a portion of the soil is removed.

The Rev. W. H. Thornton says on this point :—

"I do not believe that there was any large quantity of heather upon the moors in old time ; it came through the agency of man, and indicates ground that has been broken. There may be some heather sparse, and poor, and straggling on unbroken ground, but you find it in perfection rather on the commons that surround the moor than on the moor itself. It is nearly fifty years since last I galloped over Oare Common at the back of Mr. Snow's house, but I have not forgotten the heather in the deer park, about breast-high, and exceedingly thick. . . . Heather implies man, and when did man begin upon the moors ? It is certainly a long time since he began to build his huts of stones, and then around them here and there he would break a piece of ground, and perhaps, so doing, destroy the often thin layer of clay which had enabled the peat to form, and then the heather came. I cannot speak of the beginnings of moor cultivation, but the ground which is now covered with rich heather on Oare Common and on

Hamildon Hill probably went out of cultivation after the breaking up of the feudal system in the time of Henry VII. A substitution of sheep for men then undoubtedly took place (very similar to what occurred in Scotland when the clans were dispersed after 1745), and the pulling down of huts and fences went on through several reigns until the process was checked by the great rise in prices after the introduction of gold in Elizabeth's reign, and was stopped by the Settlements Acts under Charles II."

Earlier, Savage had arrived at similar conclusions. Referring to Luxborough, he observes :—

" It seems from what has been said of the value of Langham in *Domesday*, and the other two manors in the same parish, surveyed at the same time, that a portion of Brendon Hill must have been cultivated with it, which, it is believed, belongs to it now ; ridges being still perceptible on many points of the hill, apparently thrown up by the plough. At the present moment [1827] Langham in point of value bears no comparison with the rest of Luxborough, although in the record above-mentioned the value is exactly equal to that of both manors. In fact there is no accounting for the difference in the value of some lands as compared with that of others now and when the survey was taken, but by supposing that then many of the highlands were cultivated that are not now, and that some of the best lowlands now were then

'Some dreary, bleak, and wild morass
Or woody forest, foeman's pass.'"

Mr. Thornton is too categorical in stating that "heather implies man" in the sense that heather is found *only* where man has tilled the soil. For, as Mr. Fortescue points out, heather grows, amongst other places, on Dunkery, which, from the nature of the case, is very unlikely to have been cultivated. Winsford Hill, on the other hand, has unquestionably been subjugated by the plough. Taking everything into account, the heather and tillage theory commends itself as probable ; and accordingly we should think of Exmoor during what may be termed its middle era, when it was a royal hunting-ground, as encompassed by land more or less cultivated, while the forest itself remained in its primitive condition.

It is possible that Exmoor was technically a forest a millennium ago, in the reign of the great Alfred. Nay, as certain of the West Saxon kings possessed palaces both at Porlock and at Dulverton, it may be more than a pleasing idea that Alfred himself, if politics and books did not too much absorb him, enjoyed the pleasures of the chase over the wild forest. Somerset, it is well known, was devoted to him, and it was from the marshes of Athelney that he sallied on his triumphant career against the Danes. However, the Danes came again, and came to stay; and Canute, the wisest of their kings, has been credited with certain ordinances entitled " The Constitutions of the Forest." These are probably a twelfth-century forgery, in which the condition of things obtaining under Henry I. is, as it were, cast back to the year 1018. The actual state of things in Canute's time has been pictured in vivid terms by John Richard Green, and the passage, being distinctly pertinent to the matter in hand, may well be quoted :—

" Even the oppressive forest laws, which have been falsely ascribed to him, witness indirectly to the growing wealth and prosperity. The greater part of English soil was still utterly uncultivated. A good third of the land was probably covered with wood, thicket, or scrub ; another third consisted of heaths and moor. In both the east and the west there were vast tracts of marsh land; fens nearly one hundred miles long severed East Anglia from the Midland counties ; sites like that of Glastonbury or Athelney were almost inaccessible. The bustard roamed over the downs, the beaver still haunted Beverley, huntsmen roused the bear in its forest lair, the London craftsmen chased the wild boar and the wild ox in the woods of Hampstead, while wolves prowled around the homesteads of the North. Forest law proves that peace, and the industry it encouraged, were already telling on this waste, for the wild deer could only be thought of when stag and

bittern were retreating before the face of man, when the
farmer's axe was ringing in the forest, and villages springing
up in the clearings.

"But the king lost more than his hunting as the forest
shrank into narrower bounds. He lost power. The common
law ran only where the plough ran. Marsh and moor and
woodland knew no master but the king, no law but his
absolute will : and it was this will which was embodied long
after Cnut's time in the form of forest law."

But if there was as yet no forest law, there were,
or were soon to be, forest officials, for in *Domesday* it is
expressly set forth that the greater part of Withypool
was held in the reign of Edward the Confessor by Dodo,
Almar, and Godric, relatives of Harold. While, however, it makes mention of foresters, it contains no
specific allusion to the forest. Probably this may have
arisen from the way the property of the Crown was
distributed. There were the royal manors of Carhampton and Williton, there were the comitial manors of
Dulverton, Winsford, and Nettlecombe, formerly possessions of Harold and his relations, which the Conqueror
now held by escheat ; and to each of these it is likely a
larger or smaller portion of the forest was attached. It
may be added that forest rights were exercised by the
first Norman sheriff of Somerset, William de Mohun,
in respect of his two demesne manors, Cutcombe and
Minehead.

The extent of the forest at this time must be matter
of conjecture. The manor of Oare doubtless lay within
the forest bounds, and the same may be true of its
neighbour, the manor of Brendon, in spite of the fact
that it belonged to the county of Devon. It may be
taken for granted that the Exmoor Forest of that day
far exceeded its ultimate limits, and appears to have
included, at any rate, the existing parishes of Oare,
Exford, Withypool, Hawkridge, and Exmoor. But,
having regard to the circumstances above noted, it

would seem not unjust to regard Dulverton, Winsford, and Cutcombe as forming part of the forest, in which case it would have covered at the time of the Conquest more than sixty-two thousand acres.

However that may be, it is beyond a doubt that, owing to encroachments for which King John and his immediate predecessors were accountable, enormous tracts were added to the forest area. Records of perambulations in the time of Edward I. point to the absorption of whole parishes, manors, and lordships much in the style that called down curses on the Conqueror for his treatment of Hampshire. Culbone, Wilmersham, Stoke Pero, Porlock, Doverhay, Bossington, Holnicote, Luccombe, Withycombe, and Exton are some of the places brought within the pale, and, with these additions, Exmoor exceeded eighty thousand acres. In the course of his oppressive proceedings King John laid the foundation of our present game laws, since at Bristol in 1208 he enacted that henceforth winged as well as four-footed creatures should be protected from capture. Prior to this interdict, everywhere throughout the land, birds had been considered common property.

John's forcible seizures affected not only commoners, turned out of their homes and made to experience all the severity and injustice of forest law, but the gentry and nobility. Their manors were confiscated to the Crown. At length, the King was checked in his career of spoliation by the joint action of barons and people, and then one of the demands made upon him was that all those afforestations perpetrated by his father, his brother, or himself should be repealed. Certain articles were drawn up, which defined the liberties and privileges they desired to have granted in respect of the forests ; and to these articles King John reluctantly set his seal at Runnymead, June 15th, 1215. The ordinances were embodied in Magna Carta, and were not,

as was once believed, a separate charter.   Before, however, steps were taken for carrying the provisions into
effect the King died.

In November, 1217, the Earl Marshal, in the name
of Henry III., then a boy of ten years, issued the first
charter determining forest law in plain terms, but the
concessions wrung from the last monarch remained
a dead letter.   Nine years later money was needed
on account of the war with France, and, in consideration
of a full fifteenth penny, the King was pleased to decree
an inquisition for disafforesting all lands and woods
unjustly annexed since the coronation of his grandfather, Henry II.   Yet, notwithstanding the publication
of this edict and the appointment of Hugh de Neville
and Bryan de Lyslee as commissioners, no real progress
was made during the fifty-six years of Henry's reign.

After the accession of Edward I. frequent representa-
tions were addressed to the Crown, calling for the
redemption of the pledges given by the King's father.
Like his father, however, the new King was not much
disposed to yield to his subjects' wishes, and during the
early years of his government his attention was distracted by the war in Wales.   In 1279 he gave orders
for the perambulation of his forests in Somerset ; and
in 1293 he published the following ukase :—

" If any forester do find any trespasser wandering within
his liberty, which is within the forest, intending to do hurt
or damage therein; and after hue and cry made to him
to stand unto the peace will not yield himself, but do flee
or resist ; in this case, if the forester do kill any such offender,
he shall not be impeached for this felony."

Such harsh words did not seem to prelude reform, but
justice was at length granted for value received.   The
King was in want of money, and, in exchange for a
subsidy, the charter of Henry III. was confirmed by an
inspeximus dated October 12th, 1297.   Copies of Magna

Carta and Carta de Foresta were sent to the sheriffs,
and they were directed by writ to acquaint people with
the King's confirmation of the same. Copies also were
to be kept in all cathedral churches and read aloud
publicly twice a year, and archbishops and bishops received authority to excommunicate offenders. The
charters were further ratified on March 8th, 1299, and,
again, on March 6th, 1300. Perambulations were then
made of all the forests in the realm, after which the final
confirmation took place, in 1301, at the Parliament of
Lincoln by the issue of letters patent. If it be true, as
asserted, that Edward on this occasion confirmed the
charters for the thirty-second time, he would really seem
to have been playing with his subjects.

Here we must pause to describe the successive perambulations. Three instances of this ceremony—a big
beating of bounds—occur at the close of the thirteenth
century, and fortunately the official records have been
preserved. State documents are not usually picturesque,
and to this rule the forest rolls are no exception. Those,
however, who know the country will find plenty of
interest in the recitals, which may suggest routes for
tourists.

In 1279 two perambulations were made, the parties
starting from opposite points ; and the following narratives are based on the reports :—

I. The northern boundary of Exmoor was at Cosgate,
then known as " Cornestake." Hence they proceeded
to Fifstake, an old mark on the highway between Porlock and Lynton, near Deddycombe, and from Fifstake
to Hawkcombe Head, and, over the top of the hill, as
far as Alderman's Barrow. Striking the water-course
(near Exford ?) they followed the stream to Road Castle,
and thence by the old highway to Hernes Barrow, which
appears to have been an ancient landmark on Room
Hill. Keeping to the highway, they reached the Wam-

barrows, on the crest of Winsford Hill, and proceeded to
Longstone, an inscribed menhir about a hundred and
twenty yards from Spire Cross (see p. 6). From Longstone they moved to a point (probably near Mouncey
Hill Gate), whence the road, now termed an "old track,"
led them over Varle Hill, and along the ridge between
Ashway and Old Ashway, as far as the Barle ; and they
kept to the Barle until they came to a place where that
river receives the Danes brook, and where to-day is
Castle Bridge. The perambulators reported that within
these limits as far as Devonshire was ancient forest,
while the country to the east was outside the forest pale.

II. The southern boundary, according to the other
party, was at Willingford, and starting from that point
they proceeded in a straight line to Hocklestone, and
from Hocklestone, still in a straight line, to Sheardon
Hutch, where Sheardon water falls into the Barle.
Going down by the bank of the stream of Lanacre
Manor, and leaving that within the forest, they moved
to Stonhuste, and thence to the Deer Mark, Shepscombe Head, Redford, and Redstone, the last a familiar
landmark on the high road between Exford and Simonsbath. Thence they travelled in a direct line to the Exe,
and from the Exe to a little stream that runs down
Orchard Bottom, pausing at Spraccombe Head, a point
above Orchard Corner. Still pursuing their straightforward route, they reached Alderman's Barrow, known
in those days as Osmund's Barrow, and went on to Black
Barrow, and from Black Barrow to the spot where the
little brook that flows down Lilycombe unites with Weir
Water by Robber's Bridge. Following the brook, they
got to Lilycombe Head, and thence by the highway to
Fistones. Finally they reached Cosgate, whence they
went down by the fosse as far as the bank of Oare
Water, on the confines of Devon and Somerset. The
"sworn men of Exmoor" then give an account of King

John's encroachments, and add their testimony that the manor of Dulverton, though lawfully acquired by the reigning monarch, is outside the pale of the forest.

The third set of commissioners, who surveyed in 1298, fixed the following limits, all on the right of which was the forest of the Lord King :—Cosgate, Fistones, Lily-combe Stream, Oare Water, Black Barrow, Alderman's Barrow, the Exe, Redstone, Redford, Shepscombe Head, Deermark (stated to be a stone), Stonhuste (here Ston-chiste), Sheardon Hutch, Hocklestone, Willingford. The lands lying to the left of this boundary, which had been afforested since the coronation of Henry II., and were now to be disafforested, are also enumerated. They include Culbone, Yarnor, Porlock, Bossington, West Luccombe, Wilmersham, Doverhay, East Luc-combe, Buckethole, Lucott, Worthy Wood, Stoke Pero, Chittesham, Holnicote, Broford, the hamlets of Ford and Stile, Hawkcombe Wood, Dunkery Heath, El-worthy, Hawkwell, La Walles, Cutcombe, Quarmunces, Almsworthy, Exford, Begger Quarme, Winsford, Withy-combe, the hamlet of How, Edbrook, Exton, Hawk-ridge, Lanacre, Withypool, Brutensworthy, West Ash-way, Liscombe, East Ashway, the hamlets of Telchete and La Merse, Dulverton, Hawkwell, and the Priory of Barlynch, with its woods, heaths, and appurtenances. Some of these places cannot be identified, but most of the names, though differently spelt, are easily recognis-able amidst the old Latin.

Thenceforward the forest area appears to have been confined within the limits last specified. It is worthy of note, however, that while, conformably to the Carta de Foresta, the whole of the encroachments were dis-afforested, the tracts which John and his predecessors had annexed did not absolutely revert to the *status quo*. They became pouraille or purlieu, and as such were subject to the view of the forest officials, who had the

D

right of entry upon, and way over, all purlieu for the purpose of recovering stray animals. On the other hand forest law, the chief grievance of the common people, halted at the forest bounds, so that, in this respect, those who dwelt in the purlieu were as well off, or nearly so, as their neighbours.

Some curious tenures are recorded as having been in force during the reign of Edward I. Thus Walter Angevin of Aure (conjecturally Oare) and Hole in the county of Devon held lands on condition that whenever the King hunted in the Forest of Exmoor, he, the said Walter, should provide him with barbed arrows. At Holnicote in Somerset one Walter Barun is certified as holding of the King *in capite* a messuage, ten acres of arable and two acres of meadow land, "by the service of hanging on a certain forked piece of wood the red deer that died of the murrain in the Forest of Exmoor; and also of lodging and entertaining at his own expense such poor and decrepit persons as came to him, for the souls of the ancestors of King Edward I."

Dogs might be kept by persons of worth, *i.e.* free-holders or farmers, for the protection of house and chattels, provided that the animals were duly "ex-peditated" or "lawed." Manwood, the great authority on all matters of mediæval forestry, informs us that "expeditation" is a coined word to define what was afterwards expressed by "mutilation." "Canute in his 31st Canon doth call the lawing of dogs *genuisciscio;* but that was a kind of cutting or laming dogs in the hams; and that sort of lawing the old foresters were wont to call hamling or hoxing. King Henry II. was the first that began to cut off the claws of the fore-feet of mastiffs, and he called that manner of lawing *ex-peditatio mastivorum.*"

How was the operation performed? Manwood shall answer. "The mastiff being brought to set one of his fore-feet upon a piece of wood of eight inches thick, and a foot square: then one with a mallet, setting a chisel of two inches broad upon the three claws of his fore-foot, at one blow doth smite them clean off, and this is the manner of expeditating mastiffs." The object of this procedure is evident. It was to render dogs incapable of hunting or molesting game. The lawing took place every third year, when the Regard of the Forest was made, before a jury of "honest men."

This brings us to the subject of forest courts, which were four in number. The first, and least important, was the Court of Attachment, or Woodmote, at which the verderers received and enrolled attachments of vert and venison and the presentments thereof. This court had power to inquire, but not to convict. Secondly, there was the Court of Swanimote, which was held thrice a year—fifteen days before Michaelmas, about the feast of St. Martin, and fifteen days before the feast of St. John. This court sat in the open air, and the verderers presided. Thirdly, the Court of Regard, held once in three years for the lawing of dogs, etc. Fourthly, the Court of Justice Seat, held occasionally before one or more of the Justices Itinerant, at which final judgments were pronounced. Such courts were held at various places, Ilchester, Somerton, Langport, Wells, and Taunton being amongst those mentioned. Records of these tribunals, extending from 1248 to 1368, are still preserved, and here and there make pleasant reading. In them we meet with but few traces of the savage vindictiveness which in earlier times had made forest law a byword. Instead of bodily disfigurement and mutilation as penalty for poaching, imprisonment was now the recognised mode of punishment. Some of the presentments are worth quoting.

"It is presented, etc.—that Thomas le Shettere of la Grutte in Molland, and William Wyme, of Bremley in the same place entered the aforesaid forest on Easter Eve, year 51 [1267] with bows and arrows, with the intention of wrong-doing as to the venison of the Lord King; and hunted one hind and afterwards chased her into the wood of Longcombe without the forest bounds, and there caught her, and carried her away to their houses in Molland; and the same men were accustomed often to enter the aforesaid forest with the intention of wrongful hunting, and were harboured in the house of John, then chaplain of Hawkridge, who consented to their evil deeds. The same chaplain came and was kept in prison. And the others did not come, nor were they attached. Therefore the Sheriff of Devon is ordered to cause them to come on Monday next after the octaves of Holy Trinity [1270]. And because the townships of Dulverton *elsewhere*, Ashway le Erceneske *elsewhere*, Hurdecombe Prior of Taunton of 40^d, did not come in full, etc., therefore they are in mercy [*i.e.* the King might decree complete forfeiture or inflict a fine]. And the aforesaid John the chaplain is pardoned for the sake of the King's soul.

"It is presented, etc.—that John Scrutenger, of Cloutsham, hunted one hind in the aforesaid forest, about the feast of the purification of the Blessed Mary, year 54 [1270]; which hind was found dead in the same forest by Walter le Clerk, son of Matthew, parson of the church of Oare; and John Elyot, servant of the same parson, took her and carried her away to the house of the same parson at Oare, who knowingly harboured them with the same venison. And he came, and being convicted of this, was kept in prison. And he undertook to have the aforesaid wrongdoers, who are of his household, on Saturday next after Holy Trinity [1270]. Afterwards came the aforesaid Walter, and John Elyot, and were kept in prison. And the aforesaid Matthew, for himself and his servants, paid a fine of 20^s; pledges Adam le Bonde of Oare and Walter of Oare."

Other typical occurrences are the following. In the ninth year of King Edward III. (1335) Richard Ganne, of Lucott, "burnt the moor of the Prior of Taunton, bordering on the King's soil of the aforesaid forest; and the flame of this fire, leaping out into the heath of the Lord King in the same forest, burnt two hundred acres of heath in the same." It is further recorded "that in the tenth year of the aforesaid King Edward [1336] a fortnight after the nativity of St. John the Baptist, Roger de Gotecoumbe [Cutcombe ?] found one stag in his rye on Molland Hill, which is two leagues and more outside the said forest, which stag

OARE CHURCH

the said Roger killed and carried away the venison for his own purpose."

In 1357 the keeper of the royal forests in Somerset was Roger Mortimer, Earl of March, and the office remained vested in his family, or in that of the Dukes of York, till 1460. The Mortimers appear to have appointed deputies, and, amongst these "substitutionary foresters," as Collinson calls them, the park rolls of Petherton have preserved the name of at least one famous individual.

"10 Ric. II.   Richard Brittle
    14   „   Richard Brittle   } By appointment of
                and Geoffrey Chaucer } the Earl of March.
    21   „   Geoffrey Chaucer, by Alianor, Countess of March.
     4 Hen. V. Thomas Chaucer, by Edward, Earl of March."

Collinson's list is somewhat longer, but as it is not quite certain that the functions of these subordinate officials (if exercised at all) extended to other forests such as Exmoor, the above entries must suffice. It is significant, however, that one of the earliest descriptions of staghunting in English is to be found in Chaucer's *Book of the Duchess*. The poet clearly knew all about it, and his accurate use of technical terms can be established by reference to somewhat later treatises.

> "And as I lay thus, wonder loud
> Methought I heard an hunte(r) blow
> To essay his horn, and for to know,
> Whether it were clear or hoarse of soun(d).
> I hearde go both up and down
> Men, horse, hounds, and other thing ;
> And all men speaken of hunting,
> How they would slay the hart with strength,
> And how the hart had, upon length,
> So much embossed, I know not what.
> Anon-right, when I hearde that,
> How that they would on hunting gon,
> I was right glad, and up anon ;
> I took my horse, and forth I went
> Out of my chamber ; I never stent
> Till I come to the field without.
> There overtook I a great rout
> Of hunt(er)s and eke of foresteres
> With many relays and lymeres,
> And hied them to the forest fast,
> And I with them.   So at the last
> I asked one, led a lymere.
> 'Say, fellow, who shall hunten here?'

Quoth I ; and he answered again,
'Sir, the Emperor Octavian,'
Quoth he, 'and is here fastè by."
'A God's half, in good time,' quoth I.
'Go we fast !' and gan we ride.
When we came to the forest side,
Every man did right anon
As to hunting fell to don.
The master hunt(er) anon, foot-hot,
With a great hornè blew a moot
At the uncoupling of the houndès.
Within a while the hart y-found is,
Y-holloa'd, and rechasèd fast
Long timè ; and so, at the last,
This hart rused, and stole away
From all the hounds a privy way.
The hounds had overshot them all,
And were on a default y-fall ;
Therewith the hunte(r) wonder fast
Blew a forloyn at the last."

Although the general meaning is evident, a few words
will render the account still clearer. We do not scruple
to add them, for there is no sort of doubt that the
passage depicts the style of hunting carried on in the
Forest of Exmoor, as well as throughout the country,
in Plantagenet days. "Embossed" signifies "plunged
into the thicket." "Lymeres" were dogs, with which
such animals as harts, bucks, and boars were roused
and pursued, while "relays" were fresh sets of dogs,
laid on after the quarry had been roused. Thus the
"lymeres" almost correspond to our modern "tufters"
and the "relays" to the "pack." A "moot" is a note
on the horn. It was the custom to blow three notes—
four, if the hounds were not soon up—directly the hart
was viewed. "Rechased" (or headed back) refers to
the practice of posting men at certain points for the
purpose of keeping the stag within bounds. If the stag
passed out of bounds, a "forloyn" was sounded to
recall the hounds. Chaucer's hounds seem to have lost
their deer. One word more. The "Emperor Octavian"
is a politic or poetical disguise for Edward III

CHAPTER III

THE DECLINE OF THE FOREST

LITTLE is known of Exmoor under the Tudors.
Preserved, however, among the family papers at
Nettlecombe, and printed in one of the volumes of the
Camden Society, is a letter from Lord Daubeny to Sir
John Trevelyan, of Nettlecombe, which throws some
light on what happened during the reign of Henry VII.,
when, it is plain, the control of the forest resided in the
Lord Great Chamberlain.

" COUSYN TREVYLION,

"I commaund me unto you in as herty a maner as I
can, and understand that upon my late writing unto you for
taking hede unto the Kinges game within the forest of Exmore,
ye have right well endeavoured you for the good keeping of
the same ; for the which I am right hertely well contented
with you, and pray you of your like contynuance of the same.
How soo be it, I am enformed that of late a little grugge is
fallen bitwene my brother Sir Hugh Luttrell and you, for that
he hunted of late in the oute wods of the said forest, and
thereupon a couple of hounds were taken up by servants of
yours from his servants. After that, Cousyn, inasmoche as
my said brother Luttrell is a borderer of the said forest, and
that ye knowe he hath maried my sister, and the man whome
I do love tenderly : my mind is and desire unto you, that ye
shuld have an yghe unto hym above all others in those parties.
And that when it shall like hym to kyll a dere, or to hunt for
his disport ; that ye suffer hym soo to do I pray you as hertely
as I can. Written at Grenewich the xx daie of Feverer. And
I pray you, Cousyn, let my said broder take his disporte, and

if he list let hym kyll one dere in somer and a nother in
wynter herafter,   " Yo^r Cousin
                                    " Giles Daubeny.

" *To my Cousin,*
    " Sir John Trevylion, *Knight.*"

On the marriage of Henry VIII. with Catherine of
Aragon, "bluff King Hal" appears to have settled
Exmoor Forest upon the Queen as part of her jointure,
for in a blank indenture, preserved at the Record Office
and dated 1520, Sir Thomas Boleyn covenants with the
Earl of Devonshire to give up certain forests, farms, and
offices held of Queen Catherine, saving and reserving
one hundred deer in the said Forest of Exmoor. Sir
Thomas Boleyn, it is thought, was descended from
Robert de Boleyne, who is mentioned in the perambulation of 1298 as holding the hamlet of Liscombe, now
a farm in the parish of Dulverton. Still more interesting
is it to recall that he was father to Anne Boleyn, the
unhappy lady to marry whom Henry divorced Catherine
and quarrelled with the Pope. It is believed that
Exmoor remained vested in Catherine till her death in
1536, when it was granted to Henry's third wife, Jane
Seymour, who died in October, 1537, soon after the
birth of her son, Edward VI.

Lord Russell superintended the Queen's interests in
Somerset, but the Keeper of Exmoor Forest at that
period was Sir Hugh Pollard. This is proved by a
memorand..m concerning a theft of money from a secret
chamber in the house of Andrew Hillersden at Exeter,
the culprits being his servant, John Holland, and William
Holland, John's brother. One clause is as follows :—
"Caused the city of Exeter to be searched for William ;
sent also to Sir Hugh Pollard, to keep the fords over
the Ex in Exmoor." Sir Hugh not only kept fords,
but kept hounds, at Simonsbath, and he is believed to
have been the first to do so.

Queen Elizabeth bestowed the right of herbage in the forest on Robert Colshill, one of her gentlemen pensioners, and there is still extant a letter in the handwriting of that famous statesman, William Cecil, Lord Burghley, in which he directs the Earl of Bedford to assist the tenant with regard to certain persons " who refuse to paye such duties for ye herbage of their Cattell in our sayd forrest as is right they ought, and as by our records we be informed in former tymes hath been answered."

Like Mr. Rawle, we had almost forgotten Leland, whose description of Tudor England is, however, of the highest interest and value. This accomplished scholar having been dignified by Henry VIII. with the title of his "Antiquary" and commissioned to make a sort of inventory of the kingdom, spent six or seven years in travelling through England and Wales, noting in his journey rivers, forests, chases, cities, castles, manor-houses, monasteries, colleges, and everything that seemed memorable. The portion of his Itinerary relating to Exmoor is as follows :—

"From Dunestorre to Exford village a 7. miles.

"Of these 7. miles 3. or 4. of the first were al hylly and rokky, full of Brokes in every hilles botom and meatly woddid.

"These Brookes by my Estimation runne toward the Severne Se.

"The Residew of the way to Exford was partely on a moore and sumwhat baren of Corne, and partely hylly, having many Brookes gathering to the hither Ripe of *Ex* Ryver.

"There is a litle Tymbre Bridge at Exforde over *Ex* Brooke, there being a smaul water.

"*Ex* risith in Exmore at a place caullid Excrosse a 3. miles of by north weste, and so goith toward Tyvertun a xij. miles lower and then to Excestre a x. miles.

"From Exford to Simonsbath Bridge a 4. miles, al by Forest, baren and morisch ground, where is store and breeding of young Catelle, but little or no Corne or Habitation.

"There rennith at this place caullid Simonsbath a Ryver betwixt to great Morisch Hilles in a depe Botom, and ther is a Bridge of Woodde over this water. This Water risith by North Weste.

"The Water in Somer most communely rennith flat upon stones easy to be passid over, but when Raynes cum and Stormes of Wyntre it ragith and ys depe.

"Alwayes this Streame ys a great deale bygger than *Ex* is at Exford, yet it resortith into *Ex* Ryver.

"The Boundes of Somersetshire go beyond this streame one way by north west a 2. miles or more to a place caullid the *Spanne*, and the Towrres ; for there be hillokkes of yerth cast up of auncient tyme for Markes and Limites betwixt Somersetshir and Devonshir : and here about is the Limes and Boundes of Exmore Forest.

"From Simonsbath Bridge I rode up an high Morisch Hylle, and so passing by 2. miles in lyke Ground, the soyle began to be sumwhat fruteful, and the Hylles to be ful of Enclosures, ontylle I cam a 3. miles farther to a poore Village caullid Brayforde, wher rennith a Broke by likelihod resorting to Simonsbath Water and Ex."

James I. revived the Tudor tradition by settling Exmoor on his wife, Anne of Denmark, who leased it to William, Earl of Pembroke. On the accession of Charles I. this lease was renewed, and liberty was granted the Earl to build a lodge in the forest at his own expense, and to inclose two hundred acres of land. This is supposed to have been the origin of the Simonsbath estate of a hundred and eight acres, held by George III. in demesne at the time of the sale of the forest in 1818. Simonsbath House was probably the lodge. Notwithstanding this arrangement, King Charles appears to have entertained the idea of turning those "great forests of Exmoor and Dartmoor" to better account. A petition was addressed to His Majesty by a person whose name has not transpired, but whose occupation was that of an ambassador ; and His Majesty was graciously inclined to grant a com-

mission for disafforesting Exmoor and letting the lands
at fourpence an acre. For some reason—probably on
account of the prior agreement with Lord Pembroke—
the scheme was never carried into effect.

Meanwhile the tithes of the forest were granted by
letters patent to George Cottington " in consideration
of a present fine paid in hand, as also a good rent "—
that is to say, he farmed them. This speculation
brought Cottington into collision with the local clergy,
the consequence being a petition to Archbishop Laud,
in which the lessee explains : " He is lately informed that
some of the clergy adjoyning to yᵉ Forest have a designe
to make it a complaint unto your Grace, and to possess
you with an ill opinion of this Patent." The Archbishop,
however, will not (he thinks) run the ship of State on
the rocks, in order to satisfy country parsons. " Your
Grace doth stand at the hellme of all our publique
affaires, but in particular of these. If you please to
consider that in favouring this Grant, you steere his
Majestie's Course, the Petitioner will never be guilty
of ingratitude toward your worth, and you create him
your ever bounden servant." How little Cottington
dreamed, when he penned these words, what a bad
steersman Laud would prove!

Early seventeenth - century notices throw an interesting light on the condition of the forest and the
habits of the country people at that period. In 1621
a dispute, culminating in legal proceedings, arose
between John Pearce, gentleman, of Northmolton,
then Forester of Exmoor, and John Slowley, yeoman,
one of the copyright tenants of the manor. The cause
of the quarrel cannot be traced, but Slowley alleged
the unlawful detention of his cattle. From the de-
positions made before the Court of Chancery we select
the following declarations.

Slowley states, with reference to Exmoor, that

" although it have the name and appellation of a forest
yet in truth it is not, neither can be, a true and legal
forrest, for that there is no game of redd deere bred
within the same, neither are there any wooden coppices,
or other shelter for the harbouring of redd deere
there."

William Hill confirms this statement. He " very
seldom sees anie red deere anytime within the com-
passes of the said Forest, unless it hath been upon
times of hunting, and he thinketh that there are none
at all bred within the forest." (On this point Mr.
Chadwyck Healey, whose recent work contains an
exhaustive account of the suit, quotes Mr. Nicholas
Snow to the effect that deer seldom or never bred
within the forest proper until fences and plantations
were made by Mr. John Knight, thus providing some
shelter.)

John Court, of Withypool, deposes that " the custom
and the usage of the said Forrest of Exmore is to make
one drift of sheepe yearlie by the fifty suitors nine days
before midsummer, and they bring all the sheepe which
they then find unshorn unto Withypool Pound, and
that the forester hath the benefit of the fleeces of
the sheep then so taken, except the sheep of the fifty-
two suitors, etc. . . . He saith that he hath heard his
predecessors of the fifty-two suit say that the custom
of the Forest of Exmore is that a sheep or pig, a goose
or goat taken pasturing in the said forest are forfeit
beasts for which there is no fine nor compensation
made with the forester, and further saith he hath known
geese forfeited in his time."

In the *Particular Description of the County of Somerset*, drawn up by Thomas Gerard, of Trent, in 1633, we
meet with the following allusion to Exmoor :—

" The farthest west limmitt of this Shire comprises a part
of the Forrest of Exmore, which hence extends itself farre

into Devon; a solitarie place it is, the more commodious
for staggs, who keep possession of it. In this Forrest and
on the utmost edge of the County Ore a little riverett
gusheth out under a large Oake called Hore, I think for Ore
oake, which immediately passing into Devon leaves its name
to Ore."

The same authority tells of wondrous mines of
alabaster at Minehead.

"Att this place in our tyme a Duch man hath found out
mynes of excellent Alabaster, which they use much for Tombes
and Chimney pieces.   Its somewhat harder than yᵉ Darbishir
Alabaster, but for variety of mixtures and colours it passeth
any I dare say of this Kingdome, if not others, for here shall
you have some pure white, others white spotted with redd,
white spotted with blacke, redd spotted with white, and a
perfect black spotted with white, etc."

In 1637 Endymion Porter, wishing to obtain a grant
of the forest, offered the King double the annual rent—
£46 13s. 4d.—paid by Lord Pembroke, the actual lessee.
It is noteworthy that in Porter's petition the manor
of Exmoor, as generally, is mentioned separately, and
stated to be in the county of Devon.   Mr. Rawle
supplies us with several particulars relating to Endymion
Porter, telling us, *inter alia*, that he was a gentleman
of the bedchamber to Charles I., who, in May, 1625,
granted him a pension of five hundred pounds for life.
Nothing is said, however, of this courtier's accomplishments, though Herrick has addressed several pieces
to him.   One of them, being short, may perhaps be
quoted :—

> " To the Honoured Master Endymion Porter.
>
> "When to thy porch I come, and, ravished, see
> The state of poets there attending thee,
> Those bards and I all in a chorus sing
> 'We are thy prophets, Porter ; thou our king.'"

In the Royal Library at Windsor is a warrant, under
the sign-manual of Charles I., to the following effect :—

" Charles R.

" Our will and pleasure is that you deliver
Vnto the bere^r hereof one fatt stagg of
this season and for soe dooing this
Shall bee your sufficient warrant.
Given at our courte at Oatelands this
5th of August 1637.

" To the ranger of our
Forrest of Exmore
for Mr Windam."

It is not known who the " Mr Windam " referred to
was, but it is supposed that he was a son either of Sir
John Wyndham, of Orchard Wyndham, or of his cousin,
Sir Thomas Wyndham, of Keyntsford, Somerset.
Edmund Wyndham, Sir Thomas' eldest son, was
groom of the chamber to Charles I., while another
son, Francis, held Dunster Castle for the King in 1645-6.
Mr. Luttrell had intended holding the castle for the
Parliament, "yet," says Lord Clarendon, "by the dexterity
of Francis Wyndham, who wrought upon the fears of
Mr. Luttrell, the owner, it was with as little bloodshed
as the others [i.e. Taunton and Bridgwater] delivered up
to his majesty, into which castle the marquis placed him
as governor who took it, as he well deserved." The
Marquis of Hertford, the nobleman in question, had
endeavoured, in September, 1643, to gain the fortress
for the Royalists, but without success ; and it appears,
from a journal of the time, that a detachment of his
army marched to Barnstaple by way of Exmoor.

" After the Marquesse of Hertford's departure from Myne-
head, about 400 of those Cavaliers marched from thence to
Dulverton, and from thence to Exford in Somerset; and on
Satturday night last came to a village called Chittlehampton,
within five miles of Barnstaple ; the Inhabitants of which
Towne were all in armes expecting them, but they durst not
approach thither, having intelligence of their readinesse; the
Towne being fortified with 16 Peeces of Ordinance, and 500
men in armes. The malignant neighbours assisted these

cavaliers with their servants, to guide and direct them in the Countrey. They were tyred out with their journeys, and if the Countrey had risen against them, they might have bin taken, all, or the most part of them."

In June, 1645, whilst Colonel Wyndham was governor of Dunster Castle, the Prince of Wales, afterwards Charles II., paid him a visit. "Lord Digby," says Clarendon, "by his letters to the prince's council signified his majesty's pleasure that the prince should stay at Dunster Castle, and encourage the new levies, it being (I presume) not known at court that the plague which had driven him from Bristol was as hot at Dunster town, just under the Castle." Prince Charles stayed only a few days, and then, escorted by three troops of Lord Hopton's Horse, travelled on horseback to Barnstaple, most probably across Exmoor Forest. In connection with this visit, it may be added that a chamber, known as King Charles' room, is still shown at Dunster Castle. Nor must it be forgotten that, after the Battle of Worcester, loyal Francis Wyndham sheltered the fugitive prince for nineteen days in his Somerset home at Trent. Ere this, Dunster Castle had been reconquered for the Parliament by the Somerset hero Blake.

CHAPTER IV

THE DOONES

WE come now to the period of the Commonwealth, which, as regards Exmoor, was marked chiefly by the "usurpation" of one James Bovey. No sooner was Charles II. restored to his throne than the inhabitants of Exmoor and the neighbourhood forwarded a petition, wherein they complained of being deprived of privileges and immunities—such as pasturing of sheep, horses, and cattle in the forest at fixed annual rates—by this Bovey, "pretending that he had purchased the same as a Chace of the late usurpers." Only for asserting their just and immemorial rights, he had impounded their cattle, arrested some of their persons, and maintained long and tedious suits at law against them. To this petition the King's practical reply was the grant of a lease of the forest, with the exception of the mines and the timber, to a staunch adherent, who had been with him during ths whole period of his exile, and had lost, it was computed, nearly a million sterling in his interest—James Butler, Marquis of Ormonde.

The mention in the grant of "all Goods and Debts of Fellons, of Deodands goods, of Fugitives, and persons outlawed," naturally recalls to our minds the tradition of the Doones, the historical foundation of which Mr. Rawle impugns. He even goes so far as to question the existence of any legend of the Doones. On the latter point, at all events, we are convinced he is greatly mistaken. It may be expedient, however, to quote his

E   49

exact words. After stating that there is no evidence
of the existence of the Doones in the national records
or in county and parochial registers, he proceeds:
" None of the old inhabitants of the district round Oare
ever heard of the Doones until after the publication
of the work alluded to [*i.e. Lorna Doone*], and the
Doone Valley is but a new name given to the lower
part of Hoccombe, where it embouches on Badgworthy
water. It is, therefore, only reasonable to assume that
this redoubtable band, together with the Herculean hero
and lovely heroine, are but the clever invention of the
novelist's brain." Mr. Rawle is sadly puzzled by
Blackmore's notes, in which he refers to certain incidents
as facts, and he doubtless esteems the author's pre-
fatory remark, that " he knows that any son of Exmoor,
chancing on this volume, cannot fail to bring to mind
the nurse-tales of his childhood," as so much pleasant
fooling.

The truth is, Mr. Rawle has not carried his researches
far enough, or he would have learnt enough to convince
him that, long before Blackmore had written a syllable
of his romance, there was in existence a well-established
tradition concerning the Doones. *Lorna Doone* was
published in 1869. In 1862 Dr. Collyns completed and
gave to the world his *Chase of the Wild Red Deer*, in
which he quotes from a West Country guide-book the
assertion that Exmoor was formerly the headquarters of
a set of freebooters, the Doones, who were supposed to
have arisen during the confusion caused by the Civil
Wars. This alone is sufficient to demolish the theory
that the Doones, with all that appertained to them, were
Blackmore's creation. But we do not propose to rest
our case merely on that. We intend to show that
Blackmore's reference to the nurse-tales of childhood is
strictly and literally correct.

It would seem, however, that the novelist was not

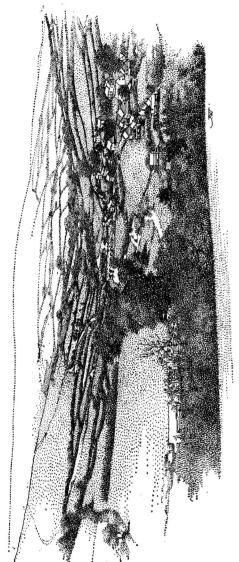

WITHYPOOL

content with childish memories. When the idea of writing *Lorna Doone* took definite shape in his mind, he made a prolonged stay on Exmoor, in order to equip himself more perfectly, and that he might compare notes with his moorland brethren—Blackmore's grand-father had been incumbent of Oare—from whom he had been so long parted by distance and necessity. The present writer stumbled on Blackmore's track, in the autumn of 1900, at Withypool. Mr. Tudball, the village postmaster, whose father was landlord of the " Royal Oak " for twenty-seven years, can vouch for the fact that Blackmore wrote part of *Lorna Doone* whilst staying at the inn. On one occasion the novelist and his wife strolled down to the bank of the stream, where Mrs. Blackmore sat down under the shade of a tree. A pretty incident ensued. As the children of Mr. Land, of King's Farm, tripped along on their way to a hayfield, she stopped them and chatted pleasantly with them. By-and-by Mr. Land himself appeared, to whom she smilingly apologised.

" I am afraid I have hindered the children."

" No matter, ma'am," replied the farmer ; " their work isn't very valuable."

Mrs. Tudball, having prior to her marriage been a dressmaker in the village, made Blackmore some shirts, and, after the visitors had left, Mr. Tudball received from them a welcome present of strawberry plants.

When Blackmore was not writing, how did he employ his time? There cannot be much doubt as to the answer. He went about, like a much humbler writer some thirty years later, talking with the villagers, and seeking to pick up scraps of information—especially, perhaps, the " nurse-tales " of which he speaks. For ourselves, we were rather fortunate in our quest, lighting on a Mr. Huxtable, who must be verging on seventy, and who was able to furnish us with some typical " nurse-tales." Huxtable's mother was a native of Challacombe, and when he was a child she used to regale him with startling narratives, of the sort children love, about the Doones. For fear of the Doones, she told him, farm buildings were arranged in a square, with communications between the different parts, so that it was possible to pass from kitchen to barn, and from stable to shippen, without going out after dark. However, one night the Doones got into a farm called Withycombe, in the parish of Challacombe, and killed everyone in the house save the mistress, who saved her life by jumping into a large butter-chest, big enough to hold five or six people and full of feathers, which she, belike, after plucking her geese, had stored up to make a bed-tick against the marriage of one of her children.

In the midst of the common, where Lanacre Bridge now stands, but where there was then only a fording-place—Lanacre Bridge will be remembered as the scene of Jeremy Stickles' adventure under very similar circumstances—Old Doone rode through the Barle at high water, and, by daring the flood, escaped his pursuers, who were close behind. The marauder, it appears, had his horses shod backwards, so as to deceive people when they were on his track. Once the Doones visited a house at Challacombe, where they got more than they bargained for. It seems that the inmates, anticipating their arrival, bored a hole through the door, and through this hole, when the robbers came up, a gun was fired at them. The shot took effect, for afterwards blood was traced in the snow as far as Chapman Barrows. Mr. Huxtable, who himself in later years took down the veritable door, was shown the hole by his mother, and she it was who acquainted him with its purpose. On another occasion, when Challacombe Revel was being held, the people heard that Doone was about, and fled to their homes in terror.

These after-gleanings — real "nurse-tales" — must satisfy everybody that Blackmore did not invent the Doones. They may be supplemented, however, by other particulars, for which we are indebted to Mr. Thornton :—

"The old people on Exmoor used to tell me that the last two of the Doone family perished in snow. Mr. Blackmore has invented a Sir Ensor Doone, but the real author of the family was, I believe, a fugitive private soldier from Sedgemoor, who only escaped hanging at the hands of Judge Jeffreys to carry on a series of petty depredations from a hovel on Exmoor. Monmouth's rebellion occurred, I think, in 1685, and it must have been in 1800, or about that time, when the last male Doone, emaciated and old, went out with his poor little granddaughter to sing Christmas carols and gather a few pence. They were found together in the snow, quite dead, on the road between Simonsbath and Challacombe, or so I have been informed.

. . . . . .

"The moors have always been the favourite resort of hunted, proscribed, and outlawed men. The records of these freebooters are for the most part lost, and what I have to say of them is disjointed and fragmentary, but Canon Kingsley had probably some foundation for his description in *Westward Ho!* of the Gubbings tribe, which infested Dartmoor in the time of Queen Elizabeth, and whose members, according to him, were completely savage.

"In my day the Warren Farm on Exmoor was bleak and bare, but tradition said that it had been the hiding-place of a proscribed nobleman, who had fled from the wrath of one of our Henrys, and who, strange to say, was credited with having been an excellent florist, and was said to have maintained a good garden in proximity to his residence. Unless the climate was better than now, he must have been a very clever man, or, at least, well accustomed to manage hothouses.

"The Doones, as I have said, were believed by my friends to have originated from a refugee soldier from Sedgemoor. They settled down in a small combe which runs up at right angles from the Badgeworthy Water, just above the old wood,

and I have ridden many a time among the foundations of
their two or three wretched huts. They increased in numbers
during the hundred years or so of their history, and became
petty malefactors and a nuisance to the neighbourhood, until
the more respectable people united and got rid of them. I
cannot remember the name of the farmhouse which stands
just above Glenthorne, on the trackway at the head of the
woods, unless it be Yarcombe, *i.e.* Higher Combe, but in 1848
an old farmer who resided there showed me an antiquated
fowling-piece with which an ancestor of his (so he declared,
with great satisfaction) had shot a Doone, who was prowling
about in his farmyard at night, literally seeking, poor beggar!
what he might devour. The Doones stole ponies, sheep, and
poultry, and were generally a nuisance."

Such legendary items are practically all that Exmoor
people can furnish out of their unassisted knowledge.
But at the eleventh hour, as it were, there comes a
gentlewoman from Scotland, claiming to be a descendant of the Doones, who tells us all about them. In the
autumn of 1901 the editors of the *West Somerset Free
Press* secured a sensational contribution (since reprinted
in pamphlet form) from a lady signing herself "Ida
M. Browne (Audrie Doon)." From certain statements
in the article we infer that, contrary to the usual order
of things, "Ida M. Browne" is the pen-name, but there
is always mystery where the Doones are concerned.
The article itself professes to be a plain historical account, and reads as if genuine. If it be a concoction,
it is one of the cleverest we have seen for some time.

The writer begins by confessing her surprise that
Blackmore should have succeeded in embodying the
traditions of her family so correctly in *Lorna Doone*,
and her yet greater surprise, on visiting the locality, to
find these same traditions well-known Exmoor legends.
She next refers us to Burke (not Edmund), who will
enlighten us as to the lineage of Moray. The Earl of
Moray, who was murdered on January 23rd, 1570, had

an eldest daughter Elizabeth, who ten years afterwards was married to Sir James Stuart of Doune. In 1581 the father of Sir James Stuart was created Lord Doune, and upon this he took the title of Earl of Moray. He is known distinctively as the Bonny Earl of Moray.

Mr. Thornton asserts that Blackmore invented Sir Ensor Doone, but we find from this account that Sir James Stuart of Doune had a twin brother called Ensor, who was proud, vindictive, and quarrelsome ; and, from the age of eighteen, the two were perpetually at variance respecting the rightful ownership of Doune Castle, near Stirling, in Perthshire. On February 7th, 1602, Sir James was assassinated by his brother's friend, the impoverished Marquis of Huntly, bribed, it was believed, by Ensor. Through the King's good offices, the murdered man's son was reconciled to Huntly, but never to his uncle, and, on the death of Ensor Stuart, the feud was kept up between the cousins.

In 1618 Ensor James Stuart, the "new pretender," adopted the surname " Doune," by which act he was supposed to assert still further his claim to Doune Castle. This was hotly resented by the Earl of Moray, who, attended by sixteen retainers, forced his way into his cousin's house at Stirling, and commanded him to leave Scotland, on pain of being held a prisoner, with his wife, in Doune Castle. Sir Ensor, as he now was (having received a knighthood from King James, as a member of his suite in his progress to London), refused to submit, and, in consequence, endured a week's captivity. Dame Ensor, however, implored him to give way, so at last, with a faithful servant, they journeyed to England to seek redress from the King. No good came of this effort, and, after waiting a long time in London, Sir Ensor, thoroughly chagrined, resolved to forsake the society of his kind. For thirteen days he travelled with his face to the setting sun. He then found himself in the valley of East Lyn, not far from Oare Ford, where was a half-ruined farmhouse. Entering this place, Sir Ensor and his wife made it their dwelling, and settled down.

Their four sons, as they grew up, developed rather more than their father's misanthropy and cruelty, and became a veritable scourge. Not a traveller was safe from their kind attentions, not a farmer but was forced to contribute to their ways and means; and when Ensor's sons came to marry, the handsomest of the village girls were either abducted or cajoled into becoming their wives. Naturally enough, their descendant does not regard their seventy-three years' residence in the West as a creditable chapter in the family history, since it was tarnished by a succession of the meanest and basest robberies like that in which John Ridd's father lost his life. This lady states that she has an old flint-lock pistol, fairly well preserved; and midway between stock and barrel are the words " C. Doone." On the reverse side is the word " Porlok," where, it is possible, the weapon was purchased. Miss Audrie Doon, however, thinks it more likely that the owner lived in the village.

Miss Doon is of opinion that the main body of her ancestors did not reside in the so-called Doone Valley, the remains of the buildings found there being merely those of cattle byres, which the exiles may or may not have used for penning the stock they had lifted. On the strength of family traditions she selects for their home a spot between Oare Ford and the source of East Lyn, in the wild and lonely combe to the right of the Oare road in its ascent towards the coach route across Exmoor. There is still in existence an old pair of bellows, bearing the inscription " E. D., Oare, 1627," whence it is presumed Sir Ensor was living near there at that date. She quotes also from a curious old diary kept by a member of the family in the eighteenth century, which contains the following entries :—

"September 3rd, 1747. Went to Barum on my way to the place they call Oare, whence our people came after their cruel treatment at the hands of Earl Moray."

"September 7th. Got to Oare, and then to the valley of the Lyn, the scenery very bonny, like our own land, but the part extremely wild and lonely. Wandered about, and thought of the old days, and of the family while there, which I gather were not peaceable."

Miss Doon therefore concludes that the upper and not the lower part of Hoccombe was the real abode of her forbears in the seventeenth century.

The spelling of the name, she avers, has varied at different periods. Sir Ensor, for some time after leaving his native land, kept the old Scottish orthography, with the "u." The "u" was afterwards changed to "o," and finally the "e" was dropped. "Lorna" she considers a pretty cognomen of Blackmore's own invention, the female name most common in the family being "Audrie," spelt in the same way as that of the patron saint of West Quantoxhead. Miss Doon suggests that, on their return to Scotland, the Doones crossed the Quantocks and were struck with the name. Perhaps so.

Sir Ensor died in 1684 at the venerable age of eighty-seven, and his remains were buried in the valley, though they were afterwards transferred to Scotland and re-interred at Stirling.

On August 4th a mysterious messenger arrived at Porlock. There was that about him which indicated that he had come a long way, and his errand was to the Doones. Where did they live? The people of the place directed him to the Oare Valley, and there an interview took place between him and Charles Doone, the son and heir of Sir Ensor. Since the banishment important changes had occurred in Scotland. James,

Earl of Moray, who had driven Sir Ensor away, had died in 1638 ; his successor, another James, was also dead, and now Alexander, the present Earl, desiring to atone for the wrongs done by his ancestors, invited the outlaws to return. The offer was met with a proud refusal, but, on reconsideration, Charles Doone, his three brothers and their families set out for Scotland. On the eve of their departure they gave a farewell feast, to which some of the Exmoor folk were asked, but hardly any dared to attend. Then, also, for the last time the flames rose high from the cradles of Dunkery Beacon.

The Doones were a month in reaching Scotland. On their arrival they were hospitably received by the Earl of Moray, who gave them lands and money. But the old resentful temper and habits of savagery, in which they had been reared, could not be extirpated in a day, and so they dwelt afar from Doune Castle, the stately heritage for which they had suffered so much in vain.

Miss Doon gives the following list of those living in the valley before their departure for Scotland :—

"Charles Doone, and his only son, Ensor, by a second wife, who died at the boy's birth.

"Bruce Doone (second son of Sir Ensor), his wife Dorothy, two sons, Angus and James, and a daughter.

"Nigil Doone (third son of Sir Ensor), his twin boys, Rupert and Charles, his wife, and two daughters.

"Rowland Doone (fourth son of Sir Ensor) and his sons, Stuart and Hugh."

There were also four menservants, sons of one Jamie Beaton, who had accompanied the exiles from Scotland. Charles Doone, who was probably the original of "Carver" Doone, is claimed as her great-great-great-grandfather by the lady to whom the world is indebted for these interesting particulars. To the question, "How came Mr. Blackmore to know so much of the history of the Doones ?" our authority can only reply by supposing that he must have got it from some Scottish family of his acquaintance.* But he did not know all, or, if he did, preferred to disguise his knowledge in the way we find in *Lorna Doone*.

With regard to Tom Faggus, Mr. Thornton observes: " I never could make out from my numerous gossips at what period they thought that 'Veggis' or 'Faggus' rode on his strawberry horse, to the discomfort of all people who were possessed of a little money in North Devon, but he was supposed to have had his head-quarters on Exmoor." Thus much is certain, that Faggus was heard of at Dulverton long before Black-more drew his portrait; and the name "Fergus," which may be found in the plaster of an old kitchen at South Court, Exford, is popularly believed to refer to the notorious highwayman.

Here are a couple of characteristic "Vaggus" stories, which are strictly traditional. He had been taken prisoner at Exebridge, near Dulverton, and begged as a privilege that he might be allowed to see his mare. The request was refused, whereupon "Vaggus" whistled, and the mare, hearing the familiar signal, broke down the stable door, and fought her way to him. "Vaggus" leapt on her back. At both ends of the bridge, how-ever, were lines of men, determined to prevent his escape. Seeing this, the highwayman turned the mare's head towards the parapet, and, jumping into the bed of the stream, was soon out of the reach of his pursuers.

The other tale relates to a farmer who was returning from Tiverton market, and having been overtaken by a smart fellow, was indiscreet enough to tell him how well he had done, and what a lot of money he had with him. His companion, amazed at his simplicity, inquired

* According to a recent paragraph in the *Daily Telegraph*, the real John Ridd, the man whose acquaintance with Exmoor was turned to such brilliant account by Blackmore, was one John Barwell, of Lynmouth, who died in 1899 in the Royal Hospital for Incurables at Wandsworth.

whether he had ever heard of one "Vaggus," who was said to relieve travellers of their superfluous coin.

"Aw, iss!" replied the farmer, "I've yeard o' un, but I ban't afeard o' no Vagguses."

"Oh, very well," said the stranger, smiling; "I thought it only fair to warn you. And, having wished the farmer a courteous good day at a cross-ways, the gentleman rode off and quickly disappeared. The next incident was the apparition of a masked figure some few miles further on, and the stern command, "Stand and deliver!"

The terrified farmer complied with indecent haste. As soon as the pelf had been made over, the mask was removed, and the features of his late companion revealed to the mortified agriculturist.

"Here!" cried "Vaggus," "take back your money, and another time, when you speak of Tom Vaggus, don't brag too loudly of your valour."

Tradition does not deal in dates—an omission, by the way, for which Miss Doon makes ample amends—but in considering the worth of this argument against the historical existence of the Doones, there is one circumstance of which we ought not to lose sight, namely, that the parish registers in the Exmoor district begin late, and have been ill kept. The Oare register begins with the year 1674, and is not only imperfect, but in places illegible. The Cutcombe register begins fifty years earlier, but for nearly a century is very imperfect. The Exford register is better, but even the Exford register is not perfect. Obviously it will not do to depend on such incomplete records as negative evidence, disproving the existence of those robbers. The fact is, sheep-stealing, till a comparatively recent period, was quite a common practice on Exmoor. In 1808 a farmer told Mr. Vancouver that in five years, thanks to the enterprise of these gentry, he had lost no fewer than a hundred and eight sheep. The formation of an organised gang during the horrible confusion arising out of the great Civil War is very far from improbable ; and here it may be observed that the legend of the Doones is not the only memory, locally speaking, of that sorrowful time. Speaking of Porlock, Savage declares that "many of the old houses are built with the chimneys towards the street—a mode of building, tradition says, of the Civil War in the reign of Charles I., and adopted for the purpose of protecting the inhabitants from the prying eyes or secret attacks of evil-disposed persons of an opposite party." The Doones were probably an exceptionally desperate and dare-devil crew, and thus left their mark on the imagination of the peasantry.

Due consideration of this evidence will, we believe, restore *Lorna Doone* to the position from which Mr. Rawle has, to some extent, ousted it—as a more developed and artistic presentment of a story which, in its ruder features, had long been associated with the bogs and fogs of Exmoor. Let us recall Blackmore's own description of his book. "The work," he says, "is called a 'romance,' because the incidents, characters, time, and scenery are alike romantic ; and in shaping this old tale the writer neither dares nor desires to claim for it the dignity, or cumber it with the difficulty, of an historical novel. And yet he thinks that the outlines are filled in more carefully, and the situations (however simple) more warmly coloured and quickened, than a reader would expect to find in what is called a 'legend.'" This account is at once explicit and true. In the foregoing paragraphs we have the background of the story, or, as it may be better to style it, the sort of rough process of which *Lorna Doone* is the consummation.

> Prose-poet of the fabled West,
>   Ere school and railway had begun
>   To fuse our shires and brogues in one,
> And equalise the worst and best ;

THE DOONES

While Devon vowels fluted yet
  By Dart and Lynn their mellow length,
  While flourished still in Saxon strength
The consonants of Somerset ;

Your Exmoor epic fixed the hues
  That lingered on by combe and tor,
  And in the hollow vale of Oare
You found a matter for your muse.

HERBERT WARREN.

CHAPTER V

AN EL DORADO

MR. RAWLE is a little inconsistent. After disavowing all belief in the existence of the Doones on account of the absence of documentary proof, he proceeds to say, "No record has been discovered as to when the parish of Oare was disafforested." His explanation of the lapse, however, is doubtless correct. Forest laws and customs gradually became obsolete, and when in 1641 it was enacted that forests in which courts had not been held for sixty years should cease to be regarded as such, it is easy to see the inevitable result. The Crown had formerly encroached on the rights of subjects; subjects now encroached on the property of the Crown, and so things went on till, late in the eighteenth century, Parliament found it necessary to interfere. In both area and value Exmoor, as well as other royal forests, had suffered considerable diminution. "Numberless unlicensed inclosures had been made, transfers effected under colour of sale, timber illegally disposed of, and numerous other irregularities committed" (Rawle).

In March, 1784, a lease of the forest was granted to Sir Thomas Dyke Acland, Baronet, for a term of ten years commencing on August 1st, 1804. According to the first report of the Commissioners of Woods and Forests, in 1787, the annual value of the property was £296 10s. 1½d., the fine paid for the last lease £510, and

F

the old rent £46 13s. 4d. This was the last of the
Crown leases. In 1815 an Act of Parliament vested in
the King certain parts of the Forest of Exmoor, and
arranged for the inclosure of the same. The area of
the forest was computed at 22,400 acres, of which a
little over one-half was assigned to the Crown. One-
eighth went to Sir Thomas Acland in lieu of tithes,
while the residue was apportioned amongst landowners
whose estates adjoined the forest, and the proprietors of
certain old inclosed tenements, who claimed for their
tenants a right to turn out and depasture their sheep
on the forest on payment of stated terms. The King's
moiety was offered for sale, and the *Taunton Courier* of
August 12th, 1818, thus announced the result :—

"Mr. Knight, of Worcestershire, has purchased the allot-
ment given in Right of the Crown on Exmoor Forest, con-
sisting of 10,000 acres, for £50,000. The property is near
Simond's Bath, and the greater part of it is to be enclosed by
a wall, in the centre of which a handsome residence is to be
built. The spot affords great facilities for the purpose, and
will, under the judicious plans in contemplation, become a
most enviable possession."

Mr. Knight was evidently full of confidence, for soon
after he purchased the Acland share for 5,555 guineas.
Moreover, by his agreement with the Government, he
was obliged to construct roads. Up to this time there
had been no vehicular traffic over Exmoor, everything
having been carried on the backs of pack-horses. All
will remember the scene in *Lorna Doone* on the arrival
of the faithful serving-man at Tiverton School—how the
Blundellites crowded against the gate in the expecta-
tion of seeing a good string of pack-horses pass ; and
Blackmore's allusions to the roads explain clearly
enough why this method of transport was preferred.

"From Tiverton town to the town of Oare is a very long
and painful road, and in good truth the traveller must make

his way, as the saying is; for the way is still unmade, at least, on this side of Dulverton, although there is less danger now than in the time of my schooling; for now a good horse may go there without much cost of leaping, but when I was a boy the spurs would fail when needed most, by reason of the slough-cake. It is to the credit of this age, and our advance

OLD BLUNDELL'S SCHOOL GATEWAY

upon fatherly ways, that now we have laid down rods and fagots, and even stump oaks here and there, so that a man in good daylight need not sink, if he be quite sober. There is nothing I have striven at more than doing my duty, way-warden over Exmoor."

Between Bampton and Dulverton things were not so bad.

" The road from Bampton to Dulverton had not been very delicate, yet nothing to complain of much—no deeper, indeed, than the hocks of a horse, except in the rotten places ! "

The reader may be tempted to think this account improbable and exaggerated, but that is only because he has had no experience of similar conditions. The state of the West Country roads in the early part of the last century (by which time, it may be supposed, there had been attempts at improvement) has been well described by Mr. Thornton, and his remarks point to very primitive arrangements :—

" The roads were in a very bad condition. The old Roman roads, long neglected, were nearly gone. The Devonshire devious ways existed, which had been formed by the feet of pack-horses, who wandered right and left to avoid soft places until a track was made, against which banks were gradually thrown up to keep the cattle from straying from the adjacent fields (thus stereotyping for ever the wanderings of the horses).

" These trackways were deeply water-worn and often shelved to a point in the centre, where large, loose stones lay roughly scattered. In my time, by day and by night I have traversed scores of such by-ways. In 1808 Mr. Vancouver, who was employed to make a report by the then Board of Agriculture, writes from experience of the horrors of a charge of pack-horses in one of these defiles. On they came without bridles or conductors, with their burdens brushing both sides of the deep-cut lane. There was nothing to be done except to turn and fly to a wider place until the string had passed on, led by some veteran charger who knew perfectly well where he was going.

" The roads twisted considerably, as I have said, by reason of the wanderings of the horses, but as moors and waste lands were gradually taken in and enclosed, they twisted more and more, because the old trackway would often, in such cases, be disregarded by those who were enclosing, and the traffic would consequently have to go round the angles of a newly made fence until the old road could be resumed. There was practically no such thing on any but a very few of the main roads as a public conveyance. Everything was done on foot or on horseback. Even the very farmyard manure, and lime, and the earth from the bottom of the steep fields, were carried on horses' backs."

Manure was, in fact, sent out in wooden vessels called "dorsels," and corn brought home on long crooks. In some places the ground was so steep that carriages simply could not be used.

The most superficial research into the habits of Old Exmoor will reveal the fact that the pack-horse was ubiquitous and indispensable. In 1765, when four of the Winsford bells were recast by Bilbie, they were broken up on the spot and the metal carried to Cullompton on pack-horses. Again, there is the legend of Mole's Chamber. On the western confine of Exmoor is a desolate building, once the "Acland Arms," with its "upping-stone" and porch still in fair preservation, while before it stretches a ruined garden. Hard by is a bog inclosed by a low wall which is broken in places—one of the sources of the Barle, and, as tradition asserts, the scene of a tragedy. Farmer Mole was returning from Southmolton market astride a horse which was laden with lime in packs. In the darkness—or perhaps he was drunk—he guided his horse into this bog, where many years afterwards the remains of man and beast were discovered as on the day of their disappearance, preserved by the antiseptic property of the peat. It is needless to add that the ghosts of Farmer Mole and his nag still haunt the locality.

Mr. Kingdon, of Simonsbath, told us that his aunt, when a young woman, drove a team of pack-horses from Southmolton to Corner Brake on Exmoor for the purpose of fetching slate. He can point out the old tracks, which do not correspond in the least with the modern roads, and are remarkable for their directness.

Mr. Thornton says that, when he went to Selworthy in 1847, the most common specimen of the equine race

was the pack-horse, or what passed as such, viz. a light
cart-horse, with active habits.   Such animals were bred
between a cart-horse and a light hackney, and, though
possessing the necessary shape, were more or less the
products of chance.   It was very different with the old
pack-horse, which was bred by a pack-horse from a pack-
mare, and might be termed in some sort a thoroughbred.   The only exceptions were those with a strain of
pony blood—smaller, but, if anything, more valuable.
Generally about fifteen hands high, it was impossible to
conceive a more useful animal.   He was "Jack of all
trades," and as country people were not so well off as
at present, they naturally looked to utility before anything else.   The conduct of the farmers in parting with
this admirable stock—some of which were fast trotters—
is hard to account for, but it is a fact that they have
been crossed up with thoroughbreds to such an extent
that they are now practically extinct.   A relic of ancient
times still survives in the sign of a public-house at
Dunster—the "Horse and Crooks."

Mr. Knight fulfilled his part of the compact, and the
roads over Exmoor will compare with any in the kingdom.   In winter they give the watchful surveyor some
trouble owing to the sudden apparition of springs,
which necessitates piping.   Nor is suitable stone for
metalling easily obtainable.   The net result, however, is
creditable both to the original makers and to those with
whom the responsibility of maintenance now rests.
Mr. Knight found a valuable ally in Parson Ralph,
of Exford, who used his influence with the farmers
of the district.   Farmers as a class are intensely conservative and not much disposed to spend money for
public purposes.   However, Mr. Ralph, himself the son
of a Cumberland statesman, exercised some kind of
witchery over them, with the result that there was soon
a marked improvement in the parish roads.   Then

Mr. Farmer, experiencing the effects in his "putts," was fain to admit that it was "a good thing done."

Under the enterprising Mr. Knight—the Cecil Rhodes of the West—Exmoor entered upon an entirely new phase. From being stationary and clannish it became painfully cosmopolitan. There was hardly an experiment which the new owner did not try, in order to make the most of his venture; and, so far as intentions went, the country was revolutionised. Instead of the pack-horse came the Arab. Cheviot sheep began to occupy the hills. Hundreds of tame deer were introduced, but as they wrought havoc on the corn, "slithering" the ears through their teeth and leaving the stalk standing, Mr. Knight repented, and the deer were killed, wherever they could be found. There were imported also black Scotch cattle, which were used in ploughing, eight in a team, at Honeymead and elsewhere, and in fetching coal from Porlock to Simonsbath in a butt. A colossal mansion was begun at the back of Simonsbath House, and, until it was dismantled in quite recent days by Lord Ebrington, the shell remained, like a ruined keep, and might have been named "Knight's Folly."

Mr. Knight, however, appears to have rested his best hopes on the mines. There is an Exmoor saying that "Mundick rides a good horse," which means that, where mundic is found near the surface, good metal lies below. At one time no fewer than four companies were simultaneously engaged in the endeavour to extract ore at a profit from the bowels of Exmoor. The Welsh Dowlais Company carried on operations at Cornham Ford and Hangley Cleave close by Span Head; the Lancashire Snider Company, in the South Forest; a Plymouth Company, at Picked Stones; and in conjunction with the Plymouth Company, Ebbw Vale tried its luck at Sparcombe (or Sparrowcombe) in the North Forest. All these attempts turned out utter failures,

There is plenty of iron on Exmoor, but the cost of removal over those soft roads was found to be prohibitive. It may be mentioned that the Wheal Eliza, as it was called, immediately below Simonsbath, was at first worked as a copper mine; and here it was that the notorious Burgess concealed the body of his young daughter whom he had barbarously murdered. The abandoned works now present a melancholy spectacle, not perhaps out of keeping with the sombreness which is characteristic of all Exmoor scenery. Besides his Scotch shepherds and Welsh and Cornish miners, Mr. Knight imported into the neighbourhood a gang of Irish labourers, who constructed what is known as "Paddy's Fence" at the foot of the Chains. He also caused to be made a large reservoir called Pinkworthy (or Pinkery) Pond, which originally covered seven acres of ground, though its present dimensions probably do not exceed one acre. From Pinkworthy Pond to Simonsbath Mr. Knight proposed cutting a canal, a section of which, about midway between the two places, was recently pointed out to us. This was one more of Mr. Knight's wild-goose schemes, which came to nothing on account of the natural difficulties and the consequent expense. Pinkworthy Pond, a few years ago, was the scene of a suicide. A farmer named Gammon, after failing to win the affections of a barmaid, rode madly off and carried out his threat of drowning himself. For a long time, however, the body could not be found, and the pond had to be emptied. As may be supposed, the incident excited widespread interest, and thousands of visitors thronged to the spot whilst the operations of dredging, etc., were in progress.

During the summer of 1855 the late Mr. James Payn, the novelist, resided at Lynmouth, and, in company with his old college friend, Mr. Thornton, went over to Simonsbath to see a horse race. Of this he afterwards gave an account in a magazine, stating that three untidy boys, mounted on three small shaggy ponies, rode away in a fog into a bog, and never came back again !

We have now to record the circumstances attending the erection of Exmoor into an ecclesiastical parish, and the building of a church and parsonage. In 1818, when the forest was purchased from the Duchy of Cornwall, it was stipulated that the new owner should assign twelve acres for church purposes. The Duchy, on its part, undertook to endow the living with a hundred and fifty pounds a year whenever the population should amount to five hundred souls. These conditions were realised in 1855, and as the five thousand pounds set apart from the purchase-money had been augmented by accumulations of interest, ample funds were available for carrying the scheme into effect. It so happened that about this time an intimate friend of Mr. Knight, the Rev. W. H. Thornton, contemplated resigning the curacy of Lynton, and on being asked whether he would care to accept the first presentation to the living of Exmoor, intimated his consent. Whereupon, as the living was in the gift of the Crown, Mr. Knight wrote to Lord Palmerston, urging his friend's claims. The famous statesman had been acquainted with Mr. Thornton's father in early life, and, partly for that reason, partly to gratify the owner of the property, readily assented to the appointment of a clergyman whose qualifications for the post were already evident, and were destined to be proved still further in connection with some trying episodes, notably the Burgess murder. Mr. Thornton returned his thanks, and the matter was settled.

The erection of the new church and vicarage was executed by contract under the Government Department of Woods and Forests, and the Commissioners sent down a clerk of the works. It turned out anything but a remunerative undertaking for the contractor, Mr. Hole,

of King's Brompton, who is said to have been practically ruined by it, while, by Mr. Thornton's account, the
clerk of the works was the reverse of efficient. After his
acceptance of the living, the incumbent—he was a "perpetual curate"—had gone for a long tour on the Conti-
nent, whence he returned eager to enter on his duties.
He found, however, that the builders were behind with
their work, and that there was no immediate prospect
of getting into residence. Accordingly he obtained
accommodation at a Mrs. Bevan's, where he was joined
by a friend, Mr. Torr, who was to act as a sort of lay
reader.

Mr. Thornton was then young and inexperienced, but
he seems to have had a capable head for business, and
as he was for ever riding over the moor, he soon discovered that something was gravely amiss. To use his
own phrase, "great rascality was being practised." At
length he said to the clerk, "Let me look at your speci-
fications." With much reluctance the official passed him
the papers, and the clergyman found that the house was
to be fitted with lead weighing six pounds to the square
foot, and with piping to correspond. On trial the
lead proved light, and as other material supplied was
similarly inferior, he ordered everything to be removed
on pain of complaint being made to the Board. As the
result he had many black looks and an insulting letter
or two, but his object seemed to be attained. The light
lead was stripped from the roofs, the weak piping dug
up, and, so far as he could discern, "dishonesty" had
ceased. But the clergyman did not know all. Where
he discovered one defect ten others escaped his notice,
so that he had later to suffer much inconvenience. For
one thing the church was faced with Bath stone. This
in itself was not a happy arrangement, since the stone
is eminently unsuitable for a site eleven hundred feet
above the sea-level. To make matters worse, however,

it was taken from the surface of an inferior quarry, thrown out of the boat in which it was brought from Bristol, and allowed to remain in the sea at Combe Martin until it became saturated with salt water.

The winter of 1856–7 was remarkable for its heavy rains and still more trying frosts, and the incumbent was distressed to find the stone peeling off in flakes. " It was enough to make me cry with vexation to see my pretty little church, my church not six months old, with a cartload of débris beneath each window, and great rifts in the mullions and window-sills."

The next visitation may have reminded Mr. Thornton of the patriarch Job. It came in the shape of a gale. Those who know Exmoor in winter, and have experienced the force of the blast, will easily credit the statement that every slate on the church and house gaped "like a sick oyster," save for some hundreds that were whirled away to a distance. It was then found that iron nails had been used in place of the copper ones for which a confiding Government had paid. Inside the house things were no better. Locks would not work, and handles, if they turned at all, turned completely off. No wonder that the incumbent despaired. Seeing no other resource, he applied to Mr. Knight, who was a member of Parliament, and through him obtained some redress, though matters were still very far from satisfactory. The church was supposed to be completed in October, 1857, when the new Bishop, Lord Auckland, an old friend of the incumbent, arrived from Wells in bad weather to perform the ceremony of consecration.

Mr. Thornton notes, with some disgust, that in order to obtain a "perpetual" curacy of the value of a hundred and fifty pounds per annum, he had to lay out nearly fifty pounds in fees and expenses. Even when this had been paid he found that the Government had left him a good deal to do. Gardens had to be made, the house

fenced round with oak posts, and rocks grubbed up to
form paths and flower-beds. Another source of expense
was the wall of the kitchen garden, and trees and shrubs
also had to be bought. " In short," says Mr. Thornton,
" the place was handed over to me incomplete, and I
not only had to complete it, to furnish the house, and
replace the fittings with good, but also to pay heavy
dilapidations when, in 1860, I resigned the incumbency."
This last injustice was, perhaps, worse than the first, and
will touch a sympathetic chord in the breasts of many
who, though they have had no experience in "hand-
selling" a living, are acquainted only too well with the
exactions of the Diocesan Surveyor.

The parish was pretty large—more than twenty
thousand acres—and, in making his calculations, Mr.
Thornton expected to have to ride twenty-five miles
in order to visit his more distant parishioners, should
his presence be required. At first, however, the puzzle
was to find them all. Hidden away in cottages situated
in outlying combes and mires, they were not easily got
at, and, moreover, were a "mixed lot"—scarcely the
sort of people the average clergyman would select as
members of his flock. "They were from all parts of
England, for the lowness of the rents per acre had
attracted broken-down farmers from afar, and the native
population was rather wild, lawless, and uncivilised."
The half-century or so that has since elapsed has
wrought considerable changes externally, and now the
Exmoor folk seem quite decent and orderly, but there
is perhaps truth in Jefferies' remark that the effects
of civilisation are largely superficial, that the people
are true descendants of their "rude forefathers." Only
they will not allow you to see it.

CHAPTER VI

THE SPORT OF KINGS

APART from Mr. Knight's experiments, the humours (or woes) of church-building, and the happily rare excitement of a murder or suicide, the annals of Exmoor consist largely in accounts of runs with the staghounds. Even when told in the graphic style of which Mr. Evered is a master, these narratives are not exempt from a certain sameness; related in the plain, business-like manner exemplified by good old Mr. Boyce, they are a weariness to the flesh, unless, of course, the circumstances are quite exceptional. Before closing this section we hope to render some account of a run which will remain forever memorable not only for staghunters and "those who know," but for the general public — the run in which his present gracious Majesty took part. Meanwhile it will be expedient to offer a short résumé of the Hunt up to the date of that episode.

As we have seen, Sir Hugh Pollard kept hounds at Simonsbath in the days of the Tudors. Between that time and the commencement of the eighteenth century there is a blank. Although the Civil War, the Monmouth Rebellion, and the Jacobite risings of '15 were disturbing factors, we cannot suppose that during the long interval staghunting was entirely suspended. We should imagine rather that the reason of the silence is the want of a *vates sacer* to chronicle the achievements of the mighty men. However that may be, when we again hear of staghunting the hounds are under the sway of Mr. Walter, of Stevenstone, an ancestor of the Rolles, and Lord Orford, who were conjointly Foresters of Exmoor under grant from the Crown. Lord Orford was succeeded in this post by Mr. Dyke of Holnicote, who also kept hounds and for many years hunted the country with great success. On Mr. Dyke's decease, his niece's husband, Sir Thomas Acland, who now assumed the name of Dyke in addition to his own, was appointed Forester or Ranger of Exmoor. He kept staghounds, and down to the year 1770 hunted the country in the most glorious style. Herein he was even outdone by his son, who bore the same name and was likewise Ranger of the forest.

From 1775 to 1784 the pack was kept by Major, afterwards Colonel, Bassett, of Watermouth Castle, who seems to have been the first person, not being a Ranger of the forest, to act in that capacity. In 1784 Sir Thomas again took the command, which he retained to the time of his death (May 17th, 1794). On the death of Sir Thomas Acland, Colonel Bassett once more became master ; and after his decease the hounds were kept by Lord Fortescue, of Castle Hill, Southmolton. This arrangement, however, lasted for one season only, the hounds being then converted into a subscription pack, of which Mr. Worth, of Worth House, Tiverton, accepted the management. In 1811 Lord Graves, of Bishop's Court, near Exeter, who had seen his first stag killed after a fine run of six hours and a half in 1805, took over the command, but his reign was of brief duration. In the following year the hounds returned to Castle Hill, and the next six years rank among the most memorable in the annals of the Hunt. We are tempted to quote Dr. Collyns' description of them :—

"Those again were glorious days. The halls of Castle Hill rang merrily with the wassail of the hunters, and many a pink issued from the hospitable seats of the neighbouring

THE HUNTSMAN AND THE WHIP

squires, on the bright autumn mornings, to participate in the pleasures of the chase. When a good stag had been killed, the custom was for James Tout, the huntsman, to enter the dining-room at Castle Hill after dinner in full costume, with his horn in his hand, and after he had sounded a mort, 'Success to staghunting' was solemnly drunk by the assembled company in port wine :—

> 'Whose father grape grew fat
> On Lusitanian summers';

after which Tout again retired to his own place, and rested himself after the labours of the day in company with one or two favourites, whose escape from the kennel had been connived at. There, before the ample fire, the huntsman dozed away the evening, and killed his deer again, while

> 'The staghounds, weary with the chase,
> Lay stretched upon the floor,
> And urged in dreams the forest race
> From Castle Hill to wild Exmoor.'

The drinking of the toast in the fashion above mentioned probably had its origin in an ancient form of a more elaborate character."

Mr. Collyns then quotes from some papers contributed, in 1824, to the *Sporting Magazine*, by a writer signing himself " Nimrod," who, with reference to this particular custom, observes :—

" In more chivalrous times, or, I should rather say, in those times when the natural ebullition of feeling was less controlled by the forms and ceremonies of society than it is at the present day, the head of the deer, after a good run, was produced in the evening with a silver cup in his mouth, out of which the favourite toast was drunk. The custom is still kept up by the huntsman, whippers-in, farmers, and others, and the operation is performed in the following manner :—The cup is placed in the stag's mouth, secured with a cord to prevent its falling out. When it is filled to the brim, the person who is to drink it holds a horn in each hand, and brings it to his mouth, when he must finish it at one draught, and then turn the head downwards, bringing the top in contact with his breast, to convince his companions that he has drunk it to the dregs, otherwise he is subject to a fine. . . . In days still more gone by a fine was

G

imposed on a man who left the field before the deer was killed."

On Lord Fortescue resigning the hounds, they reverted to their former position as a subscription pack, under the direction of Mr. Stucley Lucas, of Baron's Down, near Dulverton. He kept the command for six years, but his style of hunting seems to have displeased certain of the landowners and subscribers, with the result that the sport was discontinued, and the noble hounds sold in London. This occurred in 1825, and the purchaser, a German baron, deported the animals to his own country.

The exact origin of the old Exmoor staghounds is obscure. Mr. Collyns is confident, however, that among the ancestors of the pack, which at the time of the sale consisted of about thirty couples, were the bloodhound and the old southern hound. They ranged from twenty-six to twenty-eight inches in height, and their colour was hare-pied, yellow, yellow and white, or badger-pied. They had long ears, large throats, deep muzzles, and deep chests. Perfect in tongue, their voices might be heard—whether hunting in the water, on half-scent, or baying a deer—at vast distances. Even when running at speed, they always gave plenty of tongue. Owing to their great size, the long heather and rough sedges of the forest offered but feeble resistance to their crossing. A painting of the hounds, whose melody, Collyns declares, will never be equalled o'er the hills and woods of Devon and Somerset, is among the most treasured possessions of his son, Mr. John Barrett Collyns.

The abolition of the old pack of staghounds did not spell a period of safety and repose to the deer, which became victims of systematic efforts on the part of poachers, the latter being aided and abetted and, no doubt in many cases, paid by the much-suffering farmer. The war was carried on so ruthlessly and persistently that in some parts of the country which these animals had made their haunts no deer were to be found. They had been either driven away or exterminated. These depredations, as well as regret for the ancient sport, led to a temporary revival of staghunting. In 1827 Sir Arthur Chichester, of Youlstone, near Barnstaple, got together a fine pack composed of drafts from various kennels of foxhounds, and this pack hunted the country with much success till the spring of 1833. Sir Arthur then gave up the hounds, and encouraged by the apathy of landowners, poachers renewed their operations, with disastrous results to the already wasted herd.

Several years passed without steps being taken for the promotion of staghunting until, in 1837, Mr. Charles Palk Collyns, of Dulverton, with the assistance of his neighbours, Mr. Stucley Lucas, of Baron's Down, and Mr. George Hall Peppin, of Old Shute, effectually appealed to the feelings of West Country sportsmen, and subscriptions were promised, enabling him to bring into the field a new pack of staghounds, for which he consented to act as treasurer. This was not the first occasion on which Mr. Collyns had exerted himself for the preservation of the sport. In 1826 he had written to Lord Porchester advocating the establishment of a pack, and had received from that nobleman a sympathetic reply, concluding with the offer of an annual subscription of thirty pounds. A similar amount was promised by Sir Peregrine Acland, of Fairfield, near Bridgwater. Although no staghunter himself, he deplored the cessation of a sport so greatly enjoyed by the poorer classes, who, he remarked, looked forward to a meet of the staghounds in their neighbourhood as a partial holiday. It was, however, no auspicious time for attempting the restoration of the Hunt, since the differences of opinion which had brought about the sale of the old hounds were still fresh and vigorous.

Even after the new pack had come into existence, Mr. Collyns found his treasurership no sinecure. In a number of cases subscriptions were promised but not paid, until in June, 1841, when the accounts were audited, there was discovered to be an adverse balance of no less than £531. This state of things naturally caused the treasurer some anxiety, and in 1842 he informed the Hon. Newton Fellowes (afterwards Lord Portsmouth), who had presided at the meeting, that, without large additions to the subscription list, the establishment could not be kept up. "So you want a stop-gap, do you?" was the reply. "Well, I stopped the gap once in North Devon [i.e. as a candidate for Parliament], and I'll stop a gap again. Rather than allow the sport to perish, or stand in peril of destruction, I will keep the pack at my own expense, except when they are actually engaged in deer-hunting, and you shall employ the surplus of subscriptions in liquidating the debts due to you."

The proposal was gratefully accepted, and in course of time the debt was reduced to £75, which sum was never paid, and apparently represents the extent to which the enthusiastic Mr. Collyns was out of pocket. While all felt thankful to Mr. Fellowes for stepping into the breach when the fortunes of the chase were so critical, it cannot be said that his management of the pack gave universal satisfaction. In fact, the evidence points to a recrudescence of the mutinous spirit that had proved fatal to the Hunt twenty years before.

The landowners, who were the chief supporters of staghunting and afforded valuable aid in the preservation of the deer, found fault with Mr. Fellowes for his practice of drawing the coverts with the whole pack, instead of "tufting," the result being the destruction of a good many "unwarrantable" stags, and of deer out of season. In 1847 he resigned and was succeeded by Sir

Arthur Chichester, son of the baronet before mentioned, who hunted the country for one year.

In 1849 an innovation was decided on. Hitherto the masters had all been local men, but in the existing circumstances it is no wonder that West Country sportsmen fought shy of the position. An invitation was sent, therefore, to Mr. Theobald, who had been accustomed to hunt carted deer in the neighbourhood of Cheltenham. That gentleman acceded to the request and brought into the field a fine pack of hounds, whose achievements, however, quite failed to realise expectations. He stayed two months, and during that time his hounds succeeded in killing just three deer.

In 1850 Mr. George Luxton, of Winkleigh, got together a pack at short notice, and with this he continued to hunt during the spring of 1851. Mr. Luxton was a good sportsman, with a competent knowledge of woodcraft, but his scratch pack proved unequal to the work it was called upon to perform. In the autumn of 1851, Captain West brought down his pack of staghounds, which had been hunting carted deer around Bath. This experiment proved more successful. The hounds were placed under the command of "Sam," who had been Mr. Theobald's huntsman, and under his tuition gradually learnt to negotiate the formidable bank-fences. They were initiated also into the mysteries of water-hunting, a form of sport by which they were at first much perplexed. Captain West, however, did not believe in "foreigners" as masters, and strongly impressed on the subscribers the advisability of choosing a leader from amongst themselves.

The Hunt was now face to face with the old problem, which, in the light of previous experience, might well have appeared insoluble. The crisis was surmounted by the sportsmanship of Mr. Thomas Carew, of Collipriest, who had won a reputation as master of the Tiverton Foxhounds. Staghunting and foxhunting, however, though allied pursuits, are not exactly identical, and John Beal, who held the horn, soon found that his undoubted qualifications for the latter did not assure an equal measure of success in the former. Yet his pluck and determination were admirable, nor did they go unrewarded, as is proved by the trophies of the chase that still adorn the hall of Collipriest. Mr. Carew having hunted for the season of 1852-3, Captain West again made his appearance amidst gratifying tokens of popularity and esteem. His pack, piloted by "Sam," was ready for its work, having become well acquainted with the country on the occasion of its last visit. The consequence was a brilliant season, marked by many a fine run across the moor and the inclosed land around.

Notwithstanding this interval of sunshine, the prospects of staghunting could not be considered otherwise than gloomy when, in 1855, renewed efforts were made for the support of a pack. A subscription list was opened, and Mr. Fenwick (afterwards Mr. Fenwick Bisset), of Pixton Park, Dulverton, having been approached, consented to take the command. To those who know the facts it is a mere truism to state that, since the first beginnings of staghunting, no mastership will compare with that of Mr. Bisset, who held the reins for the long period of twenty-six years. The element of time, however, constitutes his least claim on the gratitude of posterity. When he assumed the management, there was scarcely a warrantable stag in the country, and only a few hinds. Thanks to his popularity and skill and the ungrudging way in which he maintained the Hunt, a very large stock of both was handed over to his successor.

Mr. Bisset's success, then, was great, and of this he owed a large—the largest part to himself. It is however, only fair to remember that he was effectively supported by a gentleman who acted as secretary during the many years of his mastership—namely, his friend and neighbour, Mr. Samuel Hayman Warren, of Dulverton, who was an excellent sportsman and a man of great geniality and tact. He was fortunate, too, in the possession of such staunch and able allies as Mr. C. P. Collyns and the Rev. John Russell, each of whom was a host in himself. Russell, particularly, was instrumental in procuring for Mr. Bisset the crowning glory of his long and happy reign. We allude to the visit of the then Prince of Wales, our present King.

In 1876 His Royal Highness promised Russell, who was his guest at Sandringham, that he would journey to the West and see for himself what the staghunting was like, of which he had heard so much from the venerable sportsman. The illness of one of his boys, and, later, the death of the Princess Alice, necessitated delays, but at length in the autumn of 1879 the welcome announcement was made that the Prince was about to pay a visit to Mr. George Fownes Luttrell, at Dunster Castle. It was not the first time that a Prince of Wales stayed at the Castle, since, as has been pointed out, Charles II. lodged beneath its roof during the Civil War. Few persons, however, were aware that His Royal Highness was in reality entertained by a very, very distant cousin. The accompanying table will prove that such was the case.

Edward I. m. Eleanor of Castile.

Edward II.

Elizabeth m. Humphry Bohun, Earl of Hereford.

Margaret Bohun m. Hugh Courtenay, Earl of Devon.

The Lady Elisabeth m. Sir John Vere, and secondly Sir Andrew Luttrell.

Sir Hugh Luttrell.

On Thursday, the 21st of August, the Prince duly
arrived, and the inhabitants of Dunster gave him a right
loyal welcome. Near Mr. Risdon's homestead had been
erected a triumphal arch surmounted by a plume of
feathers. A little further on was another arch, and at the
"Luttrell Arms" yet another, this last being a very fine
specimen interwoven with heather-blossom, laurel, oak,
etc. Everywhere floated flags and bannerets, on some
of which was inscribed the motto *Ich dien*, while at the
entrance to the castle was a handsome castellated arch.
Volunteers were drawn up outside the railway station,
and, on the appearance of the Prince, accompanied by
Mr. Luttrell and Viscount Bridport, presented arms.
The royal party drove to the Castle in a carriage and
pair, and were followed by a cavalcade of Mr. Luttrell's
tenantry, numbering about one hundred.

The next day the Prince proceeded to the meet,
which was at Hawkcombe Head, in a carriage with four
horses and two postillions, the other occupants being
Mr. Luttrell, the Rev. John Russell, and Prince Louis of
Battenberg. The pack, consisting of the old and some
young hounds, was already at the rendezvous in charge
of Arthur Heal, and looked in fit condition to sustain
its high reputation. The field included many well-
known local sportsmen, such as Mr. Stucley Lucas,
of Baron's Down, Mr. Warren and Mr. Collyns, of
Dulverton, Mr. and Mrs. Froude Bellew, Earl Fortescue,
Lord Ebrington, Mr. Joyce, Mr. Chorley, Mr. Nicholas
Snow, Captain Acland, and Sir Thomas Dyke Acland.
Neither the late Sir Thomas Acland nor his predecessor
was much interested in staghunting, and, indeed, the
former is said to have declared that this was the first
time he had hunted a stag, and that he would never
hunt one again. We do not know what truth there
may be in the story, but as the majority of runs take
place over the Acland estates, the family, one may

ENTRANCE GATEWAY, DUNSTER CASTLE

presume, is still friendly to a sport in which former generations of the name gained such renown.

The Prince, who was dressed in plain clothes, chatted freely and appeared charmed with the beauty of the landscape—those ridges fringed with dark woods, those lofty headlands, the sunlit surface of the Severn Sea and, beyond, the white cliffs of Wales. There was a brief halt for luncheon, and then the huntsman trotted off with the tufters to try Westcott brake. The harbourer knew he had a warrantable stag there, but it was a long time before the cunning animal could be roused, and then he resorted to every artifice rather than face the crowd. First he put up a hind and then a young male deer to take his place while he lay close beneath the shadow of the dense foliage. After it had been tried for nearly two hours to force him thence, the attempt was abandoned.

Mr. Warren now resolved to try Mr. Snow's deer-park at Oare, where stags had been seen quietly browsing in the still evening. There a good run might almost be accounted a certainty, and thither the huge field trotted hopefully. They were not kept long in suspense. A few hinds, with calves by their sides, were the first to appear. Then, simultaneously, three lordly stags broke cover and went away with their long leisurely stride moorwards. Forthwith the pack was laid on the line of one of the animals, and settling down, began to run at a speed that compelled the horsemen to a fast gallop, if they wished to catch them.

Floundering through a bog, plunging down precipitous steeps to the romantic valley of the Doones, labouring up a rugged hillside—galloping was indeed no joke, and those who had started badly were glad to find the chase returning somewhat. A momentary pause, and then onward they swept past the deserted castle of the

Doones and over the heart of the swampy forest, where many got nasty falls in the treacherous boggy grips cut for draining. Without a moment's respite for drawing rein or breathing their horses, you might see them speeding over a lofty ridge knee-deep in heather or in long, thick grass, like that of an Indian jungle, and a minute later stumbling among the slippery boulders in the bed of a torrent. What wonder if the best were panting hard and the worst tailing far behind before the confines of the forest were cleared? After that there were two or three miles of good galloping over short heather where it was feasible to keep with the hounds.

The Prince of Wales, with Mr. Chorley as his pilot, rode well in front, and scarcely a dozen of those who had started were still with the pack when, within a few miles of Lynton, the deer, refreshed by "soiling" in the cool stream, turned short back and galloped straight over the hills towards Badgeworthy Water. By this movement hundreds of followers were let in again, but after a mile or two had been traversed, the pace began to tell. Once more a keen breeze blew fresh as the field galloped over the wide expanse of moor; and the sight of the hounds racing their game in front thrilled the nerves to rapture. Dashing down through the stunted oaks of Badgeworthy Wood, the excited horsemen heard the hounds crying loudly in the valley below, and knew by this token that the end was not far off. The deer sought to breast the steep hill, but, his limbs failing him, he returned to the stream. He ran up and down a few times; then he made his last gallant stand. In a moment more all was over. The Prince, receiving the knife from the huntsman, gave the *coup de grâce*, and was duly "entered" by Mr. Joyce. It may be observed that the Prince stuck the deer instead of cutting its throat, and thus established a precedent that has been followed since. A pleasant day and a glorious finish

SOME HUNTING TYPES

realised the fondest hopes of those who wished the Prince to carry away a favourable impression of Exmoor staghunting. His Royal Highness departed on the following day for Plymouth.

To trace the history of the chase after this unique event would be somewhat in the nature of an anticlimax. By way of conclusion, however, it may be stated that Mr. Bisset resigned in 1881, and was succeeded by Lord Ebrington. Lord Ebrington made way for Mr. Bassett, and Mr. Bassett for Colonel Hornby, all of whom maintained the high traditions of the Hunt. For some seasons the mastership has been held by Mr. R. A. Sanders, of Exford, who has shown equal capacity with his predecessors in the same post.

Part II
ANIMALS

CHAPTER I

DEER

"THERE is no more beautiful creature than a stag in his pride of antler, his coat of ruddy gold, his grace of form and motion. He seems the natural owner of the ferny coombes, the oak woods, the broad slopes of heather. They belong to him, and he steps upon the sward in lordly mastership. The land is his and the hills, the sweet streams, and rocky glens. He is infinitely more natural than the cattle and sheep that have strayed into his domains. For some inexplicable reason, although they too are in reality natural, when he is present, they look as if they had been put there and were kept there by artificial means. They do not, as painters say, shade in with the landscape. He is as natural as an oak, or a fern, or a rock itself. He is earth-born—autochthon—and holds possession by descent. Utterly scorning control, the walls and hedges are nothing to him—he roams where he chooses, as fancy leads, and gathers the food that pleases him."

This is one of the many fine passages in Jefferies' classic work on red deer. The naturalness of the deer, his greater naturalness than sheep and cattle, evidently impressed itself on Jefferies, though, as we see, he finds the reason inexplicable. Perhaps this was only a phrase, for he had already instanced a remarkable fact—namely, the parallel growth of fern and antler—as well as the various ways in which the brake is bound up with the existence of the deer. The naturalness of the stag is thus completely accounted for. He is part of the moor ; he is perfectly adapted to his environment. There is also another consideration, at which Jefferies merely hints. It is this : that the West Country deer are the only large animals which, in England, are suffered to remain wild. They always have been wild, and wild they still are. So far as civilisation is concerned, they have never been brought under its yoke, except in isolated cases—and then only partially—where specimens have been domesticated. They usually prove troublesome pets. The late Mr. Lyddon, of Edbrooke, Winsford, kept a tame deer, which walked into the house, lay down by the fire, rose, and walked out again at its own sweet will, but it proved such a pest that he had no choice but to get rid of it. Another tame deer resided for a time at Pixton, Dulverton, and accompanied one of the manservants on messages, leaping the gates which were closed—sometimes for merriment—to prevent his following. This stag took to assaulting the park deer, the result being that he, too, came to an untimely end. It is needless to insist that exceptions like these do not disprove the assertion that the red deer, as a class, are essentially wild animals.

When we talk of " deer," we seldom reflect that the word was formerly used in a general sense, though rather perhaps of wild than of tame animals. " Animals," " beasts," " brutes " are all terms tracing their origin to Latin sources. " Deer," which meant the same thing, is, for us English at any rate, much older. It is a distant cousin of the Greek θήρ, and daughter of the Saxon *deor*, whilst amongst its kinsfolk are the Gothic *dyr*, the Swedish *djur*, and the German *thier*. Even in *King Lear* we find the word used in its ancient sense :—

> " Mice and rats and such small deer
> Have been Tom's food for seven long year."

On the strength of this evidence we think it may be said that the naturalness of the deer, as the animal *par excellence*, was dimly present to the minds of many before Jefferies, though never so charmingly expressed.

The distinguished naturalist describes the stag's coat more than once as tinged with gold. No doubt the colour of the hair varies to some extent with the time of the year, and during the bright summer months the play of the strong sunlight produces an effect as of alchemy. We have before us, however, a tuft of stag's hair plucked from the carcass of a deer killed in the autumn of 1900 in the Exe near Dulverton. In this two shades are discernible—russet and drab, and that seems to be the prose of the matter. Poets sing of "red" gold; and, conversely, Jefferies, who had much of the poet in his composition, discourses of the stag as "golden." In both cases, it seems to us, there is an element of imagination, which, desiring to glorify the particular object, borrows a suggestion of richness not actually there. Dr. Collyns' account of the colour is as follows:—

"Generally speaking, the stag and hind are in colour upon the neck, back, sides, and flanks of a reddish brown. The face is of the same colour, shaded off with a grey or ashen hue upon and about the jaws. A dark brown stripe of wiry hair extends from the top of the neck, between the ears, to the shoulders, and this was sometimes called the mane of the deer. About and around the short tail (or 'single,' as it is technically termed) the colour is light brown, fading into buff between the haunches and over the belly. The buff colour is generally of a lighter shade in the male than in the female deer. The throat of the stag is furnished with coarse hair, which at the end of autumn increases in growth, and forms a thick ruff during the winter. Occasionally, though very rarely in this country, deer have been found of a light cream colour, and nearly white, but these specimens are so unusual that they may be considered as *lusus naturæ*—almost, if not altogether, as apocryphal as the 'hart with the golden horns,' after which Merlin and his companions

> 'Rode
> Through the dim land against a rushing wind
>
> .   .   .   .   .
>
> And chased the flashes of his golden horns,
> Until they vanished at the fairy well
> That laughs at iron.'"

The Exmoor deer are much finer animals than the fallow deer which are found in parks, and even than the red deer of North Britain, though, it is believed, not equal to some of their own ancestors, which carried a more imposing "head." The stag's "head"—which term, to an Exmoor man, applies to the horns rather than to what supports them—is the most noticeable thing about him. And it is the glory of the stag alone, the hind not having this armament. The deer, however, is unlike other horned animals, inasmuch as his horns are not permanent. They are excrescences which have, so to speak, an independent existence. They come and go, like "butter-teeth," and are attached to the deer's head, instead of being, like the bullock's, deeply and firmly rooted. Still, the new horns grow rapidly, and are quite firm when the stag is hunted and during the trials and turmoils of the rutting season.

The stag begins life with no horns at all. He is born a little dappled calf, but the white spots and the dark stripe down his back soon disappear, and the infant deer becomes of one colour throughout. Authorities differ as to whether both stag and hind are born dappled, or the stag only, but in the opinion of a former huntsman there is no distinction between the sexes in this respect. Park deer, it is well known, vary considerably as to colour, but the wild West Country animals, which refuse to cross with fallow deer, always come true to their dun or red. It deserves to be noticed that, while the young of the fallow deer are described as "fawns," those of the wild deer are seldom or never called by this name. They are regularly known as "calves." Dr. Collyns laid down that hinds invariably drop their calves between the seventh and twenty-first of June. Mr. Fortescue, however, considers this rule too absolute, even allowing for two exceptions of calves dropped in September. After adducing evidence to the opposite effect, he concludes that "calves have been dropped at all periods between early spring and early winter, but that very late calves are less uncommon than very early ones."

Usually calves are dropped singly, but occasionally it happens that a hind has two calves at a birth. At one time an opinion prevailed that hinds never produced twins, but, after carefully testing the evidence of experienced foresters, Dr. Collyns was induced to accept the opposite view, in support of which he narrates the following story :—

"One of the instances occurred in my younger hunting days. An old forester, or harbourer, who knew and was known by most of the deer in the neighbourhood of Dulverton (for he spent the greater part of his time in watching the deer in the woods and wilds), told me, and I can place reliance in the statement so made by him, that he knew a hind which produced twin calves, both males. He saw them within a very short time after they were born, with the hind, saw them suck her on the day of their birth, and was constantly in the habit of watching them as they grew to maturity. The twins were always together, and, in their close resemblance to one another, very Dromios. They grew into goodly stags, and at eight years were found together by the staghounds in the same wood. They ran together for nearly eight miles, when they were much pressed, and parted company, I believe, for the first time in their lives. The pack settled on one, ran into, and killed him. The next hunting morning the survivor was harboured by the old forester, who had almost witnessed the birth of him and his twin brother. At his urgent request the then master laid the pack on this stag, hunted and killed him, though there was many a better stag in the neighbourhood. The old harbourer expressed his pleasure at the circumstance, as he was confident that the survivor would have pined and died from the loss of his brother and companion."

Hinds, when about to calve, seek the cover of the fern, which grows in wild luxuriance all over Exmoor, and in the fern the young animals repose through the

long hot days. When night comes, hind and calf leave
the moors for the cultivated country. The mother
plants her fore-feet on the top of the wall, while with
her hind-feet she treads in the earth, thus forming a step
by which the calf climbs after her. The hind shows
her maternal instinct by carefully choosing spots suitable for the calf, not yet strong enough to leap on to
the top of the wall—a thing he will do at one bound
when he becomes a stag. Hinds, having once made
a passage through the beech hedge that surmounts the

"YUR, I ZAY! GET OUT O' BED AN' RIN, THEE LAZY LITTLE TOÄD"

wall, invariably keep to it, and the gap thus caused is
called a "rack." Except in the rutting season, stags
and hinds do not consort, but run in separate herds.
The young male deer run with the hinds, though they
are distinguished from the females, not only by the
darker colour of their necks and chests, but by their
broader heads. With the growth of their antlers, they
are either expelled by the hinds or join themselves to a
company of stags.

When a hind, with a calf running by her, finds herself
hunted, she lifts him up with her head and throws him
several yards off the line, where he lies perfectly still

until she returns for him, if she is ever permitted to
do so. A year or two ago we were told by the late
father of the harbourer, Goss, close under Haddon, that
a short while previously a calf butted aside by his
mother was discovered and cruelly mangled by the
hounds, which were whipped off by the huntsman, but
too late to save the young creature's life. Sometimes,
in consequence of a mistake, the hounds pursue a year-
ling, which sets off at a fast pace—faster than a grown
deer—and in a straight line. This is but natural, as the
young animal has not yet acquired a knowledge of the
country, and literally does not know where to turn.
When such an accident happens the poor beggar
receives scant pity from the dogs.

In strictness a male deer is not supposed to be hunted
until he is four years old, when he is said to be runable
or warrantable. Before deer became so plentiful, this
rule was rigidly enforced, but the necessity of thinning
the great herds, which make such inroads on the
farmers' crops, has rendered the Hunts less nice in
observing it. The young stag, after leaving the hinds
and before becoming his own master, serves a sort of
apprenticeship with an older stag, with whom he feeds,
ranges the country, and lies in cover. The value of this
arrangement is seen when the "tufters" appear and
invite the warrantable stag to break cover. This he is
unwilling to do, knowing the peril, so he drives out his
young companion in the hope that he will be accepted
as a substitute, and lies down in his bed.

Although we commonly speak of stags and hinds
without much regard to their age, it was formerly the
custom, and the custom has not yet died out, to assign
different names to them at different periods of life.
Manwood in his *Treatise on the Laws of the Forest* gives
the following account of the ancient terminology :—

"And because of all other beasts of venery the hart is the

noblest and the most worthiest beast, and taketh the first place, I will first begin and speak of the terms belonging to him, and therefore you shall understand that at the first year you shall call him a hind calf, or a calf; the second year you shall call him a brocket; the third year you shall call him a spayad; the fourth year you shall call him a staggard; the fifth year you shall call him a stag; the sixth year you shall call him a hart.   But here note that some ancient writers do report that in times past the foresters and woodmen were wont to call him a stag at the fourth year, and not a staggard, as we do now.   And also at the fifth year they did call him a great stag.   And so they were wont to give him a difference by this word stag, and great stag.   And whereas some do think that a stag, of whatsoever age he be, shall not be called a hart until the king or queen do hunt him; that is not so, for they are all greatly deceived that so do think; for after the fifth year of his age, he should no more be called a stag, but a hart.   But, as Budaeus saith, at six years of age then you shall him call; so that, if a stag come to be six years of age, then he is a hart.   But if the king or queen do hunt or chase him, and he escape alway alive, then after such a hunting or chasing, he is called a hart royal."

The terms now or lately in use in the Exmoor country are as follows : The male deer is called for the first year a " calf."   In the second year he is styled a " knobber," " knobbler," or " brocket."   In the third year he becomes a " spire," or " pricket."   In the fourth he develops into a " staggart."   In the fifth he is a " stag," or " warrantable deer"; and in the sixth a "stag," or "hart," names which he continues to retain to the last.   In the old days, the terms applied to hinds were the following : In the first year, a " calf" ; in the second, a " brocket's sister " ; in the third, a " hind."   On Exmoor female deer are now called " hearsts " in the first year, and " young hinds " in the second.

Formerly a system of nomenclature was in vogue based on the number of points.   The *Book of St. Albans*, in giving directions how to know the horns of a stag, informs us—

" Thou shalt call the head of a hart antler, royal, and sur-royal; and when you may know him by the top, you shall call him forked a hart of ten; and when he beareth three on the top, you shall call him a hart of twelve; and when he beareth four, you shall call him summed a hart of sixteen; and from four forward you shall call him summed of so many as he carrieth, how many soever they be."

Although it is not usual nowadays to speak of a " hart of ten " or a " hart of twelve," save in poetical descriptions of staghunting, virtually the method is observed when we talk of a " forester " as having all his rights and so many " on top."

By reason of the changes that occur in the size and shape of the horns—changes inseparably connected with the growth and decay of the deer—some authorities have held that the age of the animal can be accurately determined by this standard. The general law of development may be thus stated : that up to a certain period the main antler, or " beam," as it is called, becomes thicker and longer, the horns have a wider spread, and the points on the top are more in number. After that period has been reached the horns begin to go back. Just, however, as Shakespeare has divided the life of man into ages, so an eminent writer has attempted to define the modifications that take place in the stag's head according to years. For the first year, it is averred, he has no horns. In his second year he throws out on each side of his head a knob of bone about two inches in height. At three there appears a spire or upright horn from six to eight inches high, while at the base of the horn project from the spire the brow-antlers. By the time he is four years old the spire has grown to about fourteen inches, and is graced, not only with the brow-antlers, but with other projections called the " bay " (anciently the " royal "). To these points at five years of age are joined—but not invariably—the " tray " antlers, with two points or crockets on the top of one horn. At six, in

addition to his "rights," the stag has two points on the
top of one horn, and three on the top of the other ; at
eight, three on the top of each horn. At the age
of seven or eight, however, the changes in the formation
of the horns are much less noticeable than before.

Mr. Fortescue opposes this method of determination,
and maintains that the growth of the horns depends on
other circumstances than mere years, such as habitat,
time of birth, quality of food, and immunity from injury
and disturbance. Altogether, it must be confessed that
it is impossible to tell a deer's age accurately by his
horns alone. The broad question whether a deer be old
or young may often be solved through their means, but
by no means invariably or infallibly. Mr. Bisset, in the
course of his mastership, marked and turned out a
certain number of male calves taken before the hounds,
whereof about one-half have since been found and
killed ; but in hardly a single case do the heads of the
three deer correspond in number of points to those
assigned to deer of their age by Dr. Collyns.

Another subject on which these authorities are at
issue is the effect on the horns of castration. "Castration," says Dr. Collyns, "has a certain effect on the deer.
If the operation be performed when the deer has no
horns, he will never grow any ; if when the horns are in
velvet, they will always remain so unshed ; if when the
horns are fully developed, they too will never be shed,
but remain in the same stage unaltered." "Partial
castration," he adds, "will probably be followed by the
same result on the side where the mutilation is effected,
but this is not asserted by experience." Upon this Mr.
Fortescue remarks :—

"Dr. Collyns is throughout incorrect in this matter. If a
male deer be castrated before he has ever grown a horn,
he will never grow one at all, but if the operation be performed
after he has grown his horns, he will continue to grow and shed

them every year. The real peculiarity of the growth of such deer's horns is that they are never perfectly developed; they are always small, always soft, in fact gristle rather than horn, and never lose the velvet. Further it appears that the operation may be so modified as either to arrest the growth of the horns or to develop them abnormally."

So far as testing the age is concerned, it is worth noting that farmers, at all events, do not consider the horns. In the autumn of 1901 the writer was in the yard of an hotel, when an Exmoor farmer entered to inspect the carcass of a deer that had been freshly killed. After feeling the body he turned to the head, which had been cut off and hung on the wall. Merely glancing at the horns, he proceeded to examine the teeth, just as he would those of a sheep, and, guided by this evidence, pronounced the animal a four-year-old.

Stags shed their horns in the spring, usually in the middle or about the end of April, but occasionally in May. Something depends on the age of the deer as well as on the state of the season. An old stag tends to cast his antlers earlier than a young one; indeed, a two-year-old deer will carry his horns a month or two longer than a senior. When the time arrives for "mewing," the stag becomes shy and secretive, retiring into the densest woods, where he will not readily be observed. It is as if he were conscious that, in losing those magnificent emblems of strength and sex, he was about to be degraded, and so were overcome with shame. The true reason, however, is probably the knowledge that, shorn of his antlers, he is no longer capable of fighting his own battles against those of his race or against the hounds.

A remarkable circumstance connected with the process is the way in which old horns disappear, and the difficulty of finding a pair. It would seem as if the stag deliberately concealed them, in order to withhold from his enemies all evidence of his dismantled and defenceless condition. One explanation is that *hinds eat the horns*. But do they? When Dr. Collyns was in Scotland, he made careful inquiries on the point, and appears to have satisfied himself that, in the Highlands at any rate, hinds certainly indulge in the practice. As he remarks, however, it is extraordinary that no mention of the fact, if fact it be, occurs in the old treatises on venery, nor is anything known of it in the Exmoor country, where harbourers and others become deeply versed in the ways of the deer. Whatever may be the truth about this species of cannibalism, persons aspiring to possess a pair of antlers are not seldom victimised by unscrupulous dealers, who not only palm off odd horns as a pair, but actually attach them to a hind's head. The head of a stag goes, as his trophy, to the master, and a genuine specimen rarely comes into the market.

Led by a sure instinct, when the new horns begin to sprout, the stag quits the tangled coverts, and seeks either the open moors or the timber woods. His reason for taking this course is that the embryo antler is so delicate and sensitive that he cannot endure the least contact with a sapling. The substance is inclosed in "velvet," which is extremely vascular, and this vascularity has to do with the rapid growth of the horns, which in four months are completely renewed.

The stag is now said to be " in velvet." and whilst in that condition he is mercifully spared the attentions of the staghunters. This is nothing but reasonable, as the animal goes in bodily fear of hurting himself, and the flies alone are a sufficient cause of torment. Staghunting is, of course, not postponed until every bit of velvet has vanished, for the opening meet takes place early in August, and it is not until the second week in September that the bone is fully hardened, so that the velvet becomes useless. When that is the case it dries and falls from the antlers in strips, and to rid himself of the tatters the stag takes to rubbing his head against trees, which he barks and ruins. A tree utilised by a stag for this purpose is called his "fraying-stock."

We referred just now to the teeth. At one year old both sexes have two cutting teeth in the lower jaw; at two years of age they have increased to four; at three there are six, and at four eight. When five years old male deer have two tusks in the upper jaw, and cases have been known of very old hinds with tusks, though not so pronounced as in the male deer.

The partiality of stags for water is proverbial; in fact, this is an attribute with which many are acquainted, otherwise quite ignorant of the ways of deer. Who does not recollect the simile in the Psalter, "as the hart desireth the water brooks," and the metrical paraphrase thereof—

"As pants the hart for cooling streams
When heated in the chase"?

It were a mistake, however, to suppose that it is only in these circumstances that deer resort to water; on the contrary, they have their regular "soiling pits," or "soiling pools," adjacent to the deep coverts in which they make their beds. After they have been out feeding by night, they first quaff the water and then wallow in the stream. The soiling pits are usually shallow, and the deer emerges covered with mud, which is afterwards rubbed off against the bushes. The animal prefers a mud bath to clear water, as the former is more cooling, and serves as a defence against the flies, which, in the heat of summer, are an insufferable nuisance to the deer.

When the hounds are after him, the stag always recollects some favourite stream, like Horner Water, whither he repairs for temporary refreshment, or in the hope of eluding his foes, or that he may make his last stand on some convenient ledge. Sometimes during the chase the deer sinks himself in a pool, in such way that only his mouth and nose appear above the surface, and there is then a fair possibility of escape. Somewhat similarly, a stag roused in the neighbourhood of Withypool Common succeeded in throwing off his pursuers by the expedient of turning a somersault into a "blind" gutter, and lying there, feet upwards, amidst the screening overgrowth.

Early in August the hunting season begins, and human cunning and endurance are pitted against the wiles and staunchness of the deer. An important factor in hunting is to know how to find the quarry. This is not a gift that comes altogether by nature, so the duty is delegated to a well-informed official called the "harbourer." As the pleasure of so many people depends on his accuracy, the harbourer is expected to be infallible. He seldom or never disappoints. When it is said that he rarely sees the deer marked down for destruction, but is, nevertheless, perfectly cognisant of its sex and warrantableness, it will appear to some as if this favoured mortal is endued with supernatural gifts and powers. That is not absolutely the case. The truth is that the traditions of the neighbourhood, a competent knowledge of woodcraft, and his own trained observation supply all that is needful. As deer travel long distances in a single night, it is not enough for the harbourer to be informed by an ally that a stag has been seen in such-and-such a covert. What the harbourer has to ascertain is that a stag will be in a particular covert on the morning of the meet, and there must be no mistake. In order that he may furnish a favourable report, preliminary operations are necessary. The harbourer himself is perfectly well acquainted with the haunts of the deer, and can count on any number of willing auxiliaries in the farmers and cottagers, the former only too ready to assist in destroying one of the pretty pests.   Thus the harbourer can learn without fail that a deer has made his bed in a certain wood on the preceding, perhaps several preceding days, but for further information convicting the stag of an intention to remain, he must rely on his own sagacity.

And here it should be said that the age and sex of deer are shown, not only by their teeth and " head," but by their " slots."   The term " slot " is sometimes used of the hoof, but, in this connection, refers to the stag's footprint.   Under favouring conditions the harbourer soon ascertains whether the stag has been in a covert or no.   At the " rack," or gap, in the fence, where the deer has broken into the wood, he finds a track moulded in the soft earth.   This track is of a size and pattern that tell their tale.   Though not unlike the footmarks of a sheep, a deer's slots are naturally much wider and longer.   The hoof-mark of a stag, too, is larger than that of a hind, and each half is longer and more pointed. Moreover, in the case of a hind, the ridge that separates the two halves is less defined.   The rounded end of the slot, representing the heel of the deer, becomes broader with age, and the toe-points spread wider apart.   A runable or warrantable stag should measure two inches at the heel, and this affords the best criterion of his age, since the width between the toes varies somewhat according to the pace at which the animal is travelling, the nature of the soil—whether hard or soft—in which the imprint is made, etc.

Supposing the slot to be of the sort desired, the next point is as to its freshness.   This question is decided by comparison of the slot with the adjacent soil.   The mark will be, perhaps, half an inch deep, and at that depth the earth may be moist, while the surface of the ground is dry.   If the bottom of the slot is still moist, and gives no signs of crumbling or cracking, it is a safe

I

inference that the deer has passed the spot recently. The explorer has now to satisfy himself that the deer has not merely crossed the covert, but is actually in harbour. Accordingly he makes a tour round the wood, carefully examining the "racks" to see if they show corresponding slots. If they show none, then he feels sure that the deer is still in the covert, where he has made his bed. Stated thus, the procedure seems simple, but, as a matter of fact, the harbourer's task is often an anxious one. The weather may seriously impede his observations. Rain will wash out a slot, while on very dry soil the print is slight and easily effaced. For every stag harboured the fee is a guinea.

Although the slot is an important, and indeed indispensable, requirement for the safe harbouring of a deer, the harbourer who knows his work can ascertain the presence of these animals by other tokens. Early in the season he will cast his eyes on the willows and mountain-ashes — the deer's favourite fraying-stocks, and, if they are ringed, he will know that there are stags in the neighbourhood. Again, the deer is a great plunderer and mischief-maker. He does more than prey on the farmer's crops—conduct which the farmer could excuse in "those fellows." But, no; that is not enough. Entering a field of oats, up wind, a stag bites off half an ear, or less, at a time. A hind, on the contrary, bites off the whole ear. This distinction was noted by an old forester, the author of the *Art of Venery*, who observes: "You may judge the hind by her feed, because she croppeth the springs round like an ox, and feedeth greedily; and, contrarily, the hart of ten doth take it delicately, breaking it off endways, to have the liquor as sweetly and tenderly as he may."

In the same manner, a stag never takes more than one bite at a turnip. He pulls it up by the root, and having tested its quality, throws it over his shoulder.

A hind, on the other hand, takes two or three bites at a root, without dislodging it, and passes on to another. Deer do not care much for barley, though they eat it occasionally. They are, however, very fond of wheat, nibbling both in the green leaf and afterwards, when the ears are ripe. Just before harvest, a party of eight or ten stags will take up their quarters

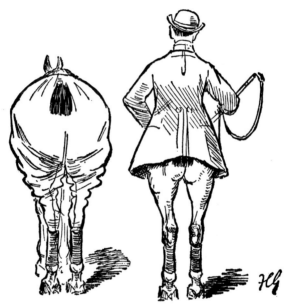

THE GENTLEMANLY 'OSS   A 'OSSY GENTLEMAN (next page)

in a wheat field, and lodge there day and night for a week. Potatoes, cabbages, carrots, and apples figure on their menu, and, marvellous to relate, they swallow apples whole. For the depredations thus caused there exists a deer-damage fund, but in view of the large number of deer now ranging the country, it may be doubted whether the money available suffices to cover a tithe of the havoc occasioned by their destructive habits. It may be added that while the local supporters of the chase do their duty, staghunting on Exmoor has been for years something in the nature of a cosmopolitan sport, and landloupers, who come to enjoy a fortnight's holiday with the hounds, besides forgetting the deer-damage fund, materially assist the four-footed marauders by the indifference some of them display to the farmer's legitimate interests.

Staghunting, which begins on the 12th of August, ends on the 8th of October, when the hounds are kennelled for a fortnight or so in order that no interference may take place with the deer's domestic arrangements. Stags and hinds do not consort together except in the late autumn, the period known as the rutting season.

The time is marked by fierce combats between rival stags, and nightly the "belling" of the stag, as he summons the hinds, is heard on the country-side. To an unaccustomed ear it is a weird and terrifying note, especially in lonely places; and even Dr. Collyns, though anything but a nervous man, was once startled beyond measure by the unearthly sound.

After a proper interval hindhunting begins and continues up to Christmas, weather, of course, permitting. It is resumed in the spring, the dates being regulated by the temperature, and ends on the 10th May. Again, at the end of July one or two hinds may be hunted to get the hounds in wind for staghunting. No harbouring occurs in hindhunting, information being obtained through gamekeepers. Unless the difference be attributed to the season of the year, a hind is stronger than a stag. She certainly runs longer and has other modes of baffling the hounds, doubling repeatedly like a hare. It is commonly observed that stags are perfectly aware when the time for staghunting is over and that for hindhunting commences, and should the hounds, whilst engaged in pursuing a hind, pass a herd of stags, the latter, it is said, will turn their heads in leisurely fashion and take no further notice.

Are stags dangerous? Despite their powers of offence, the answer is, in a general way, No! When a deer becomes conscious that a man is in his neighbourhood, his instinct is to make off. A gamekeeper, let us say, wishes to obtain a close view of a stag, which he sees approaching, and hides behind a hedge. For some time the deer follows unsuspiciously a straight course across the adjacent field, when all at once he stops short, lifts his nose, and immediately wheels about. No animal could be more timid or inoffensive. But the story is different if the stag finds himself in a "tight place." We have been told by a native of Red Deer Land that he was in a field when a hunted stag arrived, and ran along the hedge for the purpose of finding a gap. The man was a little in the way, and the stag, he declared, made a distinct "vage" at him with his horns. Luckily he eluded the blow. Formerly, there was an idea that a wound of this sort is necessarily fatal. As the *Art of Venerie* has it :—

> "If thou be hurt with hart, it brings thee to thy bier;
> But barber's hand will boar's hurt heal, thereof thou
> need'st not fear."

Experience has proved that the horns of the deer are not poisonous, but, of course, he is capable of inflicting severe, and even mortal, injuries with his formidable brow-points. It is a not at all uncommon occurrence for the younger and more adventurous hounds to be killed in attacking a stag at bay. A few years ago a good hound was so destroyed in the Union Ham at Dulverton, and it was remarked that he rolled over without so much as a whimper. Collaring a deer, when set up by the hounds, makes a great demand on a hunter's skill and resolution, and the operation is never attempted without the help of a line which is thrown over the deer's horns, and by which he is at last firmly secured. Then you will see the hounds, which hitherto have kept for the most part at a respectful distance, swarm up and bite the poor animal's nose and ears, and indeed any portion of his anatomy to which they can gain access. Once we saw a hind drowned in deep water through the efforts of the vengeful dogs. A hind, having no horns, can do nothing but kick; and a stag, when in the water, will sometimes use his heels with effect in the short rushes that precede his final stand. Not long ago there flourished in the deep woods round Haddon a deer which was known as the "Fighting Stag." He had an especial aversion for the harbourer's horse, and, whenever he caught sight of him, started off towards him with the intention of commencing a duel. We have never heard what ultimately became of him, but, being so inconvenient, we should think it highly probable that he has been marked down and yielded up his valiant ghost, perhaps in his own Haddeo.

When the late Sir Thomas Acland died, the opening meet of the Devon and Somerset Staghounds was at Haddon, but the regular trysting-place is Cloutsham Ball, and the event never fails to attract a huge mob of picnickers, who arrive from every point of the compass, in waggonettes, drags, dogcarts, etc., usually requisitioned at Dulverton, Dunster, Minehead, and other centres, several days in advance. Spreading themselves in picturesque groups round white cloths, they may be seen quaffing their cider or champagne, and discussing their ham and chicken, full of animation at the prospect of witnessing the sport, while everywhere you hear the kindly West Country drawl, as friends exchange greetings. By-and-by the master rides up, while the huntsman kennels his hounds in

the outbuildings of Cloutsham Farm, a picturesque
homestead nestling among orchards, where hospitality
is freely dispensed.   Then the harbourer appears with
conscious smile, though preserving an official reticence,
which is indeed necessary in the presence of so many
curious folks.   However, he has a stag, and a heavy
one, harboured down in Horner, and the huntsman,

AFTER A HEAVY DAY

having received instructions to begin, drafts three
experienced couples from the pack to act as tufters.
With these he makes his way down the circuitous paths
that intersect the woods, and ere long disappears from
view.   No strangers follow, for that, it is understood,
were a breach of etiquette that might endanger the
success of the move if the wrong deer broke from the
covert.   Woe betide the luckless individual that tallies

a young brocket, when a warrantable deer is in lair;
and yet such a mistake might easily arise, as a stag
will drive every hind or male deer from the thicket,
before emerging himself, and only practised eyes can
distinguish for certain the true quarry as, with his wide
antlers, he sweeps through the tangle of bushes. So
the novice must be content to wait, listening to the
huntsman's horn and the bay of the tufters, until, the
view holloa having come from a trusty throat, the pack
is laid on, and the whip and one or two followers set off
to stop the tufters. The rest of the chase shall be told
in the language, not of the everyday sportsman, but of
the imaginative Charles Kingsley :—

"Nay, I never rode with those staghounds, and yet I can
fill up his outline for him, wherever the stag was roused. Do
you think that he never marked how the panting cavalcade
rose and fell on the huge, mile-long waves of that vast heather
sea ; how one long brown hill after another sunk down greyer
and greyer behind them, and one long grey hill after another
swelled up browner and browner before them ; and how the
sandstone rattled often beneath their feet, as the great horses,
like Homer's of old, devoured up the plain ; and how they
struggled down the hillside through bushes, and rocks, and
broad, slipping, rattling sheets of screes, and saw beneath their
stag and pack, galloping down the shallow glittering river-bed,
throwing up the shingle, striking out the water in large, glisten-
ing sheets ; and how they, too, swept after them down the flat
valley, rounding crag and headland, which opened one after
another in interminable vista, along the narrow strip of sand
and rushes, speckled with stunted, moss-bearded, heather-
bedded hawthorns, between the great, grim, lifeless mountain
walls ? Did he feel no pleasant creeping of the flesh that day
at the sound of his own horse's hoofs, as they swept through
the long turf with a sound as soft as the brushing of women's
tresses, and then ring down on the spongy, black, reverberating
soil, chipping the honey-laden, fragrant heather blossoms, and
tossing them out in a rosy shower ? Or if that were too slight
a thing for the observation of an average sportsman, surely he
must recollect the dying away of the hounds' voices as the

woodland passes engulfed them, whether it were Brendon or Badgeworthy or any other place; how they brushed through the narrow forest paths, where the ashes were already golden, and the oaks still kept their sombre green, and the red leaves and berries of the mountain-ash showed bright between the forest-aisles; and how all of a sudden the wild outcry before them seemed to stop and concentrate, thrown back louder and louder as they rode, off the same echoing crag, till, at a sudden turn of the road, there stood the stag beneath them in the stream, his back against the black rock with its green cushions of dripping velvet, knee deep in the clear amber water, the hounds around him, some struggling and swimming in the deep pool, some rolling, and tossing, and splashing in a mad, half-terrified ring, as he reared into the air on his great haunches, with the sparkling beads running off his red mane, and dropping on his knees, plunged his antlers down among them with blows which would have each brought certain death with it, if the yielding water had not broken the shock. Do you think that he does not remember the death? The huge carcass dragged out of the stream, followed by the dripping, panting dogs; the blowing of the mort, and the last wild halloo, when the horn-note and the voices rang through the autumn woods, and rolled up the smooth flat mountain-sides; and Brendon answered Countisbury, and Countisbury sent it on to Lynmouth Hill, till it swept out of the gorge and died away on the Severn Sea?"

CHAPTER II

PONIES

IT is scarce possible, in the animal world, to behold anything prettier than a drove of Exmoor ponies— tiny, graceful creatures—on their way to Killerton or Bampton Fair. There is an old Exmoor word, used also on the Quantocks, which exactly describes the impression on the mind of the beholder — namely, "drift." Etymologically, this is no doubt a variation of "drove," which is all that the natives intend by it, but how infinitely more picturesque! As you watch them, the ponies, with their light, easy motion, do indeed drift along in a brown stream until they turn the corner and are seen no more.

Being what they are, it is no wonder that they have found an entrance into fiction. Major Whyte-Melville's *Katerfelto* includes an account of an animal purporting to be the ancestor of all true Exmoor ponies now in existence. Well-informed persons allude to this story as a legend, by which term may be intended a myth or unsubstantial tale that has been floating about the moor ever since the days of the wizard, and the wizard was a genuine charlatan when George III. was King. This version is not quite accurate. The story contains elements of fact and elements of romance. Whyte-Melville, whom all the world remembers as a great hunting-man as well as a successful writer of fiction, was often in the Exmoor country during the season, and generally, we believe, stayed at Rhyll, East Anstey, where he was the guest of Mr. Froude Bellew. By a stroke of good fortune he made the acquaintance of the Rev. George Owen, of Calverleigh, who concealed under a somewhat careless exterior an unusually gifted mind and a well-stored and retentive memory. Like most strong characters, Mr. Owen had his whims, and, for some inscrutable reason, he had a great aversion to imparting information that might be used for articles or books. Mr. "Otter" Davies found out this, to his cost, when he called upon him for particulars concerning his lifelong friend and whilom schoolfellow "Jack" Russell. If he got anything out of him at all, it must have been painfully little. Whyte-Melville managed considerably better. Resorting to Protean tactics—sportsman or author, as the case required—he jogged homewards with the parson, after the death, and gleaned all manner of valuable lore, which he afterwards wove into his novel. Among other items he heard of a small stallion called "Katerfelto," and the property of a Sir Thomas Acland contemporary with the wizard. The neighbouring squires cast longing eyes on the perfect little horse, and made many a bid for him, but the baronet steadily refused to sell. At length one of these gentlemen, rather than be baulked of his wish, resorted to an indefensible ruse. He *borrowed* Katerfelto, and, after keeping him some time, wrote to Sir Thomas, regretfully informing him that the stallion was dead, and inclosing a certificate. The owner, however vexed he may have been, accepted this assurance, but Katerfelto was not dead. He survived for many years, and became the sire of a numerous stock, some of which "Master George" (as the moormen, mindful of other days, persisted in dubbing him) had proved.

Russell's biographer seems to have been wholly ignorant of this story—small blame to him if he were, seeing that Mr. Owen declined to enlighten him—and offers quite another version.   Speaking of Mr. Peter Tanton, one of Russell's staunchest supporters, he observes :—

"He was the owner of a celebrated grey mare by 'Crick-neck,' her dam being a grey Exmoor by 'Katerfelto.' This last horse, the sire of such wondrous stock, and the hero of that attractive story written by Whyte-Melville, is said to have been captured after his long run on Exmoor; and then bought, according to a tradition still prevalent in the region of Hather-leigh, by the Rev. John Russell, sen., the rector of Iddesleigh, and Russell's father, in whose possession the horse died."

The reader may be left to make his own election between these two versions.   The writer, as knowing the parties, naturally prefers the former.   In all fairness, however, it should be stated that Mr. Russell, sen., was not the guilty squire, the rival accounts being locally, and in every other sense, distinct.   It appears not unlikely that the idea of making Katerfelto an Arab may have occurred to Whyte-Melville through what he had heard of Mr. Knight's well-known predilections.

The real origin of the Exmoor pony, like that of the Dartmoor pony, the Shetland pony, the Welsh pony, and any pony, is a difficult question, which must be solved apparently in one of three ways.   Either the pony is, and has always been, a separate species of the *genus* horse; or he is the primitive type, from which the horse under favourable conditions, and by natural or artificial selection, has been evolved; or, thirdly, he is the result of a process of degeneration brought about by bad climate and scanty food.   For our part, without setting ourselves against the doctrine of evolu-tion, we are disposed to believe that the Exmoo. pony, like the red deer, is strictly indigenous.   Probably the breed is as old as the first human inhabitants, and in the earliest times was far more widely diffused.

The Exeter *Domesday*, referring to Hernole (*i.e.* Oule Knowle, in the parish of Carhampton), records that one Roger has there "seven wild horses." The expression has been interpreted as relating to brood-mares turned out into the woods, but, even if this interpretation be correct, the mares may have been of the Exmoor breed. So, too, in certain proceedings instituted in 1598 in the Court of Chancery by Thomas Webber and James Darche of Luxborough against John Baker of Withypool, John Thomas of Bishop's Nympton, and one Chubworthy, the point was raised, to whom— whether to Sir John Poyntz, Knight, or to Peter Edgcombe, Esquire—the revenues should be paid by the country people who had or should put their "rother-beasts [horned cattle], horse-beasts, sheep, swine, etc.," to depasture in the Forest of Exmoor. Here, again, it is uncertain what is meant by "horse-beasts," but it seems reasonable to conjecture that the term included, if it did not denote, Exmoor ponies.

Perhaps it is safe to allege that the history of the ponies begins, in quite modern times, with the purchase of the Crown lands by Mr. Knight. Before the year 1818 this form of property seems to have been little regarded. The animals were taken for granted as fauna of the district, and there was an end of the matter. When, however, Sir Thomas Acland found himself outbid for the possession of the forest, his interest in the ponies appears to have received a sudden stimulus, and it is due to the measures then taken by him that the purity of the breed has been maintained. In 1818 the ponies running wild on the moor are said to have numbered four hundred, and, with the exception of twenty, the entire herd was sold by auction. These twenty ponies were reserved that they might form the nucleus of a new herd, and for that purpose they were sent to Old Ashway, a farm of Sir Thomas Acland

hard by Winsford Hill, where there is a fine stretch
of moorland. From these animals are descended the
only pure Exmoor ponies, and as a guarantee of their
quality they are branded on the near quarter with
an anchor, for well-nigh a century the official mark
of the herd.

Till a few years ago the care of the ponies was
inseparably associated with the family of Rawle. Mr.
Hancock tells a charming story of the first keeper, who,
for all his illiteracy, was one of the shrewdest of mankind and thoroughly respected by his neighbours in
every rank of society.

"John Rawle, who took charge of the ponies reserved from
the sale in 1818, was quite a character. He was a man of
great strength, and could go into a herd of ponies, and bring
out in his arms any one of the little whinnying creatures, a
feat which required skill as well as strength, for the ponies
fight very fiercely with their tiny fore-feet. Rawle entertained
for the head of the Acland family the sentiment of a feudal
retainer for his chief. It is said that when he accompanied
Sir Thomas on any expedition, and his master entered a house
for refreshment, Rawle stood at the door like a sentry, watchful
and immovable, however long the delay, till "his Honour"
reappeared. Sir Thomas's wish was law to him. One day
the last baronet [grandfather of the present Sir C. T. D.
Acland] said to Rawle—

"'I want to send two ponies to the Duke of Baden; will
you take them?'

"Rawle's travels had before been probably confined to
Minehead on one side and Barnstaple on the other, and he
could neither read nor write well, if at all; but he replied
without hesitation—

"'If it please your Honour.'

"His troubles on the journey to Baden were manifold, and
they were increased by the arrival of a foal *en route*. He had
only a pass for two ponies, but he succeeded in hiding the tiny
baby pony under the straw of its bed when the Custom House
officer came on board. He reached Baden at length in safety,
and delivered his charge to the Grand Duke's servants. And

the very next morning before light he started for home; 'his Honour began black game shooting on September the 1st, and he must be present.' He made his way straight back to Sir Thomas's shooting quarters without stopping to see his wife on the way and reported the safe delivery of the ponies. 'But, please your Honour,' he added, 'the folk out there be the stupidest set of fools I ever did see. They couldn't understand a single word an honest man said to 'em.'"

John Rawle was succeeded by his son Richard, "a worthy chip of the old block," whose children, it is said, caught the ponies and rode to school on them. The present herdsman is Mr. Parkman.

Probably, however, no living man knows much more about Exmoor ponies than Mr. Daniel Evans, the kindly and genial host of the "Royal Oak," Winsford, who is himself a breeder, and who for upwards of thirty years has officiated as auctioneer to the late and the present Sir Thomas Acland at the historic Bampton Fair. Postponing for the present a description of that important fixture, we may here discuss some of the points of the breed, for it should be understood that an Exmoor pony is a creature with distinctive traits, many of which a judge of horses would approve, but not all.

First as to colour. Chestnut and roan are at once excluded as foreign to the true Exmoor, and black may be placed in the same category. Brown, with a mealy mouth, or bay, is the approved colour. Some Exmoors are of a very dark brown, while others are very light bay, with a still lighter shade under the belly and inside the arms and thighs ; and, accompanying this, is a dark list or stripe down the back. Ponies with this marking are said to be of an unusually high quality. It is very necessary that the ponies should be of a "whole" colour, by which expression is signified the absence of a white star or "blaze" on the forehead, as also any white about the feet and legs. Should a pony display this objectionable characteristic, it would be summarily rejected for breeding purposes. The only exception to this rule, if exception it can be called, is dapple-grey, which, though not common, is legitimate. Other points are good quarters, in which unfortunately many of the ponies are deficient, sloping shoulders, small ears, a broad forehead, and dilated nostrils. There is an Exmoor saying, " A long horse, with a short back ; or a tall horse, with short legs," and the meaning is that the bodies, like that of a cart-horse, should be thick through. The coat is extremely long and thick, the mane full and shaggy, and the tail long and sweeping. The average height of the ponies is about twelve hands. Thirteen hands would certainly imply a tall pony. These particulars apply, of course, to the full-grown animal. The foal or " sucker," as the phrase is hereabouts, is really an equine curiosity.

" In the sucker," says an able writer in *Murray's Magazine*, " the shaggy coat is more wool than hair. So long and thick is it indeed that it has a regular wave in it ; the head is disproportionately big, and except for the shapely ears, more like a donkey's than a horse's. The tail, which often actually sweeps the ground, has a regular bunch in the middle of it, while the feet beneath the long hair on the coronet seem so small and so pointed that one looks instinctively to see whether the hoofs are not divided. Altogether, one might say without exaggeration that anyone coming unexpectedly upon a young sucker, not knowing what he was likely to see, would be much more likely at the first glance to think he had seen a goat than a horse."

Should it meet with good food and grooming, the adult pony, with its clean legs and long, springy pasterns, soon develops into a miniature thoroughbred, and is then a very handsome animal. Surefooted, strong, and handy, with fair usage it will keep free from splint, curb, or spavin, and its dainty hoofs are more lasting than " cups of steel." Ponies are so common in the district that even the humblest use them, and it is said that there are children on the moor who have never seen a donkey. Should one pass in a travelling tinker's van, they will turn and gaze at it as a rare and curious animal.

On Winsford Hill the ponies enjoy complete liberty, subsisting on the rough herbage, supplemented in winter with a few oats. They make pretty figures amidst the heather, and seldom trouble to do more than turn their heads, unless an admirer offers to approach them too closely. Then, speedily showing a clean pair of heels, they scamper off to a fresh post of observation. The writer once had a small patrol at a disadvantage. Descending the road which leads from Spire Cross to Torr Steps, he came upon a dozen or more ponies bivouacking in Old Ashway Farmyard. He drew near enough to have been able to take an excellent "snap-shot," if only he had brought his camera with him, but unluckily he had left it behind. As he advanced, first one, then another of the group wheeled about, until in a few moments the whole number were leisurely trotting down the lane. However, they could not go far, as the way was barred by one of those gates which forbid egress into more civilised parts. So there they stood herded together like a flock of sheep, and awaiting the next move on the part of the enemy. The lane, as it happens, is pretty wide at this point, and the enemy, standing back, civilly afforded them an uninterrupted retreat. The ponies took the hint, and, with a bound, one by one ran the gauntlet. It was a charming adventure.

A most satisfactory description of pony life on the moor was contributed to the *Pall Mall Magazine* for October, 1896, by Miss Evelyn March-Phillipps, a lady who is favourably known for her writings on the Italian masters of painting. It seems almost a pity that so excellent a piece of work should be lost in the pages

K

of a periodical, for, apart from a few errors due to insufficient revision, it is a most pleasing and artistic presentment of a fascinating theme. In the course of her article the accomplished authoress draws a picture of the pony at home.

"The ponies tend to run in droves, especially when scared, and this makes them easier to manage ; but even those who know their haunts may ride for an hour without finding one. At last all are gathered within the low stone walls of the yards at Ashway, where stands the herd's cottage, below Mouncey Hill and above where the Barle flows under the great Druidical boulders of Torr Steps, the witches' bridge. Behind the little pastures the purple folds of moorland stretch away to the sky, with Dunkery Beacon's dark ridge towering over all. The grass and bracken are turning orange, and here and there in the hollows the low wind-swept beeches gleam gold and russet in the October sunshine. In a small yard against an old barn or barton are penned up the fathers of the flock—spirited little fellows, with high crests and sweeping tails, plunging, fighting, rising to bite one another's manes. Hard by a whole bevy of ponies frisk and scamper round a larger yard, while in a third the little mares move placidly, their foals stepping demurely at their heels, with pretty baby dignity. The foals look very tiny, and the legs are not so long and lanky in proportion to their height as those of foals usually are. Their small bodies are covered with a thick fur-like coat, and their short, rough manes stand crisply erect, while the bright mischievous eyes of the full-grown ponies gleam through shaggy locks, tumbling in all directions."

The ponies are at home for a special object, *i.e.* for the annual stock-taking. The herd numbers about a hundred, and it is obvious that, unless precautions were taken, they would increase and multiply till difficulties would arise about their "keep." Hence it is the custom to assemble the ponies at Old Ashway once a year, when all above two years old, not already so marked, are branded with the anchor—the Holnicote token. The future sires are selected, and faulty animals no longer allowed to run with the herd. About a score are drafted for sale at Bampton Fair, while the best of the mares and foals are despatched to Killerton Park, near Exeter, where the pasturage is richer and the climate warmer than on bleak Exmoor.

The general policy of the Acland family has been to preserve with vigilance and care the purity of the strain —a policy which cannot be too highly extolled. It must be conceded, however, that, for many purposes, strength and speed do not compensate for lack of inches; and not a few adult ponies do not exceed eleven hands. To remedy this defect experiments have been made in crossing, but without permanent success. The best cross is that between an Exmoor sire and a Devonshire pack-mare. Even that has not proved in all respects satisfactory. The fact is the Exmoor strain is uncommonly tough, and though the first generation may be an improvement, the second is apt to disappoint, the foal usually displaying all the faults of the Exmoor with its characteristic excellences. Despite these failures, hope has not been abandoned, but the method now in favour is that of *cultivating* the ponies.

"For the last thirty years," says the present baronet, "we have been in the habit of taking about twenty of the best mares, with their foals, down to the better climate and grass at Killerton, where the young ones spend a year or so. And the result has been twofold. First of all, 'emollit mores, nec sinit esse feros'; and secondly, the chests are widened, and, as a direct result, the shoulder rendered more sloping and the humerus more upright, and the action improved. But the quarters are entirely another matter, and I am afraid many of the tails come out as low down in 1900 as they did in 1870. Experience has taught us that the original strain of blood is as good as any cross we can devise, and that no cross will combine good qualities through two generations with any degree of certainty."

Mr. Knight was by no means so anxious as the Aclands about maintaining the purity of the Exmoor pony, and his herd at Simonsbath was the subject of far more persistent crossing than that at Old Ashway. His attempts, too, seem to have been more fortunate. The native stock was crossed with a small thoroughbred and a horse brought from the East—a Persian or Gulf Arab; and thus was produced a stud of very beautiful ponies, many of them fourteen hands and over, and from their cleverness and docility fit for anything—harness, polo, service as children's hunters, or as light-weight hacks. These advantages were not gained without sacrifice, since the hybrids, with their admixture of warmer blood, were less hardy than the original Exmoor. Indeed, the herd could no longer stand the severe winter on the moor, but required to be fetched in and fed in paddock or strawyard. On the death of Sir Frederick Knight, his successor, Lord Ebrington, became possessor of the herd, but we understand from Mr. Molland, his lordship's agent at Simonsbath, that all Sir Frederick Knight's half-bred ponies have been sold. The old system, however, is still in vogue, and recently an Arab stallion was borrowed from the Duke of Connaught's stables. The animal has since been returned, leaving two half-bred stud ponies as mementoes. Of both Sir Frederick's and Lord Ebrington's ponies it may be affirmed that sweeter specimens of their class have yet to be found. A few of the best are reserved for private customers, but a large draft of yearlings is sold every autumn at Bampton Fair.

Bampton Fair is one of the few institutions of the sort that continue to flourish with undiminished popularity. This circumstance is the more remarkable in that Dulverton Fair, once highly prosperous, is now completely extinct, while Tiverton Fair, erewhile Bampton's most formidable rival, has all but reached the same inglorious pass. A meagre crowd still assembles on Lowman Green about two o'clock in the afternoon, when a dozen cart-horses are put through their paces, but anything more woeful and moribund than Tiverton Fair, as a going concern, it is impossible to conceive. That things were very different formerly is evident enough. It was at this fair, at the beginning of the last century, that young Russell invested in a mare—"a brown mare with big limbs and a brown head"—which took him to his first meet of the staghounds. In 1814, Tiverton Fair—then known as the "Howden of the West"—consisted of a goodly show of Exmoor ponies, Devonshire pack-horses, and half-bred hunters, while the human element included dealers like Rookes, not above cheating inexperienced youngsters. This rivalry is now entirely a thing of the past. Bampton Fair has outlived all its competitors, and, in the opinion of competent judges, far from receding, is becoming better and better year by year. Even Bampton Fair, however, is not in every respect what it was. When the nineteenth century was young, no fewer than thirteen thousand sheep were congregated in the town, whereas of late the number of sheep sold has dwindled to little more than two hundred. This is a serious falling off, but is not perhaps of capital importance, while the entries of ponies and horses show, as they do, a constant tendency to increase.

The origin of the fair is lost in antiquity. Apparently the first mention of it occurs in the reign of Henry III., when it was granted to the rector and his successors. The fair was to be held at the chapel of St. Luke, which stood at the north-east angle of the parish church, and on the festival of that saint, for three days. It is now held, as has long been the case—possibly since the adoption of the Gregorian or New Style of reckoning—on the last Thursday in October, and all over the town. The present owner of the fair is the lord of the manor.

According to the recollections of the oldest inhabitants, theirs has never been much of a pleasure fair, and
its features remain stereotyped.   The latter circumstance
helps to account for its permanence and stability, since
nothing is more harmful to fairs than tampering with
traditional arrangements.   If, for instance, the residents
determined to banish the fair from the streets, it is
tolerably certain that, from that moment, the institution
would begin to decline.   The fatal step, however, is not
likely to be taken—at any rate, for the present.

Despite its monotony, Bampton Fair possesses per-
ennial attractions.   Year after year one notes the same
faces, and the owners have not come for business
necessarily.   They hear the fair "a-calling," and the
subtle temptation masters them.   To persons who have
never witnessed it, the fair may be recommended as an
extraordinary treat.

"Let a visitor go to Bampton Fair," says Mr. Baring-Gould,
"and see the pranks of these wild, beautiful creatures, and
note as well the skill with which they are managed by the man
experienced in dealing with them.   Such a sight will remain in
his memory, and when he gets back to town, he will have
something to talk about at dinner, and if he has a bit
of descriptive power in him, he will hold the ears of those
who are near him at dinner."

Within the last five years Bampton town has been
much modernised, and it is no longer the quaint old
place that it was when first we knew it.   The revival
of work on the Cyclopean quarries has brought many
changes in its train, and brand-new buildings, totally at
variance with the former aspect of the town, meet one
at every turn.   Gone is the ruined forge, with its moss-
grown roof, that not so long ago adjoined the bridge,
and, from its low situation, was clearly there when cart
traffic passed over the ford.   Gone, too, are certain
thatched cottages on the hill where buyers and sellers

BAMPTON, LUKE STREET

[p. 135

mostly did congregate. Lovers of the picturesque, however, may count on seeing a gorgeous display of Virginia creeper on the walls of the more reputable dwellings, and if from the bridge they will gaze southwards in the direction of a "hatch" or flood-gate, where, many years ago, some eloping ponies were "suspended" in the Batherum stream, they will doubtless be pleased with the bold background of Bowbier Hill. That way lies the magnificent valley of the Exe. In the other direction the scenery is pastoral and mellow, orchard alternating with pleasant lea. There are no better apples than grow on lichened trees yonder, and at this season of the year masses of gold and red may be seen lying on the ground prior to being removed to cider-pound.

These accessories the visitor will probably mark on the day before the fair, for on the day itself there is so much bustle and excitement as to allow of few intervals for quiet observation. Bampton long bore the name of a sleepy town, but even in its sleepiest times it always woke up on the eve of the fair, when droves of ponies came trooping through the ancient streets to their temporary quarters, tiny "suckers" wedging themselves between more mature companions, and in the extreme rear, dominating the detachment, a sturdy moorman, cased in mackintosh and bestriding a high horse—mackintosh, since nine times out of ten the fair is held amidst fog and drizzle. Apart from the influx of the ponies, the air is thick with omens—premonitory signs of something about to occur. For one thing the inhabitants are busy fortifying their abodes against defilement. A house in Briton Street, erst dedicated to middle-class education and a famous seminary of its sort, has a neat arrangement of posts and chains, while in some cases front gardens with iron railings keep the beasts at bay. Elsewhere, however, helpless shops and

decent, whitewashed tenements are strongly barricaded
—a by no means unnecessary precaution, seeing that
the press of human beings, to say nothing of four-footed
intruders, sometimes amounts to a "dranget." "Dranget"—a word seldom heard nowadays—was thus defined
in our hearing by an elderly native : "It do mean a
crowd of vokes, where you can't go vore nor back."
That exactly describes the situation at Bampton Fair
on certain occasions when the fair is at its height.

Besides householders, others will be observed engaged
in a somewhat similar occupation, namely, setting out
the sheep-pens. This duty falls to the lot of Mr. Samuel
Gibbings, as lessee of the fair, and is, we believe, quite
independent of the manorial customs which still obtain
at Bampton. At the occasional court-leet or "law-day,"
which comes off when the lord of the manor is con-
vivially or hospitably disposed, there is kept up a
delightful old tradition, that of "shoeing the colts."
This means the extraction of half a crown from those
making their first appearance at the function, while
others pay a shilling, the amount thus gathered being
spent in refreshment. The appositeness of this custom
to a town whose chief glory is its horse fair does not
require pointing out.

It is not at Bampton only that the approach of the
fair arouses interest. For Exmoor people it is naturally
of vast importance, but throughout the county of Devon
and over a good part of Somerset the event is heralded
with pleasurable anticipations. Horses are, of course, a
subject of never-ending talk with country gentlemen and
farmers, and the gipsy fraternity also may be relied on
to calendar the occasion. But the odd thing is that in
the larger towns even the factory girls, whose knowledge
of horseflesh is probably not one of their most valued
accomplishments, may be overheard remarking to each
other, "Bampton Fair to-morrow!" The results of this

BAMPTON, NEWTON SQUARE

[*p.* 137

widespread interest are seen when the curtain again rises. Bampton has no special reason for being abroad at an abnormally early hour, and Mr. Thornton is, we think, rather hard on the denizens when he records that, having ridden down from Exmoor in company with Mr. Knight, he "despised the Bampton people, who were only just leaving their beds and peeping at us from the windows as we rode by." This, however, was a generation or more ago, when the virtue of early rising was more highly esteemed.

Shortly after eight the first train arrives—an up-train from Exeter. It is like a centipede, and accounts for the whole length of a liberally devised platform. The doors fly open, and then a motley crowd, composed of all sorts and conditions of men—tinkers, tailors, soldiers, sailors, gentlemen, farmers, etc.—surges up the steep way-out. Meanwhile a posse of Bamptonians watches the swarming immigrants from the 'vantage-ground of the railway bridge. The feminine contingent naturally chooses a later train, but there *is* a feminine contingent, and a tolerably strong one. In 1887, according to *Murray's Magazine*, ladies were conspicuous by their absence—at all events, from the thoroughfares.

"From end to end the long village street was blocked with horses and with cattle, with sheep and with men. We say 'men' advisedly, for out of doors not a woman was to be seen. That they had not forsaken the place altogether was evident, as girls' faces might be seen gazing eagerly from every upper window, and at a later period of the day, when business had given way to pleasure, they came forth in crowds from their retreats. But an unwritten law appeared to prescribe that in the morning women should keep out of the way."

No such unwritten law prevails now, possibly as the consequence of physical education, and of the greater freedom of manners which marked the *fin de siècle* girl. In any case, a fine show of health and beauty may be seen at ten o'clock on Mr. Blackford's grand stand, of which ladies occupy the front seats.

Mr. Blackford represents a firm of auctioneers established at Southmolton, which long enjoyed the privilege of selling Sir Frederick Knight's ponies, and is now retained in a similar capacity by Lord Ebrington. Besides these, however, he has other entries, and the orchard behind the Tiverton Hotel, in which he holds his sales, is always a centre of attraction. The ponies are herded in a big pen overlooking the steep lane, on the opposite side of which are the celebrated quarries. Thence they are introduced into the sale-ring one by one, and made to show off their points, on which the auctioneer discourses with phenomenal fluency and in a variety of picturesque phrases, broken by effective asides. Many of the bystanders have come furnished with sticks—a fact of which the candidate is speedily made aware if lack of caution or embarrassment of mind should bring him within range. Indeed, the old habitué considers it his duty to lay his stick across any animal he finds in his way. He does this quite mechanically, except when a rush of ponies elevates the occasion into a great smiting carnival, the result being a mêlée, in which everyone must look out for himself. What with these periodical charges, in which the ponies are precipitated at lightning speed through the congested square, and the ranks of horses tethered tail outwards and free to resent provocation by a kick, it is really a wonder that accidents are not more common. As a fact few accidents occur, and those few, almost without exception, through drunkenness or idiotic *horse-play*.

In the sale-ring the little frightened pony is like a cork in a bucket of water. Round and round he goes, and to and fro, utterly mystified as to what is expected of him, and wholly a creature of impulse. However, intending buyers follow his gyrations without difficulty, and concurring in the auctioneer's estimate, "strong as a castle," bid briskly. After a while the hammer falls, and then a space is cleared for the pony's escape. Out he flies amidst a rain of blows, and is immediately lodged in the "sold" ring. There he is joined from time to time by one after another of his companions who have passed the same ordeal and won like approbation.

How highly some of these ponies are appreciated will appear from the following narrative—Mr. Thornton's :—

"We walked out to the paddock to see the ponies, for Mr. Knight had forty or more for sale by auction there that day. He told me that his Worcestershire friend, Sir Thomas Sebright, wished him to send up two good ponies for his wife, and he asked me to help him to select them. They were all unbroken, and he had never seen them before, although they were his property. We chose, say, Nos. 13 and 27, and he requested me to buy them for him at the sale. This I presently accomplished, but I had to pay about sixty guineas before I could secure them. Mr. Knight was wondering how his friend would like the price, when a tall man approached us and bitterly complained that he had come all the way from Birmingham to buy ponies, only to find the best bought in by the owner. He said he was a horse-dealer. Mr. Knight replied that there was reason in his complaint, and that he might have the ponies at the price. The man took them, and, I afterwards heard, lost them in Birmingham, where the little beasts broke away from the station, and were only with difficulty recaptured. The ordinary price of an unbroken four-year-old was about ten pounds, so that I congratulated myself in selecting beforehand the longest-priced ponies on record. That day at Bampton I made the acquaintance of Mr. Leech, the artist for *Punch*, who was accompanied by Mr. Higgins, the terrible 'Jacob Omnium' of those days, and the friend of Thackeray."

A few years ago a pair of ponies was bought for Lord Rosebery by his agent, Mr. Fraser, but we did not happen to hear the price. Sixty pounds for a pair of *unbroken* ponies is doubtless, as Mr. Thornton

suggests, a "record," but animals that have been broken
and appeared nicely groomed have probably realised
even higher prices. In this connection a Withypool
farmer once ruefully remarked to us on the value of
a name. He could raise the ponies, he said, but, when
he had raised them, of what use was it for him to
expect the money, or half the money, that would be
cheerfully given to a nobleman or gentleman of note
in racing circles?

Mr. Thornton's allusion to Leech reminds us of
another artist, whose massive head, square shoulders,
and pointed beard, some ten or fifteen years ago, were
often seen in the streets of Bampton, whither he was
attracted, not by professional reasons, but by the fact
of a married daughter, Mrs. Guinness, residing in the
town. We refer to the late Mr. Stacy Marks, the
eminent bird-painter. Mr. Marks did not take kindly
to Bampton, as anyone may find who will be at the
trouble of consulting his *Pen and Pencil Sketches*, in
which he has published his impressions of both town
and fair.

In writing of Bampton Fair it would be unpardonable
not to say something about Mr. Daniel Evans and his
mart. Until the resuscitation of the lime and stone
industry obliged him to move on, Mr. Evans annually
located himself in the yard opposite the Tiverton Hotel,
amidst picturesque surroundings, but rather cramped.
His rostrum is now erected in Orchard No. 2, where
he likewise has a sale-ring, and his mealy-mouthed
ponies—all pure Exmoors—are secured in pens. It is
not too much to say that for many people his familiar
figure has become symbolical of the fair ; but, besides
being a symbol, "Sir Thomas' poor auctioneer"—
Mr. Evans does not look poor—is one of the most
entertaining of men, with a fund of good stories, wherewith he contrives to relieve the monotony of business,

MR. PUNCH, HAVING HEARD OF THE EXCELLENT QUALITIES OF THE EXMOOR PONIES, PROCURES
A FEW FOR THE LITTLE FOLKS

He once told an interested audience of the gentlemanly
habits of a stallion called "South-hill." In the paddocks
round Ashway, where this pony ran with the mares,
he was frequently seen to rise on his hind-legs, open
the gate with his fore-paws, and keep it open while
the ladies of his seraglio passed through to the moor.
We observe from Miss March-Phillipps' article that this
story, which first became known to us in the manner
stated, was corroborated by the pony-herd and other
eye-witnesses.

The fun of the fair, if it does not begin, certainly
grows apace with the removal of the ponies, which
takes place in the afternoon. Prior to the construction
of the Exe Valley Railway, the nearest station was at
Tiverton, and thither, over a length of seven weary
miles, struggling, panting men might be seen urging
the reluctant steps of an animal as stubborn as an ass
and a vast deal more spirited. The Exmoor pony,
though some have praised his docility, does not entirely
merit the compliment—least of all in his wild, un-
tutored state. In Mr. Blackford's yard a "sucker," held
by two men, was awaiting its turn to be sold, when,
without the slightest warning, it fixed its hind-legs
against a hurdle, rose on end, and turned a somersault. Its keepers, dragged after it, were pitched into
an adjoining plot. There are plenty of caprioles and
caracoles in wide Brook Street, where sometimes the
drag is applied by a sturdy fellow swinging at the
pony's tail, and naturally it is fine comedy for the spectators when the little fellow succeeds in throwing his
keeper and sousing him in a sea of mire. The 'prentice
hand does not at once succeed in grasping the situation,
and what wonder? As has been well said, "Exmoor
ponies throng the streets, flood the pavements, over-
flow the houses, pervade the place. Wild as hawks,
active and lissom as goats, cajoled from the moors, and

tactfully manœuvred when penned, these indigenous quadrupeds will leap or escalade lofty barriers in a standing jump or a cat-like scramble, whilst the very 'suckers' have to be cajoled with all the Daedalian adroitness with which the Irish pig has to be induced to go whither he would not."

What becomes of the ponies? Some, it may be hoped, revisit their native wilds as boys' hunters, a rôle for which they are excellently adapted. With short steps lightly will they cross the most dangerous bog, and the most dangerous bog, we take it, is the Devil's Stable, the worst part of the fatal "Chains." A contributor to *Outing* observes :—

"He who would ride with, and not follow, the hounds must ride a native horse, one of those untiring little horses born on the hills, whose only sign of bondage is the brand with which, once in a lifetime, they are marked. Very hardy they are, and sure-footed, picking up their living on the trackless moor or rugged mountain - side. Their eye can detect beneath the treacherous surface the hidden bog; they alone know the stride which will carry them lopsided around the steepest hill; their foot can. as it were, clutch the very ground. With them there is no fear of hind legs flying up; and their unflagging pluck will carry them through the hardest and longest day."

There is a good deal of truth in this glowing description, but Exmoor ponies cannot be recommended for adult equestrians. Farmers do indeed ride them from point to point, but, thus weighted, who could expect the diminutive mounts to live with the hounds? On the other hand, in the opinion of a competent judge, the most perfect mount for a ten- or eleven-stone man is a cross between an Exmoor pony and a thoroughbred. Sir Frederick Knight used to say that in the old days Mr. Edward Sandford, Rector of Combe Florey, owned such a galloway, which, in a chase over Exmoor with the staghounds, was unapproachable. The three Knights, with Charles on his " Commodore " and Frederick on his celebrated steeplechaser " Tory," would race after the reverend gentleman, but, if he had a fair start, would race in vain.

Some of the ponies—indeed, most of them—are sent to less congenial spheres. One of them was " spotted " a few years ago, driven by a costermonger near the Imperial Institute, while a considerable ratio, alas ! drag out a toilsome existence in mines.

CHAPTER III

SHEEP

THE origin of the Exmoor horned sheep is shrouded in mystery. Probably a race of mountain sheep has for ages upon ages climbed the bleak hillsides, but neither plain record nor vague tradition points us to its primitive home. To-day, at all events, the blackcock and the wild red deer hardly appear more proper to the locality than the hardy little sheep which roams about the moor. Experts, however, who have made a comparative study of the subject, are of opinion that the Exmoors belong to the same old stock as the Portland and Dorset, nor have they to search for a missing link. Speaking of the sheep that once lived and thrived on the Mendip Hills, that great authority Youatt remarks, " These sheep appear to be an intermediate race between the Exmoor and the Dorset." More diminutive than the Dorsets, with smaller horns and white faces, the Mendip sheep, says Youatt, would lamb quite as early, and, when required, bear two crops a year. Exmoor ewes are frequently applied to the production of fat lambs, and, with plenty of good food, are unusually prolific. Such sheep may be seen with two or three lambs running at their sides, for, as nurses, the Exmoor ewes are simply unsurpassed.

Although we have no early notices of the sheep, there is ample evidence to show that for centuries they not only constituted the most valuable asset of the hill

farmers, but were the main support of the neighbouring
towns. A wool-pack figures in the Minehead coat-of-
arms, and there must be few visitors to Dunster who
have not been struck with the delightfully quaint old
yarn-market, occupying the centre of the street, and
built by George Luttrell in 1609. Octagonal in form,
with little dormer windows for admitting light into the
interior, it is the sign and symbol of a vanished industry
which was at one time considerable. According to
a local tradition four-and-twenty master clothiers, hailing from Dunster, were in the habit of attending the
fairs at Bristol and Exeter. "Dunsters" are referred to
in an Act of Parliament of James I., which requires
"that every broad cloth, commonly called Tauntons,
Bridgwaters, and Dunsters, made in the western part
of Somersetshire, or elsewhere, of like making, shall
contain, being thoroughly wet, between twelve and
thirteen yards, and in breadth seven quarters of a yard
at the least, and being well scoured, thicked, milled, and
fully dried, shall weigh thirty pounds the cloth at the
least." In Savage's time the only memorials of the trade,
apart from the yarn-market, were some fulling-mills in a
state of decay, the ruins of a factory at Frackford, the
parochial books, and certain terraces on the south side
of Grabhurst, where stood the tenter-racks for drying
the cloths. To-day apparently the remains are even
more scanty.

In the olden times the Whit Monday fair and the
weekly markets, which were held on Friday, were the
largest in this part of the county. Thither flocked
the farmers' wives and daughters, in order to sell to the
clothiers the yarn which the busy fingers of the women,
from the mistress to the 'prentice maid, had spun from
the masters' wool in the intervals of their household
duties. An Exmoor farmer told us recently that, when
he was a boy, black sheep were appreciated, as their

wool yielded grey yarn.   He was compelled to deplore,
however, that the spinning-wheel, formerly so familiar
an object in farmhouses and cottages, had almost, if not
entirely, ceased its revolutions.

A good amount of Exmoor wool probably found its
way to Tiverton, of which town Blackmore (or John
Ridd) observes that its chief boast, " next to its woollen
staple," was " the worthy grammar school, the largest in
the West of England, founded and handsomely endowed
in the year 1604 by Master Peter Blundell, of that same
place, clothier." That an Exmoor boy should be sent
to Blundell's School for instruction was perfectly natural.
Addressing the members of the Somerset Archæological
and Natural History Society, in 1900, Mr. Edmund
Buckle, the diocesan architect, remarked that " he had
already mentioned the poverty of most of the churches
they had visited during the previous two days, and that
it was hardly natural that they should have elaborately
carved work in the churches about Exmoor.   But,
although Exmoor was in itself a poor district, he took
it that all the hills around must have been covered with
sheep ; and Tiverton was the great market for the sale
of the wool. . . . Tiverton appeared to have been an
exceedingly thriving town, dependent chiefly on the
woollen trade, and the merchants of Tiverton spent
their money very freely for public objects.   The school
they had just been to was an example of that, founded
by a merchant who had started from Tiverton ; Greenway's almshouses were another ; and there were at least
two other almshouses, and one other school, founded by
Tiverton merchants.   The Greenway's almshouses they
had just passed were founded by the same man who
had built the whole of the magnificent south side of
St. Peter's Church on which they were now looking with
admiration."   Greenway's Chapel, it may be observed,
is scored with carvings of wool-packs and galleys in

which the wool was exported to foreign countries, principally Spain and the Netherlands.

The history of the Exmoor sheep does not perhaps go back beyond the year 1794, when Arthur Young, in his *Annals of Agriculture*, briefly alluded to them. During a visit to Monksilver some specimens were brought under his notice, and he records that at Southmolton market they were sold as hoggets at from 9*s.* to 16*s.* each. Kept on the hills for two or three years, they were afterwards fattened and sold without their wool.

OLD BLUNDELL'S SCHOOL, TIVERTON

The weight of the fleeces ranged from 3 lbs. to 4 lbs., and that of the carcasses from 16 lbs. to 18 lbs. per quarter. The weight of the fleece is now about 1 lb. heavier. Billingsley, in his official report to the Board of Agriculture, declares that although vastly inferior to the old Bampton breed, as subject in their youth to a precarious existence on the hills, yet, in the opinion of many sensible farmers, they were altogether a profitable stock.

The condition of matters in the middle of the last century is lucidly set forth, in the *Journal of the Royal*

Agricultural Society for 1850, by the late Sir Thomas
Acland, one of the principal breeders :—

"The hill-country farmer generally keeps a breeding flock
of horned ewes and a flock of wethers, which run on the hill
summer and winter. The number of his ewes will be limited
by the extent of his water-meadows, on which he relies in
great measure for the keep of his couples after the lambs are
dropped. The number of hill-wethers depends on the extent
of the common right attached to the farm. About the
twentieth of June all the sheep are gathered for sorting and
shearing. The mouths of the sheep are examined, and those
whose teeth are broken are drafted and kept back from the
hill to be sold or fatted off. The ewe hoggets replace the
draft ewes, and the wether hogs of the former season are
shorn with the hill-wethers, and turned off to the hills after
being signed with some large mark which can be known at a
distance. They cost nothing but an occasional gathering
until next year, and the only profit they yield is about 5 lbs. of
wool. In their fourth or fifth year they may be brought on to
grass. They are also used as labourers on the farm, to eat the
grass in the fall of the year, and are sometimes marched in
close phalanx up and down a ploughed field to tread in the
wheat. The ordinary sheep of the country, when fat, do not
weigh above 11 lbs. or 12 lbs. a quarter. Where pains have
been taken to improve a flock, they may reach on an average
16 lbs. or 18 lbs. a quarter, and some are brought up to 24 lbs.
a quarter when fed on the Bridgwater marshes. There is also
great difference in the quality of the wool of a common and
of a well-bred sheep. It is the practice of farmers, who have
good land as well as common, to put their draft ewes with a
small-headed and high-proof Leicester ram, to sell the lambs
fat in May, and the ewes as soon as they get fat. There are
great objections to horned sheep. It is almost impossible to
prevent them from being infected with the scab while they are
on the open hill; they also acquire such restless habits that
they are always breaking the fences when brought into the
enclosed ground. In fatting them much judgment and
practical knowledge is required, for they do not get on well
in hot weather; and it frequently happens that when they are
first put on turnips they lose ground, or 'pitch,' as it is called,
for two months in the autumn, and are slow in regaining it

afterwards. For these and other reasons farmers who occupy good land in the vale with their hill-farms, are getting tired of their horned sheep, and use their hill-farms only as summering ground for knot sheep and bullocks."

The half-century that has elapsed since these words were written has been marked by important changes in the management of sheep. The price of mutton has gone up, and the price of wool has gone down, the consequence being that flockmasters have aimed rather at the quick production of flesh than at a cheap and easy supply of wool. Even this mountain breed has been, as far as possible, adapted to the prevailing conditions either by the use of long-wool or "improved" rams, or by feeding. On Winsford Hill, at Anstey, at Withypool, and at Molland, fine specimens of "improved" Exmoors may be seen. Killed at two years and a half, their mutton is superb, and only to be had at high prices. Care is taken of the lambs till they are hoggets. They are then turned out to common with the older sheep, and later are taken in to be fed. The ewes are fattened only when broken-mouthed. The highly bred sheep attain 19 lbs. per quarter, and at Christmas wether sheep have been known to reach 28 lbs. per quarter. The common sort of Exmoors fatten to about 15 lbs. per quarter. A farm bailiff of the district was once heard to remark, "You may as well try to fatten a hurdle as one of the old running wethers of the common Exmoor breed," the reason being that habits formed in a semi-wild state on the moor operate as a hindrance to profitable feeding afterwards. For three or four years the wethers are allowed to run on the hills, and the only asset derived from them is their wool. At the end of that time, however, their mutton is of the very best quality.

Although Exmoor mutton is superior, and obtains a higher price per pound than that of sheep producing a greater proportion of meat from a given quantity of food, still the farmer is apt to consider himself a loser, and is frequently heard to say, " I want more weight in my flock." As against this, competent authorities affirm that three sheep weighing 100 lbs. each would eat no more than two weighing 150 lbs. each. This fact ought to be very full of comfort to hill farmers, the climate of whose district renders it imperative that it should carry Exmoor sheep on account of their hardy nature. That they are extremely hardy admits of no question. No amount of bad weather has any effect on them, and they live to a great age. Lambing usually takes place from March to the middle of April, and weaning about Midsummer, when the lambs are kept for some weeks in the inclosures. Turned on to the hills early in the spring, they remain there all the year, except when they are brought in for shearing. The Exmoor is not only larger than the Welsh mountain sheep, but is in every sense a better animal. The likeliest quarter in which to obtain them would be Winsford Fair, which is held about the middle of August. Since the breed is not regarded as adapted for general use, the demand for rams is limited, but, owing to the care bestowed on them of recent years, good rams not seldom fetch from ten to fifteen guineas.

When required, ewes will lamb sooner than at the period named. In fact, the lambing season may be said to begin in January, and continue through February and March; and the early lambs are commonly the best for rearing. In his prize *Essay on Mountain Sheep* (1866) Mr. Dixon observes :—

"The original Exmoors milk better than the 'improved,' and old ewes especially. There are instances of ewes rearing three lambs well after the first fortnight. The ewes are always brought down to the lower ground to lamb, and get a few turnips and oats; and then come in again from the hills in

November to the poorest enclosed lands.   They are put to the
tups at two years, and are generally drafted after three crops
of lambs, though some old favourites go on for longer."

On account of their good nursing capabilities, which
have gained them a reputation as mothers of fat lambs,
draft ewes of the Exmoor breed are in demand in other
parts of the country, where they are frequently tupped
with Leicester rams.   For rearing purposes also this
cross is freely adopted, and not a few small farmers,
who have no large run of common, find cross-breds
more profitable than Exmoors.   While in the purely
hill districts the Exmoors hold their own, farmers have
sought since the Commons Inclosures Act to produce a
larger sheep by crossing them with the Leicester.   In
this they have succeeded, but at the cost of stamina and
numbers.   The notts, as they are called, are without
horns, and ewes of this description have found favour
with some (Cornish) farmers, while others have used
the tups as well.

In its own district the Exmoor sheep is reputed to
be better suited to the local conditions than any im-
portations, such as Black Faces, Cheviots, and Welsh
sheep, with all of which experiments have been tried.
The late owner of Exmoor, Sir Frederick Knight, did
not share this opinion, holding that, in both wool and
flesh, his Cheviots were to be preferred to the native
breed.   It must not be forgotten, however, that around
Simonsbath the country has been more extensively
reclaimed than elsewhere, and turnip and rape crops
are therefore more plentiful.   Mr. Dixon's verdict that
under high pressure well-bred Exmoors have done
wonders is even truer to-day than it was thirty-five
years ago.   The methods employed for their improvement have been a judicious selection of rams, a comprehensive weeding of ewes, and careful matings; or,
in other words, the principle of breeding in and in has

been adopted. Mr. John Coleman, late of *The Field*, thus sums up the result :—

"Whatever may be thought of the Exmoor, sufficient merit is exemplified under cultivation to invest the sheep with high claims for perpetuity of existence. The improvement of the sheep has recently progressed quite as fast as the reclamation of the hill commons; and if sufficient quality and capability to put on flesh rapidly can be imparted to this hardy and prolific stock, for the future requirements of agriculturists on this elevated tract of country, we may hope that it will be one of the few mountain species that the hand of civilisation will spare."

All who have seen, and seen to admire, the dainty little animals browsing on their native hills will certainly echo this hope, and the wish will be seconded no less warmly by those whose palate has been gratified with their gamy mutton. An old friend of ours informs us that in his early days the horned wethers roamed the common-right hills all the year till, at the age of eight or nine, they became broken-mouthed, and a little corn was given to them in preparation for the Christmas market. Their haunches, after hanging from one to three months, according to the weather, formed a "nectar" of mutton, such as, he assures us, present-day *bons vivants* know nothing about. The same gentleman regrets the degeneracy of lambs' tails pie due to the introduction of tailing in the spring before their full flavour is acquired. Formerly the process took place in late autumn. With reference to lambs' tails pies, the good old Sir Thomas Acland (grandfather of the present baronet), when genially reproached by Lady Acland at Holnicote for keeping her waiting at luncheon, as genially replied: "I have been feasting at Farmer Peek's on the flesh of living animals."

That reminds us that sheep-shearing used to be a time of great festivity in Exmoor farmhouses, as was natural enough when wool fetched two shillings per pound, and the sale of the fleeces accounted for more than the rent. Whether the occasion is still kept up with equal hilarity now that the price of wool has dropped to sixpence, or less, may be doubted ; anyhow, this is Miss Alice King's description of the gay doings that went on in the fat years of long ago :—

"The sheep-shearing is always kept as a much-observed festival in a West Country farmhouse. Vast meat-pies and plum-puddings are prepared in its honour by the farmer's wife, and she piles her thick clotted cream high on the top of the junket, that most characteristic of all West Country dishes. Her daughters meanwhile are engaged in their part of the arrangements for the evening. At the door of the house is placed a table on which are put all sorts of articles for the toilet, such as brushes, combs, etc.; at the side of the table is set a large tub of fresh water, in which float all sorts of fragrant herbs, spicy thyme, and sweet-scented boy's love and marjoram. Here in this *al fresco* dressing-room the young men will make themselves neat and spruce before they go indoors to the feast, and the perfumed herbs in the tub will remove from their hands the strong odour of the sheep's fleeces more effectually than any soap prepared by Rimmel or Briedenbach. Occasionally a youth, as he plunges his fingers in the tub, will start and cry out; the damsels have been minded to play their swains a mischievous and not too kind trick, and have hidden nettles under the herbs. How the bright eyes of the girls—those dark eyes which are such a special trade mark of native beauty round about Exmoor and North Devon—dance with fun as they peep from the woodbine-framed casement above, and watch the result of their artifice ! The lads know well enough that they are being spied, and think it best for the dignity of their manhood to suppress as quickly as they can all signs of discomfiture, and to enter the house with a jaunty air, unmindful of their tingling fingers. Then the feast begins in good earnest. The cider cup goes round, the old folks make jokes, the young men make love, songs are sung by any member of the company who may be possessed of musical talent. The song which is most popular on these occasions, and which it is generally the custom to sing, is one the chorus of each verse of which consists in the imitation of the noises made by the

various farm animals, such as the bleating of the sheep, the
lowing of the cattle, the neighing of the horses, etc. It
has an irresistibly comic effect to sit in the midst of a circle
of grown-up men and women, all gravely engaged in trying
to produce these strange sounds."

Another song, which is sometimes heard at sheep-
shearing, and also at Christmas parties, extols the very
particular merits of the Exmoor horned sheep. We
regret that so far we have not succeeded in recovering
the words of the song, though, *pace* the late Sir Thomas
Acland (see p. 150), we are quite of opinion that they
deserve an appreciative ditty all to themselves. Whatever may be said about their restlessness and inability
to fatten, these animals are among the most handsome
of their kind. Especially noticeable are the curves of the
horns, an element of beauty in which the Dorset rams
undoubtedly vie with the Exmoors. The Exmoor rams,
it may be observed, are more pugnacious than their
rivals, and occasionally the combats, in which the horns
are, of course, the principal weapons, are desperate
in the extreme. Exmoor sheep have a peculiar tuft
of wool on the brow, and the fleece grows so close
to the face or cheeks as sometimes to envelop the
whole features, except the nose. Another feature in
the Exmoor is its extraordinary rotundity of form
combined with short, yet open legs. Of the well-bred
flocks it is said that they are closer to the ground
than any other breed of sheep. As they have white
faces, legs, and fleeces, they have been styled "little
white ivories." Mr. H. H. Dixon summarised their
points as follows :—" A fine curly horn ; a broad square
loin ; round ribs ; a drum-like, not a square carcass,
on short legs ; and close-set fleece, with wool well up
to the cheeks." Although standing moderately on their
fore-legs, they fail somewhat behind the shoulder, where
even the improved sheep do not girth very well, and

they are rather faulty about the neck. In the case of wethers the horns should lie back, while those of the ewes are often hoop-shaped.

Speaking generally, the chief merits of the Exmoor breed consist in their round barrels, their fine-flavoured mutton, their speed, and their good constitutions. The sheep need good constitutions, since in winter it is no uncommon experience for them to be buried for days together in a snowdrift. The writer of an article in the *Cornhill Magazine*, entitled " Winter on Exmoor," thus describes the difficulties of the shepherds and the dangers of the sheep at that season of the year :—

" The resident has a long winter to go through before the snow finally melts from off the hills of Exmoor. For nearly three months after Christmas we were snowed up, the drifts being in some places tremendous. Then when the carpet of snow is so thick and soft that one cannot hear the sound of his own steps, and all is still in the fields around, the withered leaves rustling on the beech hedges give forth a weird, mysterious sound, as of something pursuing one along deserted roads.

" Now the shepherds have a hard time in collecting and often digging out their sheep. A whole flock will sometimes be buried out of sight by a heavy fall during the night, and their guardians have to tramp miles through the blinding drift before their place of sepulture can be found. The collies find the place at last and begin to sniff, and whimper, and burrow in the snow. A long iron rod, thrust downward, verifies the sagacity of the dogs ; then off come the coats, and half a dozen shovels in sturdy hands soon clear away the snow, and discover the palpitating flock in a cave hollowed out by the steam of their own breath, with possibly one or two of the weaker brethren smothered or trampled beneath the feet of their frightened comrades. The cautious shepherd, when he sees the heavy banks of cloud laden with snow driving up low over Dunkery, and covering the hills with a dusky pall, knows it is time to be stirring, and will endeavour to collect his flock into some fold-yard on one of the outlying farms ; or, at least, into the dark plantations beside the Barle, where he will hang bundles of hay to the lowest branches of the dwarf oaks and firs, so that they need not stray forth again to search for food on the frozen moor."

As a description of sheep-rescue, however, nothing can equal Blackmore's chapter, "The Great Winter," as graphic and impressive as any in his fine romance. At the risk of repetition, we will venture to quote a paragraph.

"Further in and close under the bank, where they had huddled themselves for warmth, we found all the rest of the poor sheep packed as closely as if they were in a great pie. It was strange to observe how their vapour and breath, and the moisture exuding from their wool, had scooped, as it were, a coved room for them, lined with a ribbing of deep yellow snow. Also the churned snow beneath their feet was as yellow as gamboge. Two or three of the weaklier hoggets were dead, from want of air, and from pressure; but more than three score were as lively as ever; though cramped and stiff for a little while.

"'However shall us get 'em home?' John Fry asked."

(The reader had better consult *Lorna Doone* for the solution.)

Mr. A. Kingdon, late of Driver's Farm, has a good record in this matter. During twenty-seven years he never lost a sheep through burial in the snow, and he attributes this fact to his regularity in looking after them twice a day. Sheep, he says, always beat back to the place where they sucked, so that we have here one clue as to their whereabouts in the event of their becoming lost. Another clue, which Mr. Kingdon discovered to be useful, was the presence or absence of the black lamb. The black lamb was the leader, and, if you had got him, you had got all the rest. These black lambs may be pure Exmoors, though it is not often that you get more than one or two in a flock. Usually black faces are characteristic of Highland sheep, some of which have been introduced into Exmoor. It

appears that many years ago a Mr. Spooner, a Scotch
gentleman residing at Wintershead, had a shepherd
named Scott, who afterwards became bailiff to Mr.
Knight, and who, first of men, imported Black Faces
and Cheviots. Lord Ebrington has a large flock of
Cheviots, and Mr. Kingdon, somewhat to our surprise,
pronounced them, on the whole, more hardy and en-
during than the Exmoors. The Exmoors, however, will
yield seven pounds of wool, where Cheviots average only
three pounds—so, at least, we understood him to say.

Writing in 1859, Professor Tanner observes :—

"The Leicester has been used with Exmoor and Dartmoor
sheep, but unless the produce has been disposed of as fat lamb,
they have not been able to withstand the cold of these districts.
But although the pure blood has not been serviceable in these
districts, yet the improved South Hams rams have been used
on the Dartmoors, and the improved Bampton rams on the
Exmoors, with the best possible success. The crosses thus
produced answer uncommonly well for early fat lambs, and
when reared for stock they are very much prized, and especially
the latter. These half-bred sheep are very much sought after
around the moors, and are kept as breeding stock. They are
exceedingly healthy, and can withstand the climate, whilst at
the same time they produce heavy sheep."

Probably there are no pure Bamptons left, and concerning the origin of the stock absolutely nothing is
known. The first printed mention of them occurs in
a letter addressed to Arthur Young in 1772 by a Mr.
R. Proctor Andernon, and published by the former in
the *Annals of Agriculture*. The Bampton is there
described as "the best breed in Devon," and is stated to
have "existed in the neighbourhood from time immemorial." Mr. Andernon's account of the sheep is as
follows :—

"They are generally white-faced; the best-bred more like
the Leicestershire than any other, but larger-boned and longer
in the legs and in the body, yet not so long as the Wiltshires,

with which they have been crossed, nor so broad-backed as the Leicesters. A fat ewe rises to 20 lb. a quarter on an average, and wethers to 30 lb. or 35 lb. a quarter on an average. 18 lb. of wool have been shorn from a ram of the breed that was supposed to be 40 lb. the quarter. The carcass is coarser than that of the Dorset, and the wool about 2*d.* per pound cheaper."

Billingsley, in his *Agricultural Survey of Somerset* (1798), writing with reference to the Taunton district, speaks of the Bampton breed as—

"A valuable sort not much unlike the Leicester, well made, and covered with a thick fleece of wool, weighing in general 7 lb. or 8 lb., and they sometimes reach even to the weight of 12 lb., and sell at about 10*d.* per pound. . . . The sale ewes," he says, "are put to the ram at about the latter end of July, and the flock ewes about a month after. Young rams are preferred, as it is supposed that the old ones degenerate in the quality and weight of their wool. The wethers of this breed, when two years old and fattened on turnips, attain the weight of about 25 lb. per quarter, and, being driven to Bristol market, a distance of nearly sixty miles, are sold without their fleeces in the months of May and June."

Vancouver, in his *General View of Agriculture in Devon* (1808), gives the following account:—

"The sheep most approved in the division of Tiverton are the Bampton notts, the wethers of which breed at twenty months old, will weigh 22 lb. per quarter, and shear to 6½ lb. to the fleece. The same sheep well wintered, and kept for another twelve months, will average 28 lb. per quarter, and yield 8 lb. of unwashed wool to the fleece. The present price of this wool is 1*s.* per pound."

Again referring to the Bamptons, he says:—

"The first cross of this breed with the new Leicester is growing greatly in esteem, from its improving the form and bringing the animal three months earlier to market; but, however desirable this cross so far may be, more of that blood is objected to on account of the extraordinary nursing and care required to be paid to the young couples; the lambs being represented as very tender and much oftener perishing through the severity of the season than the genuine offspring of the native sheep."

In 1855 Wilson wrote in the *Royal Agricultural Society's Journal* of the Bampton variety :—

"Like most of the old indigenous breeds of the county, it has gradually been displaced by the improved breeds; and now it is very difficult to find the pure Bampton unmixed with other blood, a few only remaining in Devonshire and West Somerset. They are usually met with crossed with the Leicester, and very much resembling them in shape, though somewhat larger in size, and hardly so fine in general character. They are without horns; and with clean faces and legs; they are hardy, but require good pasture. At two years old, if well kept, they average 120 lb. to 150 lb. each. The meat is juicy, but like that of all large sheep, inferior in quality to the smaller breeds. The wool produce is good; the fleece, averaging 7 lb., is rather coarse in quality. They are so intermixed with Leicester blood as to partake more of the character of that breed than of the old stock; crosses with the Lincolnshire and with the Exmoor breed are also met with."

There is no direct evidence to show that the Bamptons have ever been crossed with Southdowns, though it is curious that a Mr. Andrew Hosegood, of Williton, told Mr. Joseph Darby some years ago that he recollected the Bampton sheep of his boyhood as having grey faces. It is clear, however, that the original Bampton sheep had a white face, as had also the Leicester and every other long-wool known to have been associated with it. Another breeder has deposed that more than half a century ago a blue tint in the face became fashionable, and so remained, until it was found that animals with this characteristic were thinner in flesh and wool, and weaker in constitution. On this discovery being made, white faces returned to favour, and are now universally preferred.

The mixture of the Bampton breed with the Leicester

M

produced the far-famed Devon Longwool. Mr. Darby, than whom is no higher authority, discriminates between the sorts in the following manner :—

"A well-bred animal of this variety differs from a pure Leicester in having a longer and larger face, with greater width at the forehead and nose, the ears longer. The frame is more bulky, and of far greater length, although not quite so round and compact, but the girth is equal to that of the Leicester. The Devon Longwool also appears higher than a pure Leicester. In good constitution and hardihood the former surpasses the latter; it will attain much greater weight of carcass, and more flesh in a given time, and it is likewise reputed to come earlier to maturity."

In conclusion a brief note may be permitted on the larger quadrupeds with their soft, rich, curly coats which may be seen, mingled with the sheep and ponies, on the Exmoor hills. The original habitat of the North Devon cattle is in and around North and South Molton, *i.e.* at the foot of Exmoor, and nowhere do they appear to greater advantage than in the bleak region for which, owing to their active habits and hardy nature, they are specially adapted. Transferred to richer districts, like Taunton Dene, the Devon becomes another animal, larger, and with long straight hair. Vancouver praised the breed as being active at work and possessing an unrivalled aptitude for fattening. At present the ox is not wanted for draught, but it is a consolation to know that, in case of an emergency, we have an animal capable of walking as fast and getting through as much work as a heavy horse.

PART III

DIALECT

CHAPTER I

A DISCOURSE AT LARGE

THE dialect spoken on Exmoor does not differ materially from that which is heard pretty generally throughout the county of Devon, to which linguistically it belongs. Experts in the Devonshire brogue pique themselves on their ability to distinguish sub-varieties. The dialect, for instance, as rendered in the environs of Exeter is not precisely the dialect as found at Barnstaple. So, too, the people that dwell in darkness in the South Hams do not conform in all points to the uses of their brethren in East Devon. That such distinctions between tweedle-dum and tweedle-dee do exist appears certain. Thus, with reference to the term *scatt* or *skatt* (a shower of rain), Mr. F. T. Elworthy avers that "scatt is not Exmoor, but Exeter dialect; in North Devon and West Somerset it is always *scad*." He goes even further, and points out that *thick* (that) is a North Devon form and *theck* a West Somerset. Mr. Elworthy, the compiler of the monumental *West Somerset Word Book*, is an authority from whom one does not willingly differ, but, we confess, he is to us not absolutely infallible. Thus he tells us that the local pronunciation of "girl" is "guur'ld." The word is not in common use Exmoor way, but we have heard it pronounced "gurdle." Still he may be right about *thick* and *theck*.

There is one matter, however, in which Mr. Elworthy, the present writer, and all and sundry are apt to be deceived. In judging written specimens of the dialect we naturally test them by the modes of pronunciation with which we are ourselves familiar. In other words, we may not sufficiently allow for dialectal changes; but that changes have taken place, not only of late years, but during many decades, is not only probable, but provable, and that is one reason why we should treat the ancient monuments of the dialect with respect. At the time when the writer first made the acquaintance of the *Exmoor Scolding* and the *Exmoor Courtship* he had never heard the word "hear" pronounced "hire"; he had always been used to "yur" as the vernacular form, and "hire," which Mr. Elworthy rightly classes as obsolescent, both read and sounded most unnatural. Since then, however, he has heard the word from the lips of an old West Country labourer, who would never say "hire" himself, but casually, as it were, let it slip out in quoting an ancient dame, dead, perhaps, these forty years—"Dost hire me?"

These reflections are suggested in part by the experience of the writer, who, a year or two ago, believed he was citing the *ipsissima verba* of R. D. Blackmore, or, more precisely, of John Fry, when he wrote "Thee beest Zummerzett, Jan Ridd." On handing his proofs, however, to a friend, who has lived in the neighbourhood of Exmoor all his life, he was horrified by the criticism, "What's this? Blackmore must have written, not 'thee beest,' but 'thee art.' Did you ever hear anybody round here say 'thee beest'?" I confessed I had not. So, without the least scruple, the correction was accepted. But what did Blackmore write? If we turn to Chapter LVI. of *Lorna Doone* we shall find out. "Zummerzett thou bee'st, Jan Ridd, and Zummerzett thou shalt be. Thee carl theezell a Davonsheer man! Whoy, thee lives in Zummerzett; and in Zummerzett thee wast barn, lad!"

We may compare with this quotation from Blackmore some remarks in a letter addressed to the *Monthly Magazine* in September, 1814.

"They also make use of the verb 'be' through nearly the whole of the present tense of the verb *to be*, as *I be, thou beest* (pronounced *bist*), etc. They terminate the preterite tense and participle past of most verbs in *d*, as 'I saw or I have seen'; *I zeed* or *I have zeed; gid* for 'gave' or 'given.' They always use *en* for 'him' (*ihn*, German) and *'em* for 'they' or 'them,' both in affirmations and interrogations, and *'er* (German *er*) is 'he' in interrogations only, as 'Did they see him?'—*did 'em zee en?* 'Did he give them anything?'—*did 'er gi 'em ort?* 'Give him'—*gi en*, etc. They change the *snt* in such contractions as 'isn't,' 'wasn't,' into 'd'n,' as 'isn't he?'—*id'n er?* 'wasn't he?'—*wad'n er?* But they say *hant er?* for 'hasn't he?' to distinguish it from *had'n er?* As to those combinations of consonants which not only require an effort to pronounce them, but are offensive to the delicate ear, they either interpose a vowel or omit one of the consonants, as 'posts,' *postes;* 'desks,' *deskes;* 'needle,' *neel;* 'with me,' *wi' me;* 'a pound of butter,' *a poun' o' butter.*"

An even more remarkable usage is that which we find in such forms as *chell, chave* (for "I shall," "I have"), and which the testimony of the *Exmoor Courtship* and similar compositions shows to have been common in past ages. Probably no one belonging to the present generation has ever heard these coalitions; certainly the writer never has. Closely allied with this peculiarity is the Exmoor variety of the personal pronoun I, viz. *Es* (North Devon *Iss*). If we understand Mr. Elworthy aright, he considers the Exmoor *Es* to be nothing more than the ordinary "us," employed as a nominative. This is still of very frequent occurrence in the West Country, but, admitting the accuracy of Mr. Elworthy's view, one has still to ask how it is that "us" has come to be employed in this way. *Em* ("them") is also used thus, and, with the analogy of the French pronouns, *moi*, *lui*, *eux*, etc., always preferred to *je*, *il*, *ils*, when the speaker wishes to be emphatic, as a guide, it may, perhaps, be conjectured that the confusion arose from a sort of false stress.   There is a tendency on Exmoor to dispense with the pronouns altogether ; for instance, *hasn't ?* ("hast not") is deemed quite sufficient, without the addition of *thee* or *thou*.   By the way, to address a person in the second person singular is regarded on Exmoor as disrespectful.   An old man of my acquaintance observed to me the other day that, when the children were growing up, his wife never said *thee*, either to them or to himself; whereas his daughter-in-law, for all her good temper, sometimes indulged in the habit. The slight censure implied was, perhaps, unmerited, as the use of the second person singular really denotes extreme familiarity ; hence the element of impoliteness in relation to a stranger.   The French have a verb *tutoyer*, exactly expressing this state of things.

However, it is not certain that Mr. Elworthy's account of *Es* is correct.   We have in our possession a manuscript copy of one of the late Edward Capern's poems, in which the "I's" have been throughout altered to *Iss*.   Evidently, therefore, in Mr. Capern's opinion—and, as a man of the people, he was likely to be a good judge of dialect—*Iss* was a more homely and idiomatic form of *I*.   It may be observed, too, that at the present day, if a cottage girl said of a young man, *Us likes en*, she would be generally understood to indicate others besides herself, although there is no doubt a convenient ambiguity in the phrase.   That ambiguity—much would depend on the amount of unction thrown into the confession—springs not so much from a regal or editorial use of the pronoun, as from the influence of an older pronoun similar in form, but of independent origin, and now entirely obsolete.   Our theory is that the forms

Iss and *Es* are ultimately the same as the German *ich*. In the writings of some of Chaucer's contemporaries we meet with *Uch*, *Ich*, which are often agglutinated to the verb in the fashion of the *Exmoor Courtship*; *e.g. Ichot=Ich wot* ("I know"); *Icholle=Ich wolle* ("I will"). *Ich*, it is practically certain, was not pronounced, at any rate in the Southern dialect, as a guttural, and thus there would be an easy transition to the still softer *Iss* or *Es*.

The *Exmoor Courtship* gives *min* as an alternative to *'em*. *Min*, we believe, is even now not quite obsolete. What does it stand for? It is a curious fact that in the poem of Robert of Gloucester, who flourished about the close of the thirteenth century, we meet with an impersonal pronoun *me*, supposed to represent *men*, and used in the same way as the French *on* and the German *man*. In the West Country there is a vocative form *min* ("Bless 'ee, I ban't a going to zay ort, min"), which seems to be an abbreviation of *man*.

The type of English spoken on Exmoor, and in the West Country generally, is that known to philology as Southern or Saxon, and was imported into this Keltic district from the kingdom of Wessex, comprising what is now Dorset, Wiltshire, etc. There the Saxons made their earliest settlements, the Angles choosing the northeast of England. The West Country dialect is soft, broad, and Doric; it has no ugly gutturals, and even the aspirate struggles for existence. Robert of Gloucester's *Chronicle*, to which allusion has been made, was written at a period when the English tongue, after a long spell of oppression, was strongly reasserting itself; and what, for us, renders his rhyme so valuable and interesting is the fact that it was indited by the learned Robert in his own dialect—the *patois* which makes some ladies shudder, and of which the very Board School children are beginning to be ashamed. It is well, no doubt, to

be perfect in the current English of the day — an
"accent" is at once detected in a London drawing-
room or a University Church—but it is surely imperative to know one's own dialect, and whatever
shame there may be in the matter should attach to
ignorance.   After all, it is a considerable accomplish-
ment to be able correctly to talk and write dialect—
especially other people's.   A kind friend tells us that
he remembers how, on one occasion, Canon Atkinson
made great fun of Charles Dickens' Yorkshire as it
appears in *Nicholas Nickleby;* and of many another
novelist may be predicated what Ben Jonson observed
of Spenser's hodge-podge—that he "writ no language."
Meanwhile rare Ben is himself by no means impeccable.
Although in his *Tale of a Tub* he makes several of his
characters pronounce their *f's* and *s's* like *v* and *z,* still
his specimens of the vernacular are not pure and un-
defiled anything.

Many will be surprised to hear that the West Country
dialect, or an offer at it, may be found in Shakespeare
also.   Yes, in *King Lear,* where (Act IV. Sc. 6) we
come on the following dialogue:—

"*Steward.*   Wherefore, bold peasant,
Dar'st thou support a publish'd traitor?   Hence;
Lest that the infection of his fortune take
Like hold on thee.   Let go his arm.

"*Edgar.*   Chill not let go, zir, without vurther 'casion.

"*Stew.*   Let go, slave, or thou diest!

"*Edg.*   Good gentleman, go your gait, and let poor volk
pass.   An chud ha' bin zwagger'd out of my life, 'twould
not ha' bin zo long as 'tis by a vortnight.   Nay, come not
near the old man; keep out, che vor' ye, or Ise try whether
your costard or my bat be the harder: Ch'll be plain with you.

"*Stew.*   Out, dunghill!

"*Edg.*   Ch'ill pick your teeth, zir: come; no matter vor
your foins."

Some people like to think that, as Sir Walter Raleigh

and Sir Francis Drake were both favourites of Queen Elizabeth, the language of the Court in that reign was, for the most part, the West Country brogue. Without going so far as that, it is possible to see in this connection the source whence Shakespeare and Jonson may have derived hints. We may even imagine that the poets were secretly gibing at those West Country heroes, whose speech, perhaps, was as uncouth as their actions were valiant.

However, the use, or misuse, of dialect by the great masters—a topic, so far as we know, still fresh and inviting treatment—is too broad a theme to be further discussed in these pages. Rather let us return to the period when no English dialect could claim preeminence—or, if any, the southern—and literary proprieties were yet to form. In Robert of Gloucester's day, and both before and after, it was an open question whether Saxon English would not win its way, by dint of literary usage, into universal acceptance as the standard type of the language. One of the earliest compositions in what is called Middle English is the *Ancren Riwle*—written long before Chaucer, about 1220 A.D.—and in this we find *for* spelt *vor* and *fifth vifte*. Again, after Robert of Gloucester had passed away, John of Trevisa, evidently a Cornishman, and a zealous champion of English as opposed to French, or the degenerate Norman that went by that name, committed such enormities as *vorth* for *forth*, *veaw* for *few*, and—oh, ye gods !—*eorneth* for *runneth*.

Still, we are not sure that as useful examples as any may not be culled from good old Robert himself; at any rate, we will seek some for the sake of those who know Exmoor and not Robert.

> " Vor if a maid troth y-plight to do a fooly deed
> Alone privily without her friends' reed,
> Thicky vorward were vor nought."

"The Duke William anon vorbed all his
  That none were so wood to robby, nor no manner do harm
  Upon the land that is was."

In both these quotations there are words that are
obsolete on Exmoor as well as elsewhere. " Forward,"
for instance, is no longer used in the sense of "agreement," but, if it were, it would be naturally pronounced
as Robert of Gloucester spells it. In the first line of
the former quotation a "had" seems to have been
omitted, as "y" (like the German *ge*) represents the
past participle, not the preterite. This old grammatical
prefix, best known to the commonalty from the term
" y-clept," has not yet disappeared in the West Country,
though the sound is here broad enough to be marked
with an *a : e.g.* " I've a-yeard they'm ago " (gone). This
a must not be confounded with *a* which is used with
present participles (*e.g.* " I be a-gwayne hawm, I be, sure "),
and which stands for " on."

" Thicky " (*thulke*, in the text), which is found also in
Chaucer, is still quite common in West Somerset. It
means, of course, "that." "Wood" for "mad" is extinct. It may be observed, however, that Exmoor way
" wood " is pronounced " ood " or " hood," which reminds
one of Robin Hood. In Professor Child's *English and
Scotch Ballads* it is suggested that the name Hood may
be a corruption of " 'ood." Peele the dramatist, in his
play of *Edward I.*, speaks expressly of " Robin of the
Wood," *alias* Hood. The point is an interesting one,
and it may be thought a slight confirmation of a very
probable theory that West Country usage is all in its
favour. We once heard a butcher's man accost a fellow-
labourer, " Well, Squire Hoodbury ! " The person's real
name was " Woodbury."

Looking back, we notice that form "robby." The
quotations from Robert of Gloucester have been
modernised somewhat, but the word "robby" is so

spelt in the text, and like spellings occur in other authors of the period. Usually, however, the word would be written "robbe." This sort of thing is common—one may almost say normal—in Chaucer, where, nevertheless, the metre is often imperative that the *e* shall be sounded. We have here, in fact, one of the few traces in English of an elaborate system of inflexions such as we still find in German, where the final *e* is never silent. It is not pretended that the *e* is always sounded in the Exmoor country. Indeed, this is seldom the case unless you can engage your native in familiar and animated discourse. Then perchance you will be able to catch such archaisms as "hidy away," "harvesty," and the like. Whilst we are on this topic, we may as well correct a little error into which Bishop Hobhouse has fallen in his valuable edition of Somerset Churchwardens' Accounts. In one place he says that the *y*, in these cases, implies a frequentative use of the verb, and even signifies a man's trade. This is going much too far. The real fact is, and this is how it should be stated, that the *y* hardly ever occurs save where a verb is intransitive or is used intransitively. For instance, you might hear it said, "I be goin out to harvesty," but seldom or never, "I be goin out to plowy thick viel." In any case, the idea of frequency does not arise, as it would be easy to prove from the accounts themselves.

"Is" in the second quotation stands for "his," and as this is only one out of many similar lapses, we are driven to conclude that Robert of Gloucester occasionally dropped his *h's*. Nowadays this is looked upon as an unspeakably vulgar habit, which we, for our part, have not the slightest wish to encourage. As, however, the afflicted letter is seldom pronounced in French and absolutely unknown in Italian, the embryo philologer will no doubt kindly explain its omission as due, not to any innate coarseness, but to the mollifying influence of a suave southern climate. To this also may be attributed the softening of *f* to *v*, and of *th* to *d*. In Robert's poetry we meet with the form "vader" for "father." We cannot recollect ever hearing "father" pronounced in that way, but "dree" for "three," and "draw" for "throw," which may be heard any day, clearly exhibit the same tendency. "Farthing," too, is generally rendered "farden" or "varden." Jefferies says that the labourer has disused the *z* openly. We gravely question whether even now—and Jefferies wrote about twenty years ago—so unqualified an assertion is safe. At any rate, older Zummerzett—the departing generation—still maintains the affinity between Zoyland and the Zuyder Zee.

Nevertheless, it appears tolerably certain that the language spoken formerly on Exmoor was of a somewhat different character from that which prevails at present. The remarks of John Fry and Betty Muxworthy in *Lorna Doone* contain forms redolent of more northerly and easterly divisions of the county, and suggest that, in those days when local jealousies were much more strongly marked, the boundary of Devon and Somerset was the boundary in some measure of the kindred dialects. Even to this day there are traces of the sort. When I was living at Bampton some eight or nine years ago, I was told by a native of the place that words were in use at Dulverton, just over the border, that were not employed in his neighbourhood. However, the Devonshire dialect seems to have encroached to such an extent that persons born and bred at Dulverton are inclined to discriminate between their own modes of pronunciation and those east of Wiveliscombe, whilst practically identifying their speech with the Bampton type. Thus, a Dulverton man solemnly assured me that you do not hear "*miden*" (for "maiden") and similar sounds until you penetrate some twelve or fourteen miles into the county. In this I have found him to be mistaken, for I have heard *mide* (for "maid"), "*ight*" (for "eight") and "*tile*" (for "tail") in Dulverton itself, the speaker being a native of the adjoining parish of King's Brompton. On the other hand "fight" is pronounced "*faight*," and "right" "*raight*," and "night" "*naight*." The forms "*reert*" and "*neert*," which are given in the *Exmoor Courtship*, are unknown to me orally.

The elision of the *r* in words like "earth," "marsh," etc., is striking. A parallel occurs in the vulgarism "*oss*" for "horse." By way of revenge an *r* is inserted where it ought not to be found; *e.g.* in "ash" (pronounced "*arsh*"), and in "splash" (pronounced "*splarsh*"). Such anomalies are very puzzling, and a support, we fear, to the class which can see in dialect-forms merely traces of ignorance. No doubt there are both ignorance and confusion, though they do not account for everything. Apart from the occurrence of strange terms like "*sar*" (for "earn") and "*gub*" ("tell-tale"), the meaning of which must be asked and learnt from the context, it would much facilitate the understanding of the brogue if it were possible to lay down certain invariable rules with regard to deviations from the ordinary pronunciation—if, for instance, one could say that all *e's* are sounded like *i's* and all *ee's* like *ai's*. Inflexible formulae, however, cannot be applied to Exmoor verbal vagaries. "Beech," says Jefferies, "is pronounced '*bache*.'" We fancy "*bitch*" is commoner; "seem," at all events, becomes "*zim*" ("*I zim*" = "I think"), "sheep" "*ship*," and "week," "*wik*." Mr. Elworthy, again, denies that "meat" is pronounced "*mëat*," but we are sure that we have heard not only words like "beat" pronounced as they are spelt, but "gate" also rendered "*gëat*," with a marked stress on

the first syllable. There is another class of exceptions.
"Heat" is pronounced neither "*hate*," nor "*hit*," nor
"*hëat*," but "*yet*." So, too, "heath" becomes "*yeth*,"
and "herring" "*yerring*." It might seem natural to
conclude from these examples that *y* is here a rough
substitute for the aspirate, but this, we are convinced,
is not the explanation. Nor does the *y* sound appear
to have arisen from a rapid pronunciation of "heat" and
"heath" as dissyllables, since this solution would not apply
to all cases. Not only is "herring" pronounced "yerring," but I have heard "eels" called "yeels," and not
long since I came upon the form "yend" (for "end")
in a transcript from a fifteenth-century Devonshire docu-
ment.* One can only suppose, therefore, that the
natives of the West had a weakness for this *y* sound.
"*Gyarden*" (for "garden") was a common affectation
in society circles at a much more recent date.

Although "gate" is pronounced "*gë-at*," "great" is
not pronounced "*grëat*" but "*girt*." Who does not
remember "girt Jan Ridd"? This difference is due
to the intervention of another law—viz. the tendency
to invert where an *r* is in question. Thus for "run"
we have "*urn*" or "*hurn*," for "red" "*urd*," and for
"bridge" "*burge*." "Hurdle," on the other hand, is
sometimes, though rarely, pronounced "riddle." The
name "Ridler," which is common in these parts, probably means "hurdler," a man who makes hurdles.
"Burge" is likewise a proper name.

One of the most interesting features in the local dialect
is the use of words — ordinary words — in a some-

* "When he came to his full *yage* the pryor marryed hym to one Ellenor
his buttelors dofter, a verye proper woman and a wyse." . . . "His
wyfe was after iiij tymes well marryed excepte her laste husbonde. She
was a myghtye woman of welthe, but her laste husebonde beynge a lustye
servynge man sone consumed hyt so that in the *yende* she was poure."
(See "Furse of Moreshead," by H. J. Carpenter, M.A., LL.M., *Transactions
of the Devonshire Association* for 1894.)

what unusual sense. We may take as instances "miss"
and "lack." The former is employed intransitively in
the sense of "to disappear"—sometimes as a euphemism
for "to die " (*e.g.* "'Twould be a sad job vor 'em, if er
was to miss"). "Lack," again, is used for "want," where
"want" expresses an intermediate idea between "wish"
and "need" — in other words occasion, which word,
by the way, is here often pronounced "*occooshun.*" A
very old man, one of the principal farmers in the parish
of Dulverton, has been heard to inquire : "*Hot did er
lack to shut var ?*" (" What did he want to shoot for ? ")
A common saying about a person who looks fat and
flourishing is : "'E don't live on deave nits," *i.e.* "deaf"
nuts, nuts that have no kernel. " Deave ea(r)th " is shillet,
while "mate ea(r)th" is that which will support life.
A mason was once describing how, being at work near
Southmolton at the time of Lord Ebrington's return
from his wedding tour, he and others waited at the railway station, prepared to drag the happy pair in a carriage
to Castle Hill. As they stood in the shafts one behind
the other, a less enthusiastic passer-by began to laugh
and make cynical remarks. "'E *allowed* us was all
harnessed in like donkeys."

A sieve is spoken of as a "*range*"; a man will tell you
that he is going to "*range*" sand, for instance. Perhaps,
however, the most extraordinary usage is the way the
term "once" is employed. It is frequently used, not
at all in a temporal sense, but as a kind of affirmative,
or as a means of strengthening and emphasising an
assertion. For example, " I only wish I had a thousand
pounds *once*" does not mean that the speaker wishes
that he had that amount (or more) at some earlier
date, but that he very heartily and particularly wishes
that he had it now. With many this is merely a
trick and crops up casually in conversation without
the least necessity. Such "expletives" are far commoner

N

in most languages than in English, so that a stray survivor becomes on that account more notable, We strongly suspect that " glen " (pronounced "*glin* ") is used in a rather irregular way. Nuttall defines a glen as a " narrow depression between hills." The West Somerset man, however, in speaking of a glen, has in his mind a steep bank which, in his own language, he might describe equally well as a " *cleave* " or a " *clift*." These last are obviously variations of " cliff," but they generally suggest—inland, at all events—not a barren rock, but a wooded ascent or a steep field. A glen in the ordinary sense is here called a " goyle," which, Blackmore playfully pretends, is Homeric.

Talking of the classics, a word frequently used in West Somerset for " dust " is "*pelm*," which might pass for an abbreviation of "*pulverem*," and accordingly we will name it Horatian. This is one of those terms the natives keep to themselves, except in moments of excitement, when the words are apt to pop out. One day an old woman was complainant in a case of assault. The chairman of the Bench was anxious to inform himself as to what precisely had happened. He was very patient.

" So then——"

" They hend pelm auver me."

" What's that ? " queried the justice.

" There's a fule, there's a fule ! " answered the crone, throwing herself backwards in a fit of laughter, and pointing with her finger. " Doan't knaw hot dirt a-drawed be 'it."

The writer was told this story in a cottage near Dulverton. Since then he has found it in Mr. Elworthy's *West Somerset Word Book*, so that it probably relates to an actual fact. Be that as it may, it provides an excellent specimen of translation from idiomatic Exmoor into a more common variety of English, though not

quite the English of the drawing-room or the Press.*
" Hend " in this neighbourhood is constantly used, not
in the old Chaucerian sense of " polite," but with the
meaning of " throw," which latter term the old lady,
being of West Somerset extraction, would have availed
herself of the privilege to pronounce "*draw*." " *To*
"*drow* " or " *drow-y* "—it is always permissible to attach
the suffix "*y* "—signifies, not " to throw," but " to dry."
No confusion arises between "*draw* " (in the sense of
" throw") and " draw " (in the sense of " pull "). " Draw,"
when it means to " pull," becomes "*dray*," just as one
speaks of a " dray-horse." By the way, it is customary to
speak of " throwing " trees, not of " felling " them.

We have spoken of contrariety in connection with the
ee sound, showing that it oscillates, in some measure,
between *ai* and *i*. By a sort of swing of the pendulum,
while "seem" becomes "*zim*," and "week" "*wik*," "hill" is
lengthened into "*heell*," and "Bill" into "*Beell*." There is
a bridge near Dulverton called Hele Bridge. It is so
spelt in the Ordnance Map, in the local newspapers, and
is, in fact, the official and generally accepted name of
the place, which happens to be a favourite meet of the
staghounds. As the bridge is approached on the Dulverton side by a long, steep hill, it is pretty evident from

---

* With reference to translation from one variety of a language into
another, the following remarks about Dr. Johnson are worth quoting :
" It is clear," says Macaulay, " that Johnson did not think in the dialect
in which he wrote. The expressions which came first to his tongue were
simple, energetic, and picturesque. When he wrote for publication he did
his sentences out of English into Johnsonese. His letters from the
Hebrides to Mrs. Thrale are the original of the work of which the *Journey
to the Hebrides* is a translation, and it is amusing to compare the two
versions. ' When we were taken upstairs,' says he in one of his letters,
' a dirty fellow bounced out of the bed in which one of us was to lie.'
This incident is recorded in the *Journey* as follows : ' On one of the beds
in which we were to repose started up at our entrance a man black as
a Cyclops from a forge.' Sometimes Johnson translated aloud. ' The
Rehearsal,' he said, very unjustly, ' has not enough wit to keep it sweet,'
then, after a pause, ' it has not vitality enough to preserve it from
putrefaction.' "

what it derives its name, but probably not one person in a hundred, when referring to the spot, has the least idea that he is talking dialect. Of course, we allude to the educated classes.

Birds have curious names in the Exmoor country. *Colley* is the local name for blackbird, and a water-ousel is known as a *water-colley*. A bat is a *leathern bird*, and the copper-finch rejoices in the appellation of *vire-tails*. Then there are queer notions as to what birds say. The note of the yellow-hammer is thus rendered, *Little-o-o-o-o-o-o-o—bread and cheese;* and the tom-tit or great tit remarks suggestively *Pint o' beer*. A *back-and-vore toad* is a description applied to a "contrary" person, one who does the wrong thing first, perversely ; *a tiddy-toddy fellow* is a man who rambles through life without clear perception of his bearings—not a daft exactly, but a weak, easy-going creature, too indolent to think, and foolishly inclined to talk.

Strangers will doubtless be surprised at hearing the older people, who alone speak the dialect with an approach to purity, sounding the *ed* in the preterites and past participles of verbs, *e.g. Just at that very moment I wakèd up*. There is a very strong partiality for the weak, compared with the strong, forms of the preterite, so that we meet with words like *hurted*, where the average Englishman would be content to say "hurt." This may be considered a note of modernity. On the other hand, old words have been preserved which the average Englishman has let slip and forgotten. For instance, the expression *tho*, which Chaucer uses in the sense of "then," is quite at home in the Exmoor country.

Most of the points to which attention has been called will be found illustrated in the following dramatic poem by Edward Capern, well known to the last generation as "the postman poet." Originally it appeared in *Tom Hood's Comic Annual*, Christmas, 1875, but, as here

printed, is taken from a corrected MS. given to me by
the writer.

"BILZVORD JISTIS"

" Gracey. Aw massey, zoce ! gude lawks, how b'ee ?
Es yurd tha nuze tu-day ?
Mally. No, Gracey, no ! Hot es it, cheel ?
Gracey. About owld Jerry Gay.
Mally. Just make a putch, an lit es yur
Hot tez—tha hozebird !—Wull,
Es allez zed he'd niver kum
Tu enny gude mazull.
Od, drat'n, he'th bin pawchin, Grace,
Or zummat, I'll be bound !
Tha lops—he's zartin to be hung,
His lik wur niver vound.
Gracey. No, Mally, et es wis 'en thet.
Mally. Nan ?
Gracey.   Zumthin wis, Iss zay !
Mally. Hot ! wis 'en pawchin, Gracey ?
Gracey.   Ees.
A gurt dale wis, ees vay !
I'll tell tha al about et, deame ;
Yu knaw tha narra drang ?
Wull, es ed jist bin up, d'ye zee ?
Tu spayk way Hurchy Crang ;
An wen es cum hout, Mall, agen,
Tha hair was lik a vilm.
' Hot iver be min 'bowt,' zez I ;
' Tha rawd ez vule o' pilm !'
'Twore zetch a sture ; es niver zeed
Tha hoi rawd zo avor—
Tha zeame ez ef owl Codden Hill
Wur tor up mool and mor.
And hot de theenk twor al abowt ?
'Tez tru, ez I'm alive !
Thay wur a-shakin Jerry, Mall,
For batin ov ez wive.
Tu du tha theeng al viddevide,
Thay gort a blanket, deame,
An in thay shuv'd 'n, nek an crap,
An mead en ot es vleame.
Ees, thare wur Jenny Mashall, vust ;
Nex Zuke an Nanny May ;
Then Honor Brooks an Dolly Prist,
An strappin Becky Day.
An Varmer Zluman, he wur thare !
Mally. An Taylor Jans, Iss wadge !

Gracey. An Kit tha Cobbler an tha Clerk ;
      Tha smith, tu, Josha Madge.
Pore Jerry, Iss shel scat ma zides
      Tu tell ee al tha vun.
Thare he wur, tumlin upzedown,
      Tha gowlin zen o' a gun.
'Aw, do ee stap, an let ma go !'
      Ha kald hout, wen a-bump ;
An up a went agen sky-hoi,
      Wance more to kum down *vlump !*
'Yu meslin ov a brute ! dest yur,
      Weth tha hang-galluz lukes ?
Wist iver zarve er zo agen ?
      Spake hout !' zez Honor Brooks.
'Quick, in a minnet !' Honor zeth,
      'Or up ee go agen.'
'No, niver, *niver*, NIVER more !'
      Zays Jerry, zore way pain.
An zo thay let'n hout, when, lor,
      Mall, zitch a zite wur zeed !
Ha lik a dug a tail-piped urn'd,
      Or vox et vule-kry speed.
Es laff'd tu zee Bet Zlitterpuche
      An thet gurt slammick, Zal,
Gie chace, an by tha scruf o' th' nek
      Jist sheake tha skarekraw, Mall.
An lor ee shude a zeed tha pegs
      A por, go wildago,
An Kitty Cole's owld dunkey, Jack,
      Way divil-glintin Joe.
On went the skeremouch beheend
      Down Ruckaborough Hill,
Till Jerry went tu hide-a-peep,
      Zumweare ba Matha's Mill !
I'll wadge a hunderd ginneys, deame,
      He'll net vorgit tha day.
Now Iss mus weesh ee wull ; tez time
      Thet Iss wur on ma way."

THE "EXMOOR COURTSHIP"

IN such a work as the present, and in the particular section now inditing, space ought to be found for one of two ancient plays—local classics they may be termed—entitled the *Exmoor Scolding* and the *Exmoor Courtship*. We say "one" advisedly, since the former is more than popular—it is vulgar. Vulgarity is, in fact, its essential quality. The *Exmoor Courtship* is much less objectionable on this score; it is only thoroughly vulgar here and there. Both pieces have been admirably edited by Mr. F. T. Elworthy in a single volume, to which the reader is referred for fuller information and more exact details than can be furnished here. Meanwhile some remarks as to the history of the compositions will not be out of place.

A portion of the *Exmoor Courtship* appeared in *Blackwood's Magazine* for February, 1819, and in the preface to this extract it is stated that probably the drama is as old as the time of Henry VII. No authority is produced for this assertion, but Mr. Elworthy is inclined to believe that, so far as the substance of the writing is concerned, it may be correct. The preface to the edition of 1778 supplies an interesting account of the origin of the play.

"The following collection was made about the beginning of the present century by a blind itinerant fiddler (one Peter

Lock of North Molton or its neighbourhood), who was a man
of some humour ; and though his skill and dexterity as a
musician is said to have recommended him to the notice of
the great, his more common converse with the lower class
of people gave him frequent opportunities of hearing and
observing their phrases and diction ; and as persons deprived
of sight have generally a good memory, he was thereby the
better enabled to retain and repeat them.   This attracted the
notice of a neighbouring clergyman, who by the fiddler's
assistance put the *Exmoor Scolding* into the form in which we
now have it, and before his death (which happened soon after
the year 1725) communicated it to the public and afterwards
gave rise to the *Exmoor Courtship*, a performance thought
deserving to be added thereunto.   But copies of the *Scolding*
were for some time both before and after this handed about in
manuscript above forty years since, and was then taken to be
the original composition of the clergyman aforesaid, few being
apprehensive of its having any other author, or how far the
person who furnished its materials might claim title thereto,
though his fame as a fiddler was not yet extinct."

According to Sir Frederick Madden, who cites " Mr.
Merrivale " as his authority, the neighbouring clergyman
was the Rev. William Hole, Archdeacon of Barnstaple.
The *Courtship* was first published in the *Gentleman's
Magazine* for June, 1746, accompanied by a letter signed
" H. Oxon," who stated that it was written by a clergyman of Devonshire, near the forest of Exmoor, but, it
was believed, had received some additions.   The pieces
appeared together in book-form, and between 1746 and
1788 ran through eight editions.   The various editions,
as well as different portions of the same edition, exhibit
a good many discrepancies, the spelling being not
always phonetic.

An

Exmoor COURTSHIP;

OR, A

SUITORING DISCOURSE

IN THE

Devonshire DIALECT and MODE

near

The FOREST of *EXMOOR*.

The Persons.

Andrew Moreman, a Young Farmer.
Margery Vagwell, his Sweetheart.
Old Grammer *Nell*, Grammer to *Margery*.
Thomasin, Sister to *Margery*.

AN EXMOOR COURTSHIP

SCENE. *Margery's* Home.

To Margery *enter* Andrew.

Andrew. How goeth et, Cozen Magery?

Margery. Hoh! Cozen Andra, how d'ye try?

Andrew. Come, let's shake honds, thof kissing be scarce.

Margery. Kissing's plenty enow; but chud zo leefe kiss the back o' ma hond as e'er a man in Challacomb, or yeet in Paracombe; no dispreeze.

Andrew. Es don't believe thate; yeet es believe well too

[Swop! he kisses and smuggles her.

Margery. Humph!—Oh! tha very vengeance out o' tha! Tha hast a-creem'd ma yearms, and a most a bost ma neck.— Wall, bet, vor all, how dost try, es zey, Cozen Andra? Es hant a zeed ye a gurt while.

Andrew. Why, fath, Cozen Magery, most marchantable, e'er since es scoast a tack or two wey Rager Vrogwell tether day.—Bet, sugs! es trem'd en and vagg'd en so that he'll veel et vor wone while, chell warndy.

Margery. How, Cozen Andra? Why, es thort you coudent a vort zo.

Andrew. Why, twos oll about thee, mun;—vor es chant hire an eel word o' tha.

Margery. How! about me?—Why, why vore about me, good zweet now? Of a ground ha can zey no harm by ma.

Andrew. Well, well, no mater. Es couden hire tha a run down, and a roylad upon zo, and zet still like a mumchance, and net pritch en vort.

Margery. Why, whot, and be hang'd to en, cou'd a zey o' me, a gert meazel?

Andrew. Es begit tha words now; bet a roylad zo that es coudent bear et.—Bet a dedent lost his labour, fath; vor es toz'd en, es lamb'd en, es lace'd en, es throng'd en, es drash'd en, es drubb'd en, es tann'd en to the true ben, fath! Bet

CHALLACOMBE MILL

stap! Cham avore ma story.—Zes I, thee, thee art a pretty
vella! Zes he, Gar, thee cassen make a pretty vella o' ma.—
No, agar, zes I, vor tha'rt too ugly to be made a pretty vella,
that's true enow. Gar, a was woundy mad thoa.—Chell try
that, zes he.—As zoons tha wut, zes I.—Zo up a roze, and to't
we went.—Vurst a geed ma a whisterpoop under tha year, and
vorewey a geed ma a vulch in tha leer.—Ad, thoa es rakad up,
and tuck en be tha collar, and zo box'd en and zlapp'd en,
that es made hes key hoppy and his yead addle to en.

Margery. Well, es thenk ye, Cozen Andra, vor taking
wone's peart zo.—Bet cham agest he'll go vor a warrant vor
ye, and take ye bevore tha cunsabel; and than a may zwear
tha peace of es, you know.—Es en et better to drenk vriends,
and make et up?

Andrew. Go vor a warrant! Ad, let en, let en go; chell
net hender en: ver there's Tom Vuzz can take his cornoral
oath that he begun vurst.—And if he deth chell ha as good a
warrant vor he as he can vor me, don't quesson et; vor the
turney into Moulton knowth me, good now, and has had zome
zweet pounds o' veather bevore ha dy'd. And if he's meended
to go to la, es can spend vorty or vifty shillings as well's
he. And zo let en go. . . . But hang en, let's ha nort more
to zey about en, vor chave better besenese in hond a gurt
deal.

[He takes hold of her, and paddles in her neck and bosom.

Margery. Come, be quite—be quite, es zey, a grabbling
o' wone's tetties.—Es wont ha' ma tetties a grabbled zo; nor
es wont be mullad and soulad.—Stand azide, come, gi' o'er.

Andrew. Lock, lock! How skittish we be now; you
weren't so skittish wey Kester Hosegood up to Darathy Vuzz's
upsetting.—No, no; you weren't so skittish thoa, ner sa
squeamish nether.—He murt mully and soully tha tell a wos
weary.

Margery. Es believe the very Dowl's in voke vor leeing.

Andrew. How? Sure and sure you won't deny et, wull ye,
whan oll tha voaken took notese o' et.

Margery. Why, Cozen Andra, thes was the whole fump
o' the besenese.—Chaw'r in wey en to daunce; and whan the
dance was out, the croud cry'd squeak, squeak (as a useth to
do, you know) and a cort ma about tha neck, and woudent be
a sed but a woud kiss ma, in spite of ma, do what es coud to
hender en.—Es coud ha borst tha croud in shivers, and tha

crouder too, a voul zlave as a wos, and hes viddlestick into the bargain.

Andrew. Well, well, es b'ent angry, mun.—And zo let's kiss and be vriends. [Kisses her.] Well, bet, Cozen Magery, oll thes while es hant told tha ma arrant; and chave an over arrant to tha, mun.

Margery [simpering]. Good sweet now, what arrant es et? Es marl what arrant ye can ha to me.

Andrew. Why, vath, chell tell tha. Whot zignifies et ta mence tha mater? Tes thes—Colus nolus wut ha' ma?

Margery. Ha ma? Whot's thate? Es can't tell whot ya me-an by thate?

Andrew. Why, than, chell tell tha vlat and plean. Ya know es kep Challacomb Moor in hond; tes vull stated: but cham to chonge a live for three yallow beels.* And than there's tha land up to Parracomb town: and whan es be to Parracomb, es must ha wone that es can trest to look arter tha gerred-teal'd meazels, and to zar tha ilt and tha barrow, and melk tha kee to Challacomb, and to look arter tha thengs o' tha houze.

Margery. O varguice! Why, Cozen Andra, a good steddy zarrant can do oll thes.

Andrew. Po, po, po! Chell trest no zarrants.—And more an zo, than they'll zey by me as they ded by Gaffer Hill tether day. . . . No, no; es bant zo mad nether. Well, bet, look, dest zee, Cozen Magery; zo vur vore es tha wut ha ma, chell put thy live pon Parracomb Down. Tes vor twenty nobles a year, and a puss to put min in.

Margery. O vile! whot marry?—No, chant ha' tha best

---

* This is an allusion, of course, to the custom of leasing property on lives. Not long since the following paragraphs appeared in the *Daily Mail*:—

"'I know of no large properties thus affected,' said Sir Whittaker Ellis yesterday, when questioned by a *Daily Mail* representative regarding the statement in *Truth* to the effect that large property interests are affected by the death of the Empress Frederick.

"'The names of the Queen, Prince of Wales, and Princess Royal were once put into leases, particularly throughout Wales, Cornwall, and Devonshire,' continued Sir Whittaker, "but they hold good till the death of King Edward. . . .

"'The practice of leasing property for the term of the lives of persons has fallen largely into disuse; in fact, I have hardly ever dealt with such a lease during my time, and I have been in business since fifty years ago, and was interested in leases before that.'"

man in Challacomb, nor yeet in Parracomb. Na, chell ne'er
marry, vor ort's know. No, no! they zey thare be more a
marry'd aready than can boil tha crock o' Zendeys. No, no,
Cozen Andra; es coud amorst zwear chudent ha tha best
square in ole Ingland.—But, come; pray, Cozen Andra, set
down a bit. Es must g'up in chamber and speak a word
or two wey Zester Tamzin. Hare's darning up of old blonkets,
and rearting tha peels, and snapping o' vleas.—Es chell come
agen presently.

Andrew. Well, do than; bet make haste, d'ye see. Meantime chell read o'er tha new ballet cheve in ma pocket.

Margery. New ballet! O good now, let's hire ye sing
et up.

Andrew. Zing! No, no, tes no singing ballet, mun; bet
tes a godly one, good now.

Margery. Why, whot's 't about, than?

Andrew. Why, tes about a boy that kill'd hes vauther; and
how hes vauther went agen, in shape of a gert voul theng, wey
a cloven voot and vlashes o' vire and troubled the houze
so that tha whatjecomb, tha white witch, was vorst to lay
en in the Red Zea; and how the boy repented, and went
distracted, and wos taken up, and wos hang'd vor't, and sung
saums and his praers. Twull do your heart good to hire
et, and make ye cry lick enny theng. Thare's tha picture
o' en too, and tha parson, and tha Dowl, and tha ghost,
and tha gallows.

Margery. Bet es et true, be sure?

Andrew. True? O la! Yes, yes: es olways look to thate.
Look see, tes here in prent—*Lissened according to order.*—
That's olways prented on what's true, mun. Es took care
to see thate whan es bort en.

Margery. Well, well, read et; and chell g'up to Zester.

SCENE. The Chamber.

To Thomasin *enter* Margery.

Margery. Oh, Zester Tamzen!—Odd! ee es a come along,
and, vath and trath, hath a put vore tha quesson to ma
a'ready. Es verly believe tha banes will g'in next Zindey.
Tes oll es ho (*hope*) vor. Bet es tell en, Marry a-ketha! and
tell en downreet es chant marry tha best man in Sherwell
Hunderd.—But, dest tha hire ma, Zester Tamzen? Don't ye

be a labb o' tha tongue in what cham a going to zey, and than chell tell tha something. Tha banes, cham amorst sure, wull g' in ether a Zindey or a Zindey-senneert to vurdest. Es net aboo two-and-twenty—a spicy vella and a vitty vella vor enny keendest theng. Thee know'st Joe Hosegood es reckon'd a vitty vella. Poo! es a sooterly vella to Andra; there's no compare.

Thomasin. Go, ya wicked cunterveit! Why dest lee so agenst thy meend; and whan ha put vore tha quesson, tell en tha wudsent marry? Besides, so vur as tha know'st, he murt take p' p'o, and meach off, and come no more anearst tha.

Margery. Go, ya alkitotle, ya gurt voolish trapes! Dest thee thenk a believed ma, whan es sed chudent marry? Ee es net so sart-a-baked nether. Vor why? Es wudent be too vurward nether; vor than ee murt dra back.—No, no; vor oll whot's sed, es hope the banes wull go in, es zey, next Zindey. And vath, nif's do vall over the desk, twont thir ma, ner yeet borst ma bones. Bet nif they don't g' in by Zindey-senneert, chell tell tha, in short company, es chell borst ma heart.—Bet es must go down to en; vor he's by ees zell oll theez while.

SCENE. The Ground-Room again.

To Andrew *enter* Margery.

Andrew. Well, Cozen Magery, cham glad you've come agen; vor thes ballet es zo very good, that et makes wone's heart troubled to read et.

Margery. Why put et up than, while es git a putcher o' cyder. Wull ye eat a croust o' brid and chezee, Cozen Andra?

Andrew. No, es thankee, Cozen Magery; vor es eat a crab as es come along; besides es went to dinner jest avore. Well, bet, Cozen Magery, what onser dest gi' ma to the quesson es put vore now-reert?

Margery. What quesson was et?

Andrew. Why, sure ya bant so vorgetvul! Why, tha quesson es put a little rather.

Margery. Es don't know what quesson ye mean; es begit what quesson twos.

Andrew. Why, to tell tha vlat and plane agen, twos thes— Wut ha' ma, ay or no?

Margery. What! Marry to earteen? Es gee tha same

onser es geed avore. Es wudent marry the best man in oll
Ingland. Es cud amorst zwear chud never marry at all. And
more and zo, Cozen Andra, cham a told ya keep company
wey Tamzen Hosegood, thek gurt banging, thonging, muxy,
drawbreech, daggle-tealed jade, a zower-zop'd, yerring, chock-
ling trash, a buzzom-chuck'd, haggaging moyle, a gurt fustilug.
Hare's a trub! And nif ya keep hare company, es'll ha no
more to zey to tha.

Andrew. Ay, thes es Joe Hosegood's flim-flam. Oh, tha
very vengeance out o' en!

Margery. No, no; tes none of Joe Hosegood's flim-flam;
but zo the crime o' the country goth.

Andrew. Ah, but twos Joe Hosegood's zetting vore in the
vurst place. Ha wull lee a rope upreert. Whan ha hath
took a shord and a paddled, ha wull tell doil, tell dildrams,
and roily upon enny kesson zoul. Ad, nif es come athert
en, chell gee en a lick; chell ly en o'er tha years; chell plim
en, chell tose en, chell cotten en, chell thong en, chell tan en;
chell gee en a strat in tha chups; chell vag en, chell trem
en, chell drash en, chell curry hes coat vor en; chell drub en;
chell make his kep hoppy. Ad! chell gee en zutch a zwop;
chell gee en a whappet, and a wherret, and a whisterpoop, too.
Ad chell baste en to the true ben.

[Speaks in a great passion, and shows with his hands how
he'll beat his adversary.

Margery. Look, look, look, Cozen Andra! Vor why vor be
ye in zitch a vustin vume? Why, es don't zey twos Joe Hosegood zes zo, but only zo tha crime o' tha country goth.

Andrew. Well, well, Cozen Magery, be't how twull, whot
caree I? And zo good-buy, good-buy t' ye, Cozen Magery!
Nif voaken be jealous avore they be married, zo they may
arter.—Zo good-buy, Cozen Margery! Chell not trouble ye
agen wone while, chell warndy. [Going.

Margery [calling after him]. Bet hearky, hearky a bit,
Cozen Andra. Es wudent ha ye go awey angry nether. Zure
and zure you won't deny to see me drenk. Why, ya han't
a-tasted our cyder yet. [Andrew returns.] Come, Cozen
Andra, here's t' ye.

Andrew. Na, vor that matter, es owe no ill-will to enny
kesson, net I. Bet es won't drenk, nether, except ya vurst
kiss and vriends. [Kisses her.

Margery. Ya won't be a zed.—[He drinks]—Well, bet

o

hearky, Cozen Andra; won't ye g'up and zee Grammer avore
ye g'up to Challacomb? Tes but jest over tha paddick, and
along tha park.

Andrew. Es caren't much nif's do go zee old Ont Nell.
And how do hare tare along?

Margery. Rub along, d'ye zey? Oh, Grammer's wor vower
hunderd pounds, reckon tha goods indoor and out a door.

Andrew. Cham glad to hire et; vor es olweys thort her to
ha be bare buckle and thongs.

Margery. Oh no, mun; hare's mearty well to pass, and
maketh gurt account o' me, good now.

Andrew. Cham glad to hire o' thet too. May be hare may
gee tha a good stub. Come, let's g' ender than.

[Takes her arm under his, and leads her.

SCENE. Old Grammer Nell's.

To her *enter* Andrew and Margery.

Andrew. Good den, good den, Ont Nell. Well, how d'ye
try? How goth et wey ye?

Old Nell. Well, vath, Cozen Andra, pritty vitty, whot
chur. Chad a glam or two about ma. Chad a crick in ma
back and in ma niddick. Thoa chur a lamps'd in wone o'
ma yearms. Tho come to a heartgun. Vorewey struck out
and come to a barngun. Tho come to an allernbatch; and
vorewey fell in upon ma bones, and come to a boneshave.
But e'er zence old Jillian Vrinkle blessed vore tes pritty vitty;
and cham come to my meat list agen. Well, bet hearky,
Cozen Andra; es hire ya lick a lit about ma Cozen Magery;
ay, and have smell'd about her a pretty while. Chawr a-told
that ye simmered upon wone tether up to Grace Vrogwill's
bed-ale.—Well, Cozen Andra, cham all vore, and so chawr so
zoon's es hired o' et. Hare's net as zome giglets, zome
prenking, mencing thengs be, oll vor gamboyling, rumping,
steehopping, and giggleting; but a tyrant maid vor work, and
tha stewarliest and vittiest wench that comath on tha way o'
Moulton, no dispreise.

Margery [softly aside to her]. Thenk ye, Grammer, thenk
ye keendly. And nif es shudent ha en should borst ma heart.
—[Aloud.] Grammer, don't tell me of marrying. Chave
a told Cozen Andra ma meend already that chell ne'er marry
vor ort es know.

CHALLACOMBE BRIDGE

Old Nell. Stap hether, Cozen Magery, a lit, and tarn these cheesen.—[Pretendedly privately to her] Go, ya alkitotle, why dedst tell zo, tha wert ne'er marry? Tha wutten ha tha lick; a comely sprey vitty vella vor enny keendest theng. Come, nif tha wut ha en, chell gee tha good stab. Thare's net a spreyer vella in Challacomb.

Margery. Bet, Grammer, wull ye be zo good's ya zey, nif zo be, vor your zake, es vorce ma zel to let en lick a bit about ma?

Old Nell. Ay, es tell tha. [Aside.] Cham agast hare'll dra en into a promish wone dey or wother.

Andrew. Well, Ont Nell, es hired whot ya zed, and es thank ye too. But now chave a zeed ye, tes zo good as chad a eat ye, as they use to zey. Es must go home now as vast as es can.—Cozen Magery, won't ye go wey ma a lit wey?

Margery. Mey be es mey go up and zee Ont Moreman, and mey be es man't.

SCENE. The Open Country.

Enter Andrew *followed by* Margery.

Margery. Ad, es 'll zee ee up to Challacomb-Moor stile. Now must es make wise chawr a going to Ont Moreman, and only come theez wey.

Andrew [spying her]. Cozen Magery, Cozen Magery! Stap a lit. Whare zo vast, mun? [She stays.] Zo, now es zee ya be as good as yer word; na, and better; vor tha zedst mey be chell, and mey be chont.

Margery. Oh, ya take tha words tether wey. Es zed mey be chell, and mey be chont, go up and zee Ont Moreman. Es zed no more an zo. Es go thes wey vor to zee hare, that es oll. Bet chudent go zo vur to meet enny man in Challacom, ner Parracomb, ner yeet in oll King George's kingdom, bless his worship. Meet tha men aketha!—Hah! be quiet, es zey, a creaming a body zo. And more and zo, yer beard precketh ill-favouredly. Es marl what these gurt black beards be good vor. Ya ha made ma chucks buzzom.

Andrew. Well, whot's zey, Cozen Magery? Chell put in tha banes a Zendey, bolus nolus.

Margery. Then es ell vorbed min, vath.

Andrew. Oh, chell trest tha vor thate. Es don't thenk

you'll take so much stomach to yer sel as to vorbed min avore zo menny vokes. Well, Cozen Magery, good neart !

Margery. Cozen Andra, good neart ! Es wish ye well to do.

SCENE. Margery's Home.

To Thomasin *enter* Margery.

Margery. Zester Tamzen, where art? Where art, a popeling and a pulching? Dost hire ma?

Thomasin. Lock, lock, lock ! Whot's the matter, Magery, that tha leapest, and caperest, and sing'st so? What, art tha hanteck?

Margery. That's nort to nobody. Chell whistly, and capery, and zing vor oll thee. Bet yeet avore oll, nif tha wultent be a labb o' tha tongue now, chell tell tha something. Zart ! whistery ! Ma banes g'in a Zendey, vath, to Andra, tha spicest vella in Sherwill Hunderd.

Thomasin. O la ! Why thare lo ! Now we shall be married near together ; vor mine be in and out agen, thof my man don't yeet tell ma tha dey. Es marl ha don't pointee whot's in tha meend o' en.

Margery. Chell g'in to Moulton to-marra pretty taply, to buy some canvest vor a new chonge.

Thomasin. Ay, ay ; zo do ; vor tha cassent tell what may happen to tha in thy middle banes.

Margery. How? ya gurt trapes ! Whot dest me-an by thate? Es scorn tha words. Ded ort hap to thee in thy middle banes? Happen aketha !

Thomasin. Hah ! Ort happen to me in my middle banes? Es scorn et to tha dert o' ma shoes, looks zee, ya mencing, kerping baggage.—Varewell !

PART **IV**

FOLKLORE

CHAPTER I

RECIPES

A N interesting and important branch of folklore is
that which concerns itself with the various ills
that flesh is heir to. Among the ills which age will
class as minor afflictions, but to which pretty maidens
object as spoiling their beauty, is " summervoy," or
freckles, and, by way of remedy or prevention, they are
wont to lave their faces in dew on three successive
morns. This, by-the-by, is an old-world belief in no wise
restricted to Exmoor and the neighbourhood. An old
quatrain has it—

> "The fair maid who, the first of May,
> Goes to the fields at break of day,
> And washes in dew from the hawthorn tree,
> Will ever after handsome be."

The details may be different, but the idea is essentially
the same.

So, too, old Pepys, writing in his *Diary* for 1667,
observes : " My wife away down with Jane and William
Hewer to Woolwich, in order to a little air, and to lie
there to-night, and so gather May-dew to-morrow morning, which Mrs. Turner hath taught her is the only thing
in the world to wash her face with, and I am contented
with it." And again, in 1669: " My wife up by four
o'clock to gather May-dew."

Somewhat similar, though attended with more risk,
perhaps, to the patient, is the process to which young

infants are subjected. At the first fall of snow which takes place after its birth, the child is borne from its comfortable cot and stood stark naked in the snow, with which it is rubbed all over. This is done to inoculate it against chilblains, and persons so treated are averred never to suffer from the complaint.

The surgeon's knife is naturally dreaded, and, therefore, it is not surprising that "miserable mortals" should have recourse, preferably, to prayer, especially as the milder remedy is believed to be equally efficacious. Thorns are removed and inflammation subdued by prayer; and a charlatan in the Exmoor country reaps a rich harvest in fees from his credulous neighbours notwithstanding the fact that his "cures" do not always preclude the unwelcome lancet. In cases of hæmorrhage this godly practitioner repeats the following charm :—

> " Christ was born in Bethlehem,
>   Baptised in Jordan.
> The waters, wild and rude,
> The Child, mild and good,
> Put Its foot into the flood,
>   And bade it turn."

Where burns are in question another form is adopted, viz.—

> " Three angels came from north, east, west ;
> One brought fire, one ice,
> The third the Holy Ghost :
> So out fire in frost.
>   Gloria Patri."

After these examples it will not excite wonder that Holy Writ is occasionally invoked for the purpose of cure. A passage of Ezekiel, for instance, is said to arrest bleeding, and, if any quotation possessed the healing virtue, must be allowed to be exceedingly well chosen. The words are : " And when I passed by thee, and saw thee polluted in thine own blood, I said unto thee when thou wast in thy blood, Live."

On Exmoor sciatica is known as "boneshave," and the local leech prescribes the following treatment of the disease. The patient has to lie beside a running stream, while someone recites the verse :—

"Boneshave right,
Boneshave stright,
As the water runs by the stave,
So follow boneshave."

The term "stave" here denotes the willows, etc., that line the bank of the stream, and evidently the notion is that the malady will be driven out and float away on the surface of the water. Many years ago, it is alleged, one John Roden tried the experiment, and paid the penalty with his life.

A similar fate nearly overtook another old man. He attempted to cure an irreducible hernia, of which he was the victim, and his plan was to go downstairs head foremost. A child suffering from congenital hernia is passed through a cleft maiden ash. The ceremony takes place on a Sunday at sunrise, the direction being from west to east, and the process symbolises a new birth to complete that which is imperfect. The writer is acquainted with a man whose brother underwent this "cure," with, he stated, a perfectly satisfactory result, and, that no doubt might remain, he gave directions where to find the tree.

Sunday is the day also for the cure of king's evil. Then it is that the seventh son (or, still better, the seventh son of a seventh son) holds his levée, and both operator and patient should have fasted from the previous eve. The cure is effected by touch and prayer. A seventh son is *par excellence* "the" doctor. One of the order has been heard to declare that in growing up he seldom tasted food on Sundays. His parents found his cures a source of much profit, and accordingly kept a strict watch over him. Belief in the supernatural

powers of a seventh son is, of course, not confined to
Exmoor, and formerly it was imagined that he could
heal the deaf, the blind, and the lame. Walter Yonge,
in his *Diary*, alludes to a story of the sort reported from
London in January, 1606–7. The Bishop of London,
Dr. Vaughan, conducted experiments with the boy,
who was of Roman Catholic parentage, but, adds
Yonge, "no miracle followeth any, so that it appeareth
a plain lie invented to win grace to the popish faction."

In a village churchyard near Bridgwater, Somerset, is
a tombstone with the following inscription :—

"Sacred to the memory of Doctress Anne Pounsberry, who
departed this life Dec. 11, 1813, aged 73 years. Stand still
and consider the wondrous works of God."

"Doctress," as used here, was not an epithet merely,
but a baptismal name, since the person in question was
the seventh daughter of a seventh daughter. Her pre-
scription for the king's evil was: "Take the legs of
a toad. Bake and grind them to powder with pestle
and mortar. Place the powder in a bag round the neck
of the sufferer."

The "evil eye" still exerts a baleful influence, and
those affected thereby are said to be "overlooked."
This disagreeable faculty is credited to people with
a squint, or, to use the local expression, a "north
eye"; and the counsel is given: "Always spit when
you meet a man with a north eye." The amulets of
West Somerset include horseshoes and probably also
some of the ornaments used by carters about their
horses' heads. In chimney corners, too, may yet be
found here and there the heart of an animal stuck with
pins, the object of which, according to the inmates, is
to "keep away they there witches." This custom
is obviously related to the practice of fashioning little
wax dolls for the purpose of attracting or estranging
love. In the reign of James I., as we learn from Lord

Brooke, the Countess of Essex repaired to one Doctor Forman, an ancient gentleman who dwelt at Lambeth and was said to be skilled in the magic art. The naughty lady, being weary of her lawful spouse and enamoured of Viscount Rochester, obtained from the sorcerer a wax doll pierced with a thorn, which, however, did not answer her intention.

For epilepsy the ordinary cure is to borrow silver coins from neighbours and friends and wear them as a necklace or bracelet for a year. But, where the subject is an unmarried girl, a variation seems usual. Instead of applying to all and sundry for silver coins, she makes the round of the parish, and at cottage and hall levies a toll of one penny, neither more nor less and always on the bachelors. Then she sets off to the nearest town and invests her gains in a silver ring, with which she encircles the finger otherwise sacred to the wedding-ring. From the moment it is *in situ* she is secure—at all events, so long as she continues to wear it.

The remedy for whooping-cough is to lay the child on the ground of a sheepfold, while goitre is cured by the touch of a corpse. A less serious but still plaguy affliction, warts, is treated in a variety of ways. For instance, you may steal a piece of meat, and bury it. Then, as the meat decays, the wart will decay in sympathy. Or you may place in a bag as many stones as you have warts, and throw the bag away. Probably some curious person will pick it up, and whoever does so will infallibly contract the warts. This method, however, is terribly selfish and unkind, so that perhaps a third expedient will be preferred—viz. that of rubbing with bean cods or celandine, to the accompaniment of prayer.

For a certain class of diseases only one remedy is efficacious. This remedy is of a mystical sort, and such as would commend itself to a Paracelsus or Cagliostro rather than to the school of Galen. First a toad has to be found, and, when one has been caught, a leg is severed from the body of the yet living animal. This is inclosed in a small bag, which is hung about the patient's neck, whereupon, to his surprise and delight, he instantly recovers.

Such at least is the belief, but, in point of fact, mystic cures are sometimes nothing more than nominal. For instance, the wife of a keeper named Larcombe had the misfortune to be bitten by a snake whilst gathering whortleberries on Dunkery. The poor woman became very ill, and her husband, in his distress, ran off to seek the advice of a "wise-woman." The ancient dame went with him to his cottage, and, having hung an amulet on the patient's neck, directed that the bed should be so placed as to point due north and south. No improvement set in, however, and the wise woman, on being apprised of her failure, accounted for it by saying that the bed could not have been set true to the north.

Evelyn in his *Sylva* remarks that in Wales the mountain ash was regarded as sacred, so much so that there was not a churchyard in which one was not planted, while on certain days of the year everybody wore a cross made of the wood. Supposed to be protection against the evil eye and evil spirits, boughs were stuck about the house, and the wood was used for walking-sticks. In the Exmoor country mountain ash is known as "quick-beam," and here also it excites superstitious feeling. Quick-beam must not be applied to ordinary uses. If a bullock is struck with it the animal will discharge blood. A friend of Savage, the local historian, was looking over a gentleman's estate, and, before mounting his horse, cut a couple of twigs from one of the quick-beam trees in the hedge. These he intended to serve in lieu of a whip. However, a labourer hailing from an adjacent village, having divined his object, interposed with the question—

"Lord bless 'ee, zur, hot a be gwain to do wi' they?"

"Going to do with them?" replied the farmer. "Why, beat my horse with them, and carry them home."

"Dooant 'ee, zur, dooant 'ee!" cried the man in alarm. "They be quick-beam."

"I know they are," was the rejoinder; "but what of that?"

"Hot o' that, zur!" answered the yokel. "Dooant 'ee knaw they be mortal unlucky?"

A somewhat similar feeling prevails with regard to the elder tree. Not long ago a visitor at a farmhouse was watching a labourer who was engaged in binding faggots for burning. This man firmly refused to include elder wood; otherwise, said he, all the cattle on the farm would die. He added, by way of explanation, that our Lord's cross was of elder. According to the *Cursor Mundi*, an early English poem which contains a cycle of sacred legends, the holy cross was composed of three different kinds of wood, cypress, cedar, and pine, together symbolising the mystery of the Trinity. They formed a single tree, which was in existence ages before the birth of Christ, and could not be used for common purposes. A priest cut it; there flashed flame. A woman sat on it; her clothes took fire. But the story of the cross is too long to be told here.

The farm-hand's warning that it is unlucky to cut quick-beam reminds us that on and around Exmoor there are countless unwritten rubrics and authentic tokens relating to luck. You are invited to a christening, and, kind-hearted person as you are, would like to bring luck with you. Very well; go to your cupboard, fetch thence a piece of bread, and crown it with a morsel of your prime cheese. Having done this, call to mind the sex of the child for whose future you are concerned, and, sallying forth, present the bread and cheese to a girl, if the child be a boy, or to a boy, if the child be a girl. By so doing you will have the satisfaction of knowing that you have done everything in your power to ensure for the infant, at whose baptism you are to assist, a happy and prosperous existence. Baptism is supposed to have a beneficial effect on a cross baby's temper.

Turning to what may be termed the veterinary department, there are farmers still left who will only approach a cow afflicted with the udder-ill backwards. Then, without looking, they sign the animal in the region of the disease with the symbol of the cross, and the result is invariably her recovery. Chain canker is treated somewhat differently. At Sandy Way a sod was cut from under the hoof of the unfortunate beast and placed with the spine downwards in the nearest whitethorn bush, there to dry gradually away with the complaint. The recipe for felon quarter-evil is to cut the sod under the foot while dew, damp and cold, yet lies on it, and bury it upside down.

There are superstitions connected with the moon. In order that you may prosper through the month, turn over your money on first seeing the new moon, but be sure that you don't see it through glass. Otherwise, says the oracle, you might reverse all the money in your possession, and still there would be no end of bad luck. Another necessary precaution is that of not pointing at the moon with your finger. If you do, you will be dogged by the worst sorts of misfortune. Hedgers should take notice that the time to make hedges is when the moon is waxing, not when it is on the wane. Indeed, hedges made under the latter circumstances will not grow. Similarly, cut stripes should be laid away from the sun—preferably, towards the north. Water that rises from a spring or runs northwards is considered good for sore eyes. An instance may be found in the parish of Old Cleeve, where water rises from two springs and takes a northward direction. Presumably, therefore, it is trebly efficacious.

May is an unlucky month. Cats born in May bring vermin—snakes, toads, etc.—into the house. It is unlucky to import May blossom into your dwelling. Though beautiful to look at and sweet of smell, it is banned equally with peacock's feathers. Then there is the old rhyme about "tucking" a baby :—

> "If you tuck him in May,
> You will drive him away."

When you first hear the cuckoo, run, or you will be afflicted with laziness all the year. This is also a favourable moment for wishing. But hear a cuckoo after Old Midsummer Day, and you will not live to hear another.

> "If you would live and thrive,
> Let the spider run alive,"

is a local distich. How many housewives pay heed to it? This reminds us that fruit-stains on linen, etc., are supposed to vanish as the season for the particular fruit passes away. Would-be housewives, in shelling peas, should watch for a pod containing nine, and hang that same pod over the doorway. Then the first man to enter will be her destined husband. If you are changing houses, and should see a flock of sheep go by, that is a good sign. Having taken possession of your new abode, you may be surprised by a cock walking up to the door and ejaculating a crow. This is a harmless token that a stranger is about to arrive. It is far different, however, when a hen takes to crowing. When an old hen forgets herself in this way, the cottager, in vague alarm at such an unnatural occurrence, usually counters the move by wringing the neck of the offender.

P

Equal, and perhaps greater, horror is inspired by cock-crowing in the dead of night. It is regarded as an infallible sign of death. It is a sign of death if a dog howls at night, if a bird taps the window, if fruit trees or broad beans blossom twice, or if bees pitch on dry wood during swarming. If a corpse is put out at a window, as sure as fate another member of the family will die before the year is out. At a funeral all should walk in couples. If an odd person follow, it is a sign of bad luck. It is an ill omen to return to the house after setting forth on a journey, but the individual may ward off the effects by sitting down again. If a white bean is found growing in the garden, or the bees suddenly die, you may know by this that some member of the family is dead. Of all signs, however, the most fatal is that which is described *par excellence* as the " death token." This consists of three raps, given at intervals of a few seconds, at your bed's head in the stillness of the night. To be awakened by such sounds is a presage of impending bereavement, which no forethought can avert. There are other signs of imminent misfortune—not necessarily death or loss of relatives—and among them are dreams. It is, for instance, uncommonly bad luck to dream about eggs, copper pence, or the parson in church with his surplice on.

That reminds one of the ghastly and horrible custom of " spirit-watching." This custom is observed on Midsummer Eve, when churches are narrowly watched. In the case of some the ghosts of all in the parish, not excluding the parson and the clerk, have been seen to enter, but it does not follow that evil consequences will ensue, except as regards those whose apparitions remain in the building. Such luckless wights will, it is believed, most certainly die, and one instance is recorded where a father became insane on remarking that his daughter's phantom stayed behind in the sacred edifice.

"When the bell tolls to denote a death in a parish," says Miss Alice King, " every old woman in the village street may be seen standing at her door, with her hand held up to her ear and with an expression of fearful and solemn meaning in her face.   These ancient dames say that they can tell, with perfect certainty, by the sound of the bell whether there will be soon again another death in the parish.   Their phrase is that 'the bell goes either lightly or heavily,' though what the difference may be no one but an old lady who has been cradled among the heatherbells is ever able to distinguish.   There is always a certain disappointment in the old crones' faces if the bell has no evil omen in its sound.   They seem to derive a kind of gloomy pleasure from the declaration of the fact that death will quickly revisit the village; and from doorway to doorway they nod and wink, and beckon to each other significantly, the meaning of the pantomime being various conjectures as to who the next person called out of this world will be.   If, however, one member of the prophetic sisterhood ventures to hint to another that she may be the party whom the omen concerns, she is greeted with some such compliment as the following :—

"'Molly, all that I can tell 'ee be that you be sure to go before I do.   You be failing fast; I've seen it for the last six months past.'

"Whereupon Molly replies in a tone of triumphant assurance—

"'But I ban't pitched away as you be, Betty.   You are safe to go first; and that's what the bell do mean.'"

On the Sunday after a funeral West Country custom prescribes that the funeral party attend morning service in the church, and in order that they may show proper affection and esteem for the dead, the mourners are expected to remain seated throughout the service, with their heads bowed in woe.   This constrained posture is maintained until the last member of the congregation has left the building, or one of the bereaved persons has succumbed to an attack of determination of blood to the head.

Amongst the treasures which every West Country

farmer of any standing keeps stored in his wardrobe is a voluminous white pocket-handkerchief. Ample enough to serve as a child's counterpane, the article naturally provokes the curiosity of a stranger to whom it may be displayed, and, when asked its purpose, the housewife proudly replies that it is "master's funeral handkerchief." It is, in fact, reserved for these melancholy occasions, and forms so essential a part of the funeral etiquette that no well-trained and self-respecting farmer would dream of appearing without it.

WITCHES AND GHOSTS

A CONTEMPORARY Italian writer, speaking of that "tragic epoch" the Middle Age, draws the following picture as typical :—

"Across the dreary landscape flits a forlorn, mistrustful phantom, which seeks and hurriedly plucks up sinister herbs with woolly stems, with leaves streaked black and red like tongues of flames. It is the pale witch, gathering henbane and deadly night-shade."

Are there witches yet left in the Exmoor country? Fifty years ago, it is said, the region was full of them. Now it might cost a stranger some research to find them; but it is safe to answer that there are. Unless the writer has been misinformed, an old lady bearing this character resides in Dulverton. It is possible, however, to be bewitched without having the least notion of the human agent, and dire sometimes are the effects.

A farmer, for instance, was in great trouble about his stock. Three or four sheep died quite unaccountably and he made up his mind that some evil influence was at work. He had seen a hare, apparently, and this hare he chose to consider as the form the witch had assumed in order to execute her fell purpose.* So he repaired

---

* That witches appear in the shape of a hare is a very old belief. Compare Ben Jonson, *The Sad Shepherd*, Act II. Sc. 2 :—

    Alken. He is bewitched.
    Clarion.   This is an argument
   Both of her malice and her power, we see.

to a "conjurer" at Waterrow, named Burge, who, before the farmer could utter a word, told him his errand, and showed him the features of the witch. The farmer returned well satisfied with his visit, for, having paid the conjurer his fee, he had been assured that ere long the old woman should be punished.

So it proved. The witch pined and pined, until she was "no otherwise than skin and bone hanged up agin' a wall." Her breast-bone projected as "keen as a knife," and when she had become so feeble as to seem incapable of moving either hand or foot, she would come down-stairs at three o'clock in the morning and sit stark naked, with her hair hanging down her back, on the cold stones of the porch. Sometimes she would be found lying on a green spot in the road, whence she would suddenly start up and spin round and round like a whirligig. Often she was carried into the house as one dead. The neighbours would finger her wrist or place their hands against her heart, and there would be no pulsation. The husband, as quiet a man as ever breathed, was remarkable only for one thing, viz. that he was always followed by a gander. He was not, however,

> *Alken.* She must by some device restrained be,
> Or she'll go far in mischief.
>   *Robin.*   Advise how,
> Sage shepherd ; we shall put it straight in practice.
>   *Alken.* Send forth your woodmen then into the walks,
> Or let them prick her footing hence ; a witch
> Is sure a creature of melancholy,
> And will be found or sitting in her forme,
> Or else, at relief, like a hare.
>   .   .   .   .   .
>
> All this I know, and I will find her for you ;
> And show you her sitting in her forme ; I'll lay
> My hand upon her, make her throw her skut
> Along her back, when she doth start before us.
> But you must give her law ; and you shall see her
> Make twenty leaps and doubles, cross the paths,
> And then squat down beside us.

In the story the reader will not fail to note how exactly the punishment is made to fit the crime believed to have any part in his wife's misdeeds; in fact, if report might be trusted, prayed ardently for her decease. One Christmas he returned to find her lying cold and motionless on the bed.

"Think her's dead now," he soliloquised. "I'll send for the doctor." Hardly had he reached the foot of the

AT THE FOOT OF PORLOCK HILL.

stairs when there was a knock on the floor, and his hopes were again blasted. In truth, the old lady did not die, but recovered and passed the residue of her days without making further attempts to frighten either waggoners or horses.

Many such stories are current. A farmer had experienced great losses amongst his cattle, and being well aware that such things do not occur save through

malign influence, went off in search of the nearest
" conjurer," or white - witch, who, it happened, lived
thirty miles away. However, he was fortunate in finding
him at home, and, in answer to his inquiries, was
informed that he owed all his trouble to the machinations of a certain old woman. This ancient dame had
long dwelt in a cottage, loosely built without mortar and
covered with rough thatch, which stood on a waste plot
adjoining the moor and directly above his homestead.
Thrusting a crown into the diviner's palm, the farmer
left the house, his eyes glowing with resentment, and his
tongue vowing vengeance on the wicked old crone.

"She shall die, the sinner!" he exclaimed. "She
shall die. Nothing on earth shall save her."

On reaching home, he, accompanied by several of his
neighbours, climbed the hill to the witch's abode,
inspired by Heaven knows what evil designs. But his
murderous intentions, if he had any, were thrown away.
When he opened the door of the hovel, he discovered
the old soul tossing in a mysterious fever, and almost at
her last gasp. This, of course, was the " conjurer's "
achievement; and, to mark their abhorrence of such
characters, when the old witch was dead, the people
came and burnt the cottage, and demolished the walls
thereof.

The true witch is not content with causing mischief;
she loves to see the mischief she has caused. Near the
north coast of West Somerset is a farmhouse where,
some years ago, there was great distress. The occupier
had experienced heavy losses amongst his cattle, and
several members of his family had been taken ill. Luck
had deserted the place, which evidently lay under some
evil spell. The usual remedy was resorted to, the
farmer's son making his way to the nearest white-witch.
This person gave him a powder, with instructions to
strew it round the place, and assured him that it would

prove an admirable prophylactic against the approach of any evil or hurtful thing. Moreover, the white-witch declared that ere long the family would behold the author of their troubles seeking to draw nigh the house. Now it so happened that in a cottage not far away dwelt a solitary old woman. Soon after the son's return, this ancient crone was descried peering through the palings by which the little garden before the house was fenced in. The coincidence, it was thought, could not be fortuitous; and the farmer, fancy-ing that he had discovered the evil of his house, ex-claimed in a rage, "Set the dogs on her!" At the same time he attempted to rise from his armchair. Singular to relate, however, some mysterious power nailed him to his seat, and in a moment or two man and chair and all began to ascend towards the ceiling. The others who were present hurried out of the room in the direction of the old woman. The withered form was already retreating, and on reaching a thick hedge, vanished completely out of sight. A little later the dogs returned with every symptom of shame and discomfiture. The story concludes with the assertion that the farmer has never recovered from the shock, but remains to this day crippled and infirm, and an imbecile.

This melancholy recital suffices to show that witches, even more than the generality of their sex, are kittle cattle to deal with, and as a rule it is sound policy if you chance to meet with one of the sort, or only a person suspected of witchcraft, to be very deferential and oblige her in every possible way. It is dangerous to receive a gift from a witch, but it is still more dangerous to refuse one. An old woman of singular appearance called once on a time at a farmhouse, where she leant over the half-door and asked for a drink of cider. Apples had been scarce that year, and her demand was refused. The old woman turned away, and as she hobbled off, muttered curses on the niggardliness of Farmer Jones and his spouse. "It won't be long," she hissed, "before you'll be sorry you didn't give me the cider." So it turned out. The farmer, hitherto a prosperous man, experienced nothing but misfortune. His stock perished, and not only his stock, but one by one his buxom daughters pined away and died.

In their contests with the powers of darkness, even when they assume the form of beautiful females, hermits are usually represented as victorious. St. Dunstan and St. Anthony are cases in point. Exmoor witches, however, have sometimes reversed this rule, and put venerable anchorites to shame. Whatever they may be in other parts of the world, on and around Exmoor witches are not necessarily old women, and the particular witch whom our story concerns chanced to be of the opposite sex. It was near the Doone Valley that the tragedy befell. There in his cell dwelt a holy man, passing his hours in devout contemplation, telling his beads, repeating his orisons, and eschewing the converse of the world. Nobody, it might be thought, could be more harmless or more secure from harm than he. Possibly for that very reason he brought upon himself the envy and malice of a certain witch, who one day drew a circle and by wicked sleight lured the holy man to enter. On realising his plight, the hermit instinctively made the sign of the cross, but too late. Like a hapless fly, he had fallen into the meshes of his adversary, and could not extricate himself. Captive and docile, he followed the witch into his hut, and was seen no more. From this story it will be gleaned what the "magic circle" portends on Exmoor. Step into it, and witch, or foul fiend, will have you body and soul. Perhaps not wholly unconnected with this belief is the fact that in the better sort of farmhouses, as well as in old manor-houses, are sometimes found, moulded on the ceiling of the hall or principal living-room, ovals. Anything that is said beneath these figures is considered sacred.

In view of the terrible punishments which it is in their power to inflict, witches and wise women are naturally regarded with no small measure of reverence. But little coal is consumed in this remote region, the customary fuel being either wood or turf. This is burnt in an open hearth, over which rises a wide chimney. When the village maiden, full of trepidation, resorts to the grey-haired sibyl for counsel and assistance, it is in the chimney that the wise-woman takes her stand, and, gazing up into the heavens, mutters her incantations to the stars. Advice, of course, is not bestowed gratis, but if the charm should prove ineffectual, the victims seldom blab. If they did, who knows but that the spell might descend on them?

Besides witches proper, there is a class of old ladies who can hardly be distinguished from them, and who in less civilised times would certainly have run a serious risk of being burnt. Partly it is their age, partly their look, partly their temper, but above all the possession of certain uncanny accomplishments, that tends to identify them with the unhappy creatures who acknowledge Satan as a master. In one of her graceful sketches of West Country life, Miss Alice King limns a delightful portrait of one of these eccentric, but doubtless very innocent, old " dummin " on her native heath :—

" It is a splendid golden day in early September, a day when summer dressed herself out in all her bravery, that we may look and admire before she glides away to make place for her sober-robed sister autumn. Up the deep lane all tapestried with feathery fern and trailing white convolvulus, all spangled with golden rod and yellow ragwort, we pass behind our guide's quaint little black bonnet and flowery shawl. She has a large basket on her arm, which signifies that she is on an excursion of business rather than pleasure. She is going to gather whortleberries, which she will make a pretty penny of in the country town by-and-by. She walks at a brisk pace, and her petticoats move with a swing and a rustle that has in it a warning sound for those used to West Country folk. Whatever she does and whatever we may think of her doings, we must not smile; if we do, the old lady will decidedly show herself 'hoity-toity,' a mysterious and terrible word, which is quite untranslatable out of West Country dialect, but which implies all sorts of nameless horrors that it is far better to dream of vaguely than to contemplate in reality.

"And now we are out on the hillside, the hillside which has spread over it such a rich and curiously woven carpet of purple heather and golden gorse, the hillside which is the ball-room of the winds, where they love to whirl in their wild waltz, playing their own wild music the while. The old lady has not the slightest eye for the picturesque, or the slightest mind for the poetical; she is simply bent on gathering as many whortleberries as she can into her basket, and hither and thither she goes from bush to bush over the heather. Suddenly as we follow and watch her, we start back; there lies a viper coiled up among the heath close to our feet. What does the old lady do? Does she scream and run away as an old lady in such a situation might be expected to do? Instead of that she does something that surprises us beyond all power of expression—she actually stoops down and picks up the viper as calmly as any other old lady would pick up a skein of wool. In mingled terror and astonishment we make a movement towards her, thinking she must suddenly have taken leave of her senses, but an authoritative gesture with her disengaged hand warns us to stand back. Then she begins to repeat in a loud distinct voice certain texts of Scripture, which she strings together with marvellous glibness, the snake resting in her hand the while as peacefully as a lap-dog in its mistress's lap. Then she lets the viper slip gently out of her hand back to the heather, the operation having apparently been equally enjoyed by it and the old lady, who now turns to us and says, 'I bears right vore, you see, and goes drough with it, but if I was to stop for so much as the crack of a sheep's tail. or say half a word out of place, the varmint would be up with his head and sting me, as sure as eggs be eggs.' On account no doubt of the frequency with which they are seen in the heather on the hills, vipers hold a somewhat prominent place in the imaginations of West Country damsels, who in their childhood have spent their time roving over the moorland. If a West Country girl dreams of one, she will tell you that it is a sure sign she has a secret enemy who is endeavouring, unknown to her, to do her harm.

"There are other West Country dames who possess an exactly similar mysterious influence over bees. An old lady who is gifted in this latter abnormal manner, will stand with a swarm of bees flying around her, and pitching occasionally playfully on her shoulder, as if she were a pillar cut out of Dunkery stone. She will even put her hand into a bee-hive, and keep it there for several minutes, and then withdraw it without the least injury. If you ask her what it felt like she replies unconcernedly, 'Why, when I have got my hand in the hive, it do zim all the while as if I was touching velvet, pretty little dears, their wings be so soft-like.'"

As Miss King reminds us, the superstition of West Country folk invests these insects with odd ways quite unrecognised by standard works on entomology. It is alleged, for example, that bees are deeply offended if anybody sees them drink. Once, it is said, an unfortunate maiden was standing beside a stream, when a bee drew near to take her evening draught. Recollecting what had been told her about the irritability of these creatures, the girl ran away as fast as she was able, and tried to hide herself in an adjacent wood, The angry bee flew after her, however, and ensconced herself in the maiden's hair, inflicting much mental and physical agony on the object of her resentment.

It is the practice in the West Country, whenever a death occurs in a family, to " tell the bees," otherwise the bees, too, will die. Apparently, in earlier times, it was believed that the bees would accompany the soul of the deceased to the other world, unless restrained by some act of propitiation. Be that as it may, the fact is well known around Exmoor that the bees must be treated on these occasions with due respect, either by turning the hives or placing crape on them. The writer is acquainted with a Dulverton man who had the misfortune a few years ago to lose his son. He requested his brother to tell the bees, but the latter, it seems, performed the duty somewhat perfunctorily, merely tapping the butts with his stick.   The consequence was that during the winter all the bees died.*

It is proper to add that such notions are not confined to the West Country. In Hampshire there is a rhyme:—

> " Bees, bees, awake !
> Your master is dead,
> And another you must take."

And in Worcestershire they say :—

> " The master's dead, but don't you go,
> Your mistress will be good to you."

Also, in some parts of Brittany it is customary to tie a small piece of black stuff to the bee-hives in case of a death, and a piece of red in case of a marriage. This is done on the plea that otherwise the bees would never thrive.

According to a Warwickshire rhyme :—

> " If your bees fall sick, and pine, and die,
> One of your house will soon in churchyard lie."

There does not appear to be any trace of such a belief in the Exmoor country, but it is a very serious matter to see yourself, *i.e.* your wraith. Not many years since a Dulverton man, riding in the direction of the

---

* The *Gentleman's Magazine* for 1859 contains the following story bearing on this usage : " In Devonshire the custom is (or was in the year 1790) to turn round the bee-hives that belonged to the deceased at the moment that the corpse was being carried out of the house ; and on one occasion at the funeral of a rich farmer at Cullompton, as a numerous procession was on the point of starting, a person called out, ' Turn the bees,' upon which a servant, who had no knowledge of the custom, instead of turning the hives about, lifted them up, and then laid them down on their sides. The bees thus invaded quickly fastened upon the attendants, and in a few moments the corpse was left quite alone, hats and wigs were lost in the confusion, and it was a long time before the sufferers returned to their duty."

station, was thrown from his horse and broke his neck. On hearing of this fatality a woman of the place delivered herself of the following comment: "I knaw'd sumfin would happen to un, 'cause er zeed hisself down thick raud a wik agone." In order to counter the ill effects of beholding one's own image, a considerable interval should be allowed to elapse before taking the same route, which by the token in question has been proved to be unlucky.

The Exmoor peasantry are fond of noting coincidences, and the results of this habit are sometimes sufficiently remarkable. Thus, in one village, it was observed that whenever the parson concluded his sermon at four o'clock, as sure as fate somebody would suffer for it. Death, illness, accident, loss of property—one of these things was certain to overtake some luckless member of the little community, and that in the course of the week. The feeling became so strong that at last the clergyman was spoken to on the subject. To humour his flock, he so arranged that his discourse should either exceed or fall short of the objectionable limit, and, as the hour approached, carefully listened for the warning note of the church clock.

That is a reminder of the immense concessions which the clergy were formerly in the habit of making to the strange fancies of their parishioners. One of their principal uses in the eyes of the laity was that of laying ghosts. When a house was "troublesome," to whom should the inmates fly but to their pastor, who, as a matter of course, knew more about the supernatural than the rest of their neighbours put together? Early in the last century the belief that parsons could lay ghosts was simply universal in the West Country, and the Rev. Richard Polwhele, in his *Traditions and Recollections*, supplies an amusing account of the supposed business of a literary club at a country house.

The club was christened " The Alps," after the initials
of the prinicipal members, Andrew, Lee, Polwhele, and
Swete, who were all in holy orders. So much by the
way. " That Haldon was haunted by infernal spirits
seems to have been the belief of the vicinity. And
the importation of four parsons in Sir R. Palk's own
carriage was a phenomenon not to be accounted for
on any other ground than their conjuring character
and their instrumentality in clearing the house from
those infernal spirits. This, accordingly, was the work
assigned us. And one of the champions, after a long
struggle, was successful in sending a devil through the
roof, and another in locking up the archfiend himself
in an iron chest, like the enchanted chest of Orismanes.
Such was the report of the neighbourhood, and even
now it is firmly believed by many people at Exeter
of no mean understanding." When stories like these
were circulated as gospel in the civilised regions at the
mouth of the Exe, it is only natural that even more
exaggerated ideas found credence at its source. What
is yet stranger, some of the clergy were every whit as
superstitious as those to whom they ministered, and
entertained not a shadow of doubt as to the reality
of their exorcisms. A parson might actually make a
reputation for himself in this line, but the country-folk
always postulated that he must be a *strong* man—
otherwise his health would suffer. The frequent
expenditure of virtue told on the most powerful constitutions. Thus a certain clergyman, who was " so
strong that he could lay any ghost," and so good-
natured as to be unable to refuse any application for
his services, found himself compelled to resign his cure
and leave the scene of his mighty works. They had
fetched him so often that he was a perfect anatomy—
nothing but skin and bone.

Sometimes the parson himself needed to be laid.

A HAUNTED SPOT, NEAR SIMONSBATH

Q

An old farmer once regaled his spiritual adviser with an account of sundry incidents connected with the departure from the world of a local clergyman. The parson died, and was buried with the solemn rites of the Church in the parish churchyard. The last farewells having been taken, the mourners slowly wended their way back to the house, when, on entering the study, they were startled to find, seated stern and silent in his armchair, the form of the old man, which, they supposed, had been left behind in God's acre. But that is not all. The apparition came again. Indeed, every evening, as night settled on the dreary moor and a white mist stole up the hillsides, the phantom returned to its place, and no prayer, no reasoning availed to move it. At last it was resolved to call in a parson, who, in his dealings with spectres, was believed to be irresistible. He arrived, and the ghost, hitherto entirely intractable, rose from his chair and followed him out of the house. The awestruck spectators watched the two figures as they crossed the meadows in the twilight and approached a bottomless black pool, bordered with gnarled old trees. Then, as with a flash of lightning, the ghost vanished, and from that hour the family abode in peace.

Not altogether dissimilar is the tale which the moorman repeats with bated breath of the wicked squire. The evil ways of the squire had long been the scandal of the neighbourhood, but at last the time came when he must go to his account. It was winter, and a terrific storm was raging. Successive claps of thunder shook the venerable manor-house, vivid flashes of lightning lit up the apartment in which the old reprobate lay a-dying, while, descending in torrents, the rain continually lashed the casements. Above the howling of the tempest were heard at times diabolical voices and pitiless laughter, as of fiends gloating over their prey. And all the

while the wretched squire, locked in mortal conflict
with an invisible enemy, exerted his fast-ebbing powers
to stave off the inevitable end. At last, in despair, he
lay back and, stammering unseemly curses, passed into
the Unseen. Ask a moorman the occasion of the
storm, and he will reply evasively, "Something they
parsons know about."

A typical instance of ghost - laying in this part of
the world is connected with the vagaries of one Master
Lucott, a buccaneer of Porlock. A week after his burial
he, or his ghost, was observed at the Weir—a circumstance which excited no little dismay in the neighbourhood. The parsons were adjured to do their office on
the runagate, and as the old salt was likely to offer
exceptional resistance, twelve clergymen were deemed
not too many for the occasion. One of the apostolic
number proved faint-hearted, but the rest persevered—
for a time—heroically with their task. They assembled
in Porlock Church, and Lucott was cursed with bell,
book, and candle. These formalities, however, proved
entirely inefficacious. To their horror the holy men
descried the pale features of the eloping buccaneer
grinning at them, with an expression of intense amusement, and, to complete their discomfiture, the phantom
presently advanced down the aisle. Upon this the
parsons decided, each on his own responsibility, that
the church was no place for them, and bolted helter-
skelter out of the building. However, the parish priest
of St. Decuman's was more politic than his brethren, and,
on his services being enlisted, resolved to take Master
Lucott by guile. He defied the blasphemous rogue to
eat a portion of the consecrated wafer, and Lucott,
having accepted the challenge, found himself shorn of
his power. Compelled to obey the priest's directions,
he mounted a horse and rode with him as far as Doni-
ford. Here, observing that a man stared at him, he

summoned all the energy he had left, and knocked out
the rustic's eye. But it was all over with him. He was
bidden to enter a small box, which the parson forthwith hurled into the sea, and Master Lucott never reappeared.

The influence of spirits is sometimes detected in cases
of sickness, and then the parson is in request as a
medicine-man. The following story, related by Miss
Alice King, will serve to illustrate the point:—

"Some years ago, a clergyman, who had been recently
appointed to a living among the hills in the heart of the West
Country, was called on to see a man in his parish, who had
been suddenly taken ill. On his arrival at the cottage, he
found that the patient was suffering from hæmorrhage, and,
turning to the man's mother, who was standing by, he said
to her—

"'You must send for the doctor at once, and as quickly as
you can.'

"The old woman shook her head, and puckered up her
face into a thousand wrinkles, as she replied, with a knowing
wink—

"'No, no! I ban't a-going to send for the old doctor; he
don't want no doctor's stuff. You just do your duty as a
parson, please, sir, and say a prayer to stop the blood.'

"The clergyman first stood staring in blank amazement at
the speaker, and then, when further pressed by her, was
obliged to confess that he knew of no such prayer, either in
the Prayer-book or out of it; after which he had to make a
hasty retreat from the cottage, for his confession of ignorance
caused the old woman to address him in terms that were by
no means complimentary or respectful.

"'Get along with ee!' she cried. 'You be either making
gammots of me, which is very onbecoming of a passon to do,
or you be no passon at all.'

"For some months after this misadventure the clergyman
could see that he had fallen in the estimation of his flock.
They did not come to church, and they treated him with
evident reserve and mistrust.

"At length his cook, who had still some belief in him,
perhaps because he paid her the compliment of eating every

day a good dinner in spite of his parochial reverses, asked him if he would go and visit her sister, who had lately fallen sick. The old woman who was nursing the patient told the clergy-man that she was very much troubled, because she could not make a certain medicine, which she had to give the sick woman, fizz up as the doctor did when he mixed it, and that she supposed it must be done by some charm which the doctor alone knew. The clergyman examined the medicine, and found it was an ordinary saline draught. He understood that the old woman's failure had arisen from her putting in the wrong mixture first. Without, however, explaining this, he mixed the draught for the patient, and made it fizz quite as splendidly as the doctor had done.

"'The minister be a powerful man after all!' exclaimed the old nurse ; 'he do know how to command the spirits.'

"After that the clergyman grew rapidly in popularity, and fully gained the confidence and affection of his parishioners."

It is a thrice-told tale, yet it seems impossible to omit in this section on apparitions the strange case of Mrs. Leakey, the whistling lady of Minehead, otherwise the chapter would be open to the charge of incompleteness. Owing to the fact that Sir Walter Scott has inserted it in his notes on *Rokeby*, this story is much better known than the majority of local legends, and in the reign of Charles I. must have attained something like general notoriety. At all events, a sort of commission, con-sisting of the Bishop of Bath and Wells, Paul Godwin, and Sir Robert Philips, sat on the matter, and deposi-tions were taken on its behalf by the grave Mr. Byam, than whom no clergyman was more respected in the West. Elizabeth Leakey, the daughter-in-law, Mr. Heath-field, curate of Minehead, and two other parsons affirmed that they had seen the ghost, and some of them averred that they had talked with her. Nevertheless, the com-missioners reported that "they were of opinion, and did believe, that there never was such an apparition at all, but that it was an imposture, device, and fraud for some particular ends—what ends they knew not." The docu-

ment, endorsed by Archbishop Laud, is at the Public
Record Office, and in the *Calendar of State Papers*,
Domestic Series, Charles I., 1637–8, is assigned to
February 24th of that year. Sir Walter, however,
appears to have derived his information from a copy of
Athenianism, a work of Dunton's, of *Dunciad* memory,
at the end of which the tale is engrossed under the title
of "The Apparition Evidences."

Coleridge once remarked, "There are three classes
into which all the women past seventy that ever I
knew were to be divided : (1) That dear old soul;
(2) that old woman; (3) that old witch." On the
evidence before us, we can hardly escape the conclusion
that Mrs. Leakey was an old witch, though during her
lifetime her acquaintances appear to have thought her
a dear old soul. The venerable gentlewoman was so
sociable that friends could not bear the prospect of
parting with her, and would say to her, and to each
other, that her death, whenever it came, would be a
general misfortune. Mrs. Leakey was of the same
opinion, and, in reply to such compliments, would
observe, in a sprightly tone, that though they might
like her company now, it would be very different after
her decease. After a while she died and was buried,
when, instead of reposing like other folks, the lively old
dame showed herself ubiquitous. By night, at noon-
day, in her own home, afield, in town, at sea, on shore,
you could never be sure of not meeting her, and all this
restlessness was produced by nothing more than feminine
worry about a necklace which, it seems, had passed into
the wrong hands. One regrets to add that the
amiability which had so eminently distinguished her
in the flesh had entirely deserted her, and when a
doctor of medicine, forgetful of his manners, neglected
to help her over a stile, she kicked him.

One of her humours was to appear on the quay and

call for a boat, but she did not confine herself to these harmless antics, and blossomed forth into an inveterate wrecker. Her only son was the owner of several vessels, with which he drove a considerable trade between Mine-head and Waterford. Should any of these vessels approach the harbour, "this ghost would appear in the same garb and likeness as when she was alive, and standing at the mainmast, would blow with a whistle, and, though it was never so great a calm, yet immediately there would arise a most dreadful storm that would break, wreck, and drown ship and goods." So she went on until her son lost all credit in the mercantile community. He was unable to freight a vessel, and, even had he been able, he would have found it impossible to get together a crew. Still the old lady was not satisfied, and, to glut her malice yet more, strangled her son's only child—an innocent babe—in its cradle.

Other particulars are humorous and incongruous. Thus we are told that her daughter-in-law was dressing her hair at a looking-glass, when the ghost peeped over her shoulder. Instead of losing her senses, which, the philosophic Coleridge declares, is the proper thing to do under the circumstances, the younger woman plucked up courage and addressed her mother-in-law, by whom she was despatched to a certain Irish prelate noted for his crimes and misfortunes. Arrived at her destination, she urged the transgressor to repent, and warned him that otherwise he would end his days on the gallows. The bishop, however, was undismayed, and answered cheerily that, if he was born to be hanged, he would never be drowned—doubtless, a hit at the shady reputation of old Mrs. Leakey.

One more ghost story, and it shall be borrowed from Mr. Thornton's interesting *Reminiscences of an Old West Country Clergyman.*

"One morning," he says, "I went bare-headed to the yard

above Selworthy Cottage to see the boy groom 'Polly' properly. It was early, let us say about half-past eight.

"'Good morning, sir,' said the boy; 'do you know that Mary Stenner has seen a ghost, and is well-nigh mazed this morning?'

"Up the hill I went at full speed, highly delighted, and ran unceremoniously into the kitchen of the farmhouse by the church. Mrs. Stenner was at that time, perhaps, thirty-five years of age, stout, ruddy, and free from fancy. But there she sat by the kitchen fire, 'in the vapours,' as our forefathers would have said. Burnt feathers, fans, cold waters without and a taste of hot waters within—all these remedies were in full requisition, and others besides them.

"'Oh, Mrs. Stenner, is it true that you have seen him?' A sigh, and a sip, and a shake of the head were given or taken. But there was no reply.

"'Oh, Mrs. Stenner, do tell me what he is like.'

"'Mr. Thornton! My dear soul! Why, did you not hear me screech? I screeched that loud! Oh dear, oh dear! I thought you would hear me. I'll never come up from Budleigh Hill after dark alone—no, never, never!'

"'Well, but, my dear Mrs. Stenner, what did you see after all?'

"'I hadn't left Budleigh Hill by two gunshots, when there it was, the nasty thing, running along by my side. 'Twas awful. It had four legs, and it was black, and had great fiery eyes as big as saucers, and it ran on until it came to where the water crosses under the road, and they things, of course, never can abide running water, so it just couldn't get across, and off it went up in the air like a flash of fire. I screeched—oh, I screeched, and I thought that the parson and you would surely be down the hill to me, and they from Budleigh would come upwards.'

"I was young then, and so I made a mistake by remarking that no doubt it was her sheep-dog that had come down to meet her—come 'against her,' as they say in Somersetshire, and given her a start. That suggestion, however, would not do at all, and I had to beat a hasty retreat. Presently, I met the sexton, John Hobbs, and made eager inquiries again.

"'I know all about it,' said John; ''tis exactly twenty-five years since we was bringing the corpse of —— from Horner

Mill to Selworthy, and the handle of the coffin against the head came loose, just exactly to the very spot where Mary Stenner met with the ghost last night. I picked up a stone and knocked it in again, and no doubt it went into the brain, and let the spirit out. Oh, yes ! I know all about it.' "

CHAPTER III

HIGH DAYS AND HOLIDAYS

CLERGYMEN appointed to West Country livings meet with all sorts of surprises, as the foregoing incidents plainly show. One vicar had been just long enough in his parish to form a favourable impression of the people, and to hope that they had formed a favourable impression of him, when an incident occurred by which he was greatly mystified and disconcerted. Hitherto his ministrations had been well attended, but, on entering his church on the first Good Friday, he found almost all the pews empty, and nobody to listen to his discourse save a few old women, most of them deaf, or, at least, hard of hearing. He naturally concluded that he had unwittingly offended his flock, and that this was a prearranged demonstration. After the service he approached one of the old women, and asked her, rather nervously, what had caused the parishioners to absent themselves. The old lady first stared in astonishment, and then, with a smile of pity at the parson's ignorance, informed him that, according to the usual custom, the villagers were planting their beans, that they (the beans) might appear above ground on the morning of Easter Day.*

* On Easter Day it was formerly the custom for young men to climb the nearest hill to see the sun rise—an act which was supposed to bring good luck. In the early part of the last century Dunkery was the favourite place of resort, probably on account of its superior altitude. " Its sides," says Miss King, "were covered with young men, who seemed to be coming from every quarter of the compass, and to be pressing up towards the Beacon."

The same parson was probably "taken aback" also on the occasion of his first wedding. Weddings in the West Country have some queer characteristics, one of which is, or was, the following. Before "restoration" became the rage, there might often be seen in the partition between the belfry and the nave a little window, through which, during the progress of the ceremony, a rustic face might be descried, intently watching. This is not the visage of a Doone or a disappointed lover, waiting for the psychological moment to wreak vengeance on the parties, but the kindly features of a ringer, whose duty it is to acquaint his fellows the instant the ring is on the bride's finger. Directly the announcement is made, the bells burst into a crashing peal and thereby assure good luck to the wedded pair. Meanwhile the officiating clergyman has to struggle through the remainder of the service—a veritable anti-climax—as best he can.

Marriage generally presupposes love and courtship, and with love is associated a very curious custom, to which Gay, in his *Pastorals*, makes the following allusion :—

> "At eve, last Midsummer, no sleep I sought,
> But to the field a bag of hemp-seed brought ;
> I scattered round the seed on every side,
> And three times in a trembling accent cried :
> 'This hemp-seed with my virgin hand I sow ;
> Who shall my true-love be, to crop the mow ?' "

The moon is up and silvering the quiet meads, when, lo ! into the churchyard steals a romantic maiden, with something in her hand. This she throws over her shoulder, repeating the while :—

> "Hemp-seed I scatter,
> Hemp-seed I sow ;
> He that is my true love
> Come after me, and mow."

She casts a rapid look behind, sees her love hasting after her, scythe in hand, and that moment must be off,

WINSFORD CHURCH

without indulging a second glance. Otherwise she will
be overtaken by the phantom, who will obey the invitation, and cut her legs with the scythe.

This, however, is not the only mode of eliciting the
precious secret. On Midsummer Eve a maiden, desirous
of learning the initials of her destined spouse, puts under
her bed a basin of water, in which are the letters of the
alphabet, floating face downwards. She goes to sleep,
and the next morning, on awaking, examines the basin,
where, if she be lucky, she will find two or three of
the letters turned over, the first letters of the future
bridegroom's Christian name and surname. Another
picturesque custom, in which the maiden is frequently
joined by the young man, is the following. The table
having been laid for supper, the doors are thrown open,
and those keeping vigil wait until the clock strikes
twelve. At the witching hour there enters a shadowy
form (two, if the young man be present) which consumes
the supper and vanishes. Where two ghosts appear, they
are, of course, male and female. If a maiden would
know the year of her marriage, at noon on Midsummer
Day she ties a wedding-ring to a hair of her head, and
hangs the ring in a glass of water. The clock now
strikes twelve, and ere the last stroke, "the ring will
have tinkled against the glass as many times as there
are years before she will be a wife." On Midsummer
Day, too, while it is chiming twelve, a maiden will
pluck a full-blown rose, blindfolded, and wrap it up
in a sheet of white paper. This she refrains from
opening until Christmas Day, when, according to some,
it will be found as fresh as when she gathered it.
Better still, if she puts it in her bosom, the young
man she is to wed will come and snatch it away.

Miss Alice King has made this custom an excuse for
a charming picture of West Country life :—

"But why is sweet Bessie, the farmer's dark-eyed daughter,

absent from her merry companions? She is sitting in yonder deep window-seat, where the moonbeams are falling softly on something she holds in her hand, while her cheeks burn and her heart beats. Let us steal across the room, and take one glance at that object which she touches almost reverently as her fingers close lightly over it. It is a withered rose. For some time Bessie has loved handsome Robin, the young Exmoor farmer, whose uncle is her father's neighbour, and there seems some reason to believe, by certain signs and tokens known in the silent alphabet of lovers, that her affection is returned. But Robin is a very shy wooer, and Bessie, like all West Country maidens, is very proud and reserved, and therefore the courtship languishes.

"Thus it has come to pass that Bessie has hit upon an exceedingly original way of making her backward suitor declare himself. Long ago, in the bright summertime, she gathered a blush rose on Midsummer Day, and stealthily, secretly, so that not even her mother could know, she laid it carefully in the inmost recesses of her drawer. She has thought of that rose all through the golden harvest weather, and dreamed of it at night, and now, on Christmas Eve, she has taken it out of its hiding-place, and to-morrow she will go to church with her withered rose in her breast. Robin is paying a Christmas visit to his uncle, and Bessie fully believes that if in reality he loves her, he will be compelled by the virtue of that charmed, withered midsummer rose to go up to her when he meets her on Christmas morning, and take it from her bosom, and this will be an infallible sign that his heart is hers, and they will be married before another Christmas Day comes round."

The present writer was in an Exmoor farmhouse not long ago, when he was informed that the farmer's son was to be married in a week's time. His sister, a nice-looking young woman, and industrious as all Exmoor people are, was to be one of the bridesmaids, and, as she had already acted in a similar capacity, her well-wishers recalled the saying that it is unlucky to be a bridesmaid three times. The fair object of these remarks, however, was quite composed and merely smiled sweetly. Possibly she had reason to surmise that at the next wedding she attended she would figure as bride, and so become ineligible.

Some years ago a lady and gentleman were staying in the West Country, when they became the parents of a fine boy. As soon as the mother was convalescent, the conversation naturally turned on the christening, and, desirous of paying a neighbouring farmer and his family, who had shown them much kindness, a marked compliment, suggested that his handsome daughter "Harts" (*i.e.* Harriet) and her lover should stand godfather and godmother to the child. What was their surprise, when, instead of the proposal being at once accepted with pleasure, the result was a scene. The farmer knitted his brows ominously, "Harts" turned deathly pale, and her maiden aunt, who was in the room, first screamed and then fainted, or, in West Country phrase, "dropped away." Meanwhile the visitors looked on gravely, and, as soon as an opportunity presented itself, expressed sorrow at having made so unwelcome a suggestion, at the same time asserting their innocence of any unkind intention. The farmer, considerably mollified by their apology, now condescended to explain that, from the point of view of the young people and their relations, no arrangement could be more sinister, since, in the West Country at least, it was the firm belief that a betrothed couple who stood sponsors to a child together would never be man and wife.

Au contraire, a West Country bride has no superstitious dislike of removing her wedding-ring immediately after the ceremony. Indeed it is taken off as soon as she returns to the house, in order that little bits of the wedding-cake may be passed through it. These morsels are eagerly appropriated by the girls, who, on lying down that night, put them under their pillows, with the certain consequence that they dream of their husbands to be. In many West Country villages

R

a pretty custom is still observed after a wedding. A chain of flowers bars the road by which the happy couple have to return to the house, and all the young bachelors of the parish turn out to guard it. Before the bridegroom is allowed to rejoin the wedding party the merry troop insist on his paying toll, whereupon, amidst jests and laughter, he is sent on his way rejoicing.

Already allusion has been made to Christmas as the time to which love-sick maidens look forward with eager anticipation. But, of course, they are not alone in this. From the gleeful children who chant the quaint carol beginning—

> " Christmas Day in the morning,
> Joseph whistling, Mary singing,
> All the bells of heaven are ringing,
> Christmas Day in the morning,"

to the old folks who sit and warm themselves by the ashen faggot on Christmas Eve, all regard the holy season with high approval and satisfaction. Even the beasts of the field, it is said, are aware of its approach, for in every cowshed the " master-bullock "—*i.e.* the finest and strongest of the cattle—will low three times at the first stroke of midnight, and then go down on his knees before the manger, as if in homage to the Babe of Bethlehem. No master or mistress allows servants or labourers to work on Old Christmas Day— that is, if their employer is wise, since the infraction of this rule is apt to bring with it the direst con- sequences. Miss King relates the following story of a " terrible near woman," whose love of money tempted her to break the time-honoured custom :—

" On the morning of Old Christmas Day, instead of putting on her best dress and bonnet, and going to church, as all West Country good Christians do, she put on her second-best bonnet and her thick grey cloak, and had the horse harnessed and put into her tax-cart, and drove to the nearest market town to sell her butter and eggs, of which she took good stock with her in the cart, neatly packed in two or three baskets. All went well with the dame at first. She disposed of all her wares in the most satisfactory way, and at a high price. The inhabitants of the town, as she went from door to door, appeared to have a special liking for the produce of her dairy and poultry-yard. It was Christmas-time, and everybody was anxious to secure good cheer for their families, and certainly in all the neighbourhood there was no such butter and thick, solid cream as the dame's—there was no denying it.

"At length, late in the afternoon, the dame started homeward, with her purse well filled and her baskets empty. It had been a beautiful winter's day, and she jogged along in much placid comfort and contentment, counting up her gains in her mind. At dusk, however, a thick fog came suddenly on, after the fashion of fogs near Exmoor, and the dame began to have much trouble to see her way in the dark lanes; but she was what is called in the West Country 'a spurrity woman,' and she kept on her way undaunted. She was within half a mile of her home, when her little horse, who had Exmoor blood in him, all at once started violently, upset dame, cart, and baskets, freed himself from his harness, and galloped home without them. The dame was picked up with a broken leg, from the consequences of which she limped all her life after. The conduct of the horse was attributed to supernatural intervention."

In connection with Christmas, it may be mentioned that in the West Country it is reckoned a crime to kill a robin. This notion is believed to have sprung from a beautiful old legend that, as the Saviour hung on the cross, the little bird toiled to extract the nails from His bleeding hands, and that some drops of sacred blood, falling on its breast, left the red stain which we now find.*

* With regard to other winged creatures, the raven is considered a bird of ill omen, possibly because of its harsh note as it cleaves the air towards the inaccessible nest it has built for itself on cliff or tree-top. At the sight of a single magpie it is proper to doff your hat, otherwise the omission will infallibly bring ill luck. The number is here of consequence, as is shown by the rhyme—

"One for sorrow,
Two for mirth,
Three for a wedding,
Four for a birth."

On the 17th of January, the eve of Old Twelfth Day, it is customary to sing to the apple trees and fire off guns, in order to ensure a bounteous crop. This practice is not absolutely confined to the West Country, though it is probably more generally observed here than in other parts of the kingdom. The ceremony, which is known as "wassailing the apple trees," is thus performed: A party of labourers, with whom perhaps is the local Vulcan or carpenter, makes the round of the orchards, starting about seven o'clock in the evening, when the men have left work. In each orchard that they enter a ring is formed, and then the quaint wassail song, of which the words are traditional and doubtless of great antiquity, is sung by the assembled band. As might be anticipated, there are different versions of the ditty in different localities, but the variations are comparatively slight. Thus in some places the first verse commences—

"It is our wassail round our town,
Cup it is white, and ale it is brown."

This unlooked-for allusion to *ale* seems at first very singular and out of place, and does not occur in all the renderings of the song. The word "wassail," however, which is derived from the Anglo-Saxon *Waes-hael* ("Health be to you"), formerly denoted a liquor composed of apples, sugar, and ale, which was greatly in request at carousals. It may be added that the term—pronounced in the West Somerset dialect "wazzayal"—is now only heard in connection with the custom of singing to the trees. After each verse the leader shouts in stentorian tones—

"Hats full, caps full, three bushel bags full!
Hip, hip, hip, hurrah!"

And the others join heartily in the acclaim.

"Formerly," says Mr. W. Elton, "an old musket was brought round and discharged at each hurrah; but of late years this has been wanting, the men perhaps not being willing to risk the vigilance of the officers of the Inland Revenue."

Mr. Elton is, we are sure, quite mistaken, if he means it to be inferred that the custom of firing at the trees has fallen into desuetude. It is certainly as common as —our own impression is, much more common than— the habit of singing to them. Labourers, it is true, no longer carry muskets or fowling-pieces, as they did once; but in most districts there is no lack of guns, and the farmers and their sons are, many of them, quite superstitious enough to provide against the omission of the ceremony.

One line of the song explains—

"And a little more cider will do us no harm."

This is evidently intended as a hint, and in the hospitable farmhouses of the West Country such a hint is invariably acted on.

"A bucket of hot cider, with toast floating on the top, is now," says Mr. Elton, "sent out by the owner of the orchard, be he squire or farmer; the toast is placed in the apple trees for robins to eat, while the cider lubricates the throats of the singers. They form a curious and picturesque sight, these men in their rough working clothes on a bright and frosty night, with the moon shining down through the bare and rugged branches of the apple trees on their scarcely less rugged features; and if by chance there be a few inches of snow on the ground, the effect is perfect. One forgets that it is the end of the nineteenth century, and you fancy yourself assisting at a Druidical function of the dark ages. The whole company then march up to the back entrance of the house, singing a verse which ends with the line—

'So open the door and let us all in.'

Upon which knocking is heard, the door is opened, and the men come in. More cider is supplied, and dancing is indulged in, usually to the accompaniment of a somewhat asthmatic accordion; if the maid-servants of the establishment are many and comely, the visit is often prolonged. Cheers

for the family bring the visit to a close, and the men troop off
to go through the business again at the next orchard   It is
astonishing that many of the older men really believe that if
this custom were omitted, a poor crop of apples would
assuredly follow; and, if a man is unpopular, his orchard is
purposely avoided."

As all who have had experience of such matters are
aware, nothing is more difficult than to secure a connected version of a rustic song.   Almost invariably
one's interlocutor can remember snatches, like the lines
already quoted, which serve to convey an idea of the
composition, but even when pieced together, do not
represent the whole.   So far as our knowledge extends,
the only extant copy of the wassail song that can be
deemed authentic and trustworthy, is that furnished by
Dr. Prior, of Halse, to the Rev. Wadham P. Williams,
of Bishop's Hull, who, in turn, communicated it to
the *Somerset County Gazette.*   It is worth quoting, as
the Exmoor version, which may yet be recovered, must
have closely resembled it.

> " Wassail, wassail, all around the town ;
> The zidur cup is white, and the zidur is brown.
> Our zidur is made from good apple trees,
> And now, my fine fellows, we'll drink, if you please ;
> We'll drink your health with all our heart,
> We'll drink to ee all before we part.

>> " Here's one, and here's two,
>> And here's three before we go ;
>> We're three jolly boys all in a row,
>> And we're three jolly boys, all in a row.

> "This is our wassail, our jolly wassail,
> And joy go with our jolly wassail.
> Hatfuls, cupfuls, dree basket, basketfuls
> And a little heap in under the stairs.

> " Down in a green copse there sits an old fox,
> And there he sits a-mopping his chops.
> Shall we go catch him, boys—say, shall we go?
> A thousand to one whor we catch him or no.

" There was an old man, and he had an old cow,
  And for to keep her he couldn't tell how ;
  So he bild up his barn to kip his cow warm,
  And a liddle more liquor'll do us no harm.

" And now we'll go whooam, and tell our wife Joan
  To put in the pot the girt marrow-bone,
  That we may have porridge when we do cum whooam.

" There was an old man, and he lived in the West,
  The price of a barrel wur what he loved best,
  He loved his old wife so dear as his life,
  But when they got drunk, why, they soon cum to strife."

CHAPTER IV.

PIXIES, BARROWS, AND THE DEVIL

IN Brittany, a little to the south of Brest, and near
the coast, are certain ruins reputed to be those
of a palace belonging to the "courils," a race of pigmies
dealing in sorceries, very malicious, and great dancers.
Often seen by moonlight skipping about consecrated
stones or any Druidical monument, they seize people
by the hand, and compel them to follow them in all
their movements. At length, after the spirits have
made them dance to the top of their bent, the mischievous elves trip up their heel, leave them sprawling
on the ground, and go laughing away. These "courils"
are evidently first cousins of the West Country "pixies,"
whose peculiarities they share.

Owing to the alarming spread of enlightenment, it is
excessively hard nowadays to get definite information
about pixies, though every now and again one meets
with a grey-beard who has heard any number of stories
of them. Not believing them, however, he has, with
mistaken superiority, refused to find house-room for
them in the chambers of his memory. So vague, in fact,
has the tradition become in districts where it was once
vivid and strong, that very soon the school-children
will stand in need of a definition. Instead of furnishing
a formal statement, it may be well to cite what is, or
ought to be, the *locus classicus* on the subject.—at all
events, portions of the charming account given by

Mrs. Bray in her *Traditions of Devonshire*, and written at a time when a vast deal more was known about pixies and their ways than is the case now. Afterwards we shall have no difficulty in showing that essentially the same ideas obtain about the little people on Exmoor as in the country around Tavistock.

"The pixies are certainly a distinct race from the fairies, since, to this hour, the elders amongst the more knowing peasantry of Devon will invariably tell you (if you ask them what pixies really may be) that those native spirits are the souls of infants, who were so unhappy as to die before receiving the Christian rite of baptism.

"These tiny elves are said to delight in solitary places, to love pleasant hills and pathless woods; or to disport themselves on the margins of rivers and mountain streams. Of all their amusements dancing forms their chief delight; and this exercise they are said to follow, like the Druids of old, in a circle or ring. Browne, our Tavistock poet, alludes to this custom when he writes—

> 'A pleasant mead
> Where fairies often did their measures tread,
> Which in the meadows make such circles green.'

"These dainty beings, though represented as of exceeding beauty in their higher or aristocratic order, are nevertheless, in some instances, of strange, uncouth, and fantastic figure and visage; though such natural deformity need give them very little uneasiness, since they are traditionally averred to possess the power of assuming various shapes at will. . . . But, whatever changes the outward figure of fairies may undergo, they are amongst themselves as constant in their fashions as a Turk. Their dress never varies; it is always green.

"Their love of dancing is not unaccompanied with that of music, though it is often of a nature somewhat different to those sounds which human ears are apt to consider harmonious. In Devonshire that unlucky omen, the cricket's cry, is to them as animating and as well timed as the piercing notes of the fife, or the dulcet melody of rebec or flute, to mortals. The frogs sing their double bass, and the screech owl is to them like an aged and favoured minstrel piping in hall. The grasshopper, too, chirps with his merry note in the concert, and the humming bee plays his hautboy to their tripping on the green; as the small stream, on whose banks they hold their sports, seems to share their hilarity, and talks and dances as well as they in emulation of their revelry, whilst it shows through its crystal waters a gravelly bed as bright as burnished gold—the jewel-house of fairyland; or else the pretty stream lies sparkling in the moonbeam, for no hour is so dear to pixy revels as that in which man sleeps and the Queen of Night, who loves not his mortal gaze, becomes a watcher. . . .

"Many a pixy is sent out on works of mischief to deceive old nurses and steal away young children, or to do them harm. This is noticed by Ben Jonson in his *Masque of Queens*—

> 'Under a candle I did creep
> By day; and when the childe was a-sleepe
> At night, I suck'd the breath; and rose
> And pluck'd the nodding nurse by the nose.'

"Many, also, bent solely on mischief, are sent forth to lead poor travellers astray, to deceive them with those false lights called Will-o'-the-wisp, or to guide them a fine dance in trudging home through woods and waters, through bogs and quagmires, and every peril; or, as Robin Goodfellow says, to—

> 'Mislead night wanderers, laughing at their harm.'

"Others, who may be said to content themselves with a practical joke, and who love frolic more than mischief, will merely make sport by blowing out the candles on a sudden, or kissing the maids 'with a smack' as they 'shriek out, Who's this?' as the old poet writes, till their grandams come in and lecture them for allowing unseemly freedoms with their bachelors. Some are despatched to frolic or make noises in wells, and the more gentle and kindly of the race will spin flax and help their favourite damsels to do their work. I have heard a story about an old woman in this town, who suspected she received assistance of the above nature, and one evening coming suddenly into the room, she spied a ragged little creature, who jumped out at the door. She thought she would try still further to win the services of her elfin friend, and so brought some smart new clothes, as big as those made for a doll. These pretty things she placed by the side of her wheel; the pixy returned and put them on, when, clapping

her tiny hands in joy, she was heard to exclaim these lines
(for pixies are so poetical they always talk in rhyme)—

> 'Pixy fine, pixy gay,
> Pixy now will run away.'

And off she went; but the ungrateful little creature never spun
for the poor old woman after. . . .

"The pixies, however much they may have been deified by
the Druids or northern nations, were never, I believe, considered as saints in any Catholic calendar, though it is affirmed
that they have so great a respect for a church that they never
come near one. Some very good people, calling themselves
Christians, do the same in these days, but whether it is from
so respectful a motive is, perhaps, somewhat questionable.
Pixies, then, are said to congregate together, even by thousands,
in some of those wild and desolate places where there is no
church. Various are the stories told about these noted personages; amongst others that in a field near Down House
there is a pit which the pixies, not very long ago, appropriated
for their ball-room. There, in the depth of night, the owl,
who probably stood as watchman to the company, would hoot
between whiles; and sounds, such as never came from mortal
voice or touch, would float in the air, making 'marvellous
sweet music'; whilst the 'elves of hills, brooks, standing lakes,
and groves' would whirl in giddy round, making those 'rings
whereof the ewe not bites,' that have for ages puzzled the conjectures of the wisest and most grave philosophers to account
for them according to the natural order of things.

"Whitchurch Down is said to be very famous for the peril
there incurred of being *pixy-led*, for there many an honest
yeoman and stout farmer, especially if he should happen to
take a cup too much, is very apt to lose his way; and whenever he does so, he will declare, and offer to take his Bible
oath on it, 'that as sure as ever he's alive to tell it, whilst his
head was running round like a mill-wheel, he heard with his
own ears they bits of pisgies a-laughing and *a-tacking* their
hands, all to see he led astray, and never able to find the right
road, though he had travelled it scores o' times long agone
by night and by day, as a body might tell.' And many good
folks relate the same thing, and how pisgies delight to lead the
aged a-wandering about after dark.

"But as most evils set men's wits to work to find out a

remedy for them, even so have we found out ours in this part of the world against such provoking injuries. For whosoever finds himself or herself pixy-led, has nothing more to do than to turn jacket, petticoat, pocket, or apron inside out, and a pixy, who hates the sight of any impropriety in dress, cannot stand this, and off the imp goes, as if, according to the vulgar saying, he had been 'sent packing with a flea in his ear.' Now this turning of jackets, petticoats, etc., being found so good as a remedy, was like a quack doctor's potion, held to be excellent as a preventive; and as some good mother may now and then be prevailed with to give her darling Dr. Such-a-one's panacea to keep off a disease before it makes its appearance, even so do our good townsfolk practise this turning inside out, ere they venture on a walk after sundown near any suspected place, as a certain preventive against being led astray by a pixy."

Here we must reluctantly cry " Halt ! " Whether it would ever have been possible, even for Miss Alice King, to piece together so delectable an image out of the scattered fragments of Exmoor myth and marvel, must be a matter of conjecture. So far as West Somerset is concerned, belief in pixies is no doubt dying out, and it may have been dying this many a day. Such traditions, however, as survive render it quite evident that the information possessed by Exmoor folk harmonises with that of their Dartmoor brethren. Not far from Dulverton Station, between the Minehead main road and Bury village, is a wood known as " Pixy Copse," curiously enough in proximity to an old British camp. Pixies, too, are said to sit on Comer's Gate, a favourite hunting fixture at the northern extremity of Winsford Hill, and within easy hail of Withypool. Some of the country people, 'tis said, fear to pass this spot after dark, having no desire to make the acquaintance of a race noted for its caprice, and wielding, as they suppose, supernatural power. It has been suggested to the writer that in the days when "fair trade" was carried on over Exmoor, smugglers, for their own ends, deliberately fostered, if they did not originate, such stories. According to Mrs. Bray, Dartmoor was infested by similar characters.

"It is nothing wonderful," she says, "that such an extensive waste as the moor, so full of rocks, caverns, tors, and intricate recesses, should have been in all ages the chosen haunt of banditti; and in former days they did not fail to avail themselves of its facilities for conveying away plunder, or personal security against detection; whilst the gentry of those times, unless in a numerous and well-armed company, feared to cross the moor, so dangerous as it was known to be from lawless men, and so reputed to be haunted by the spirits and pixies of credulity and superstition."

Nothing seems more likely than that robbers and smugglers should have exploited these fancies, or that peasants, in their ignorance, should have confused the machinations of adventurers with the whims and wiles of aerial beings. At the same time it is well to remember that pixies are usually associated in the popular imagination with mists and fogs, and it is probable that some tales, at any rate, if not most, drew their origin from mistaken impressions of objects seen through this distorting medium. In one of the early chapters of *Lorna Doone* we meet with a case in point. A heavy fog encompassed the wild hills, as John Fry and his young charge were riding Oarewards, when, by the fierce light of Dunkery Beacon, they descried the cavalcade of the Doones in the hollow below. Fry's philosophy was to let their horses go, while they themselves lay flat on the ground. John Ridd, however, on perceiving a young maiden slung across a miscreant's saddle-bow, cast prudence to the winds.

"It touched me so to see that child a prey among those vultures that in my foolish rage and burning I stood up and shouted to them, leaping on a rock and raving out of all possession. Two of them turned round, and one set his carbine at me, but the other said it was but a pixie, and bade him keep his powder. Little they knew, and less thought I, that the pixie then before them would dance their castle down one day."

Regarding the imagined dislike of pixies for consecrated places, we are able to confirm the assertion by a story told us not long ago by an erstwhile inhabitant of Exford. At Knighton, in the parish of Withypool, whilst the church bells were ringing, the King of the Pixies went into the farmhouse and requested the farmer to lend him his "plough and tackle" —*i.e.* his team of pack-horses and their crooks. "I want," said he, "to take my wife and family out of the noise of the ding-dongs." From the same informant we learnt that farmers were accustomed to lay in a floorful of corn overnight, and the pixies would come and thrash it. The Knighton family were inquisitive, and one night, on peeping through the key-hole, found that the pixies had no clothes on. Out of gratitude for their services, they left a suit of clothes in the barn, whereupon the pixies, insulted, went away and never came again. This, it will be observed, is a fair parallel to Mrs. Bray's anecdote of the foolish old lady.

In Prebendary Hancock's *History of Selworthy*, on which we have already drawn for sundry valuable particulars, we have come across some odds and ends about pixies, which prove, among other things, that the Exmoor tribe did not always go naked. Probably their nakedness at Knighton is accounted for by the arduous nature of their occupation.

"At D—combe, 'there in the meadow,' the pixies light fires and dress their children, and in the same meadow there is a post which none can pass at night, because a shapeless thing with rattling chains springs out against the passer-by. [Probably a malefactor had been hung in chains there—a human pixie.] The pixies were active in our district in days gone by. If some favoured houses were left ever so dirty, they were found cleaned up in the morning. Even the unfinished operations of brewing have been found completed. The little people came through the key-hole, and expected to be paid by a basin of bread and milk being set for them in a corner. In some houses it was the custom to put a pail of clean water, towels and soap ready, for the use of the pixies. A woman of Minehead who had a relation that had dealings with the pixies, saw this relation one day in Minehead market filching pieces of meat from the stalls. She went up to him, and spoke to him. 'Which eye,' he asked, 'did you see me with?' She told him. Straightway he blew upon it, and she became blind in that eye. A luckless person saw twenty-four pixies 'down to Great Gate.' They discovered her watching them, and in revenge they led her about all night over the moor, and about the woods, till with the break of day they left her. This was the fate also of Farmer B., returning from Minehead market. He was led about the fields and moor until morning. But another man, thus mischievously troubled, bethought him of a sure remedy in such cases; he took off his coat, and turned it, and got home at once without difficulty."

Another story in the same work apparently relates to pixies. Much pleasanter than the foregoing, it tells how a lady living in those parts was driving home from dinner in an old-fashioned gig that was fashionable then.

"A bright moon made the bright, clear summer night still clearer; and as the carriage approached an open part of the road, proceeding at a rapid pace, the lady saw a group of little children, prettily dressed, dancing across the road. 'Take care,' she said to the driver; and he, fearing he would drive into them, at once slackened his speed, saying, 'All right, I see them.' But the figures became indistinct and disappeared as the gig drew near."

As has been said, it is extremely difficult to learn anything definite about pixies nowadays. If you ask an oldster for information, his answer will be something like this: "Pixies used to carry little lanterns, that's what I used to yur um zay yeers ago." On one occasion, however. the writer was more fortunate, and he learnt something about pixies which may almost be termed sensational. In the " Ring of Bells," at Challacombe, he met with a Northmolton man, who had spent several years of his life as a shepherd on Exmoor. This man deposed that in his parish there were such beings as *pixy-men*. It was a common saying amongst the farmers that if you wanted a field of corn reaped properly, it was best to get it done by the pixies. Accordingly, a bounteous supper both of meat and drink was taken out to the field, and left there. The next morning it would be found, sure enough, that the work had been done, and done thoroughly. A day or so later, however, a deputation would call at the farmhouse, and a local labourer, touching his cap, would explain that he was the chief of the pixy-men who had partaken of the supper and reaped the field of corn. The farmer thereupon bestowed a gratuity on the party, who were, generally speaking, well rewarded for their pains. If such organised hypocrisy was at all common, one can understand why faith in the pixies has fallen into disrepute.

Exmoor and Brendon, with their borderlands, are remarkable for the vast number of cairns to be found on them. These objects serve as landmarks, and figure conspicuously in the geography of the district. Chain Barrow, Chapman Barrows, Black Barrow Down, Alderman's Barrow, One Barrow, on Exmoor, and the Wambarrows on Winsford Hill, are instances proving to what an extent these memorials of the past, these "graves of the giants," have affected the nomenclature of the country. But, besides these which have and give names, there are many nameless barrows, most, if not all, of which have at some time or other been opened. Such at least is the opinion of an antiquarian friend of ours, who has passed all his life in the neighbourhood of Exmoor. The son of the late owner of Exmoor, Sir

Frederick Winn Knight, expressed, it is said, an intention of examining the barrows on succeeding to the estates, but, owing to his untimely death, the design was never carried out. That some of the cairns have been rifled is an historical certainty, but it is probable that the predatory instinct has been checked in many cases by the superstitious feeling with which these places of sepulture are regarded by the peasantry. A few years ago it was whispered at Dulverton that a local gentleman—none other than Mr. Arthur Locke, the then secretary of the Devon and Somerset Staghounds—had "seed something" near the Wambarrows. We have never inquired of the genial squire whether there was any truth in the story, having, perhaps hastily, assumed that it was apocryphal, but it is a fact that the spot is supposed to be haunted by a black dog—first cousin of the Irish manthè dog. Not far from the Wambarrows are the ramparts of an old British fort, Mouncey Castle, which has also its legend—namely, that on a certain night of the year a chariot passes round the hill, and disappears into the cairn in the field below.

"On the distant hills," says Richard Jefferies, "the only break to the slow curve of their outline is caused by an occasional tumulus. There are no copses on the summits of the ranges, only tumuli here and there, singly or in groups. The contents are not so well known as elsewhere, for there is a prevalent dislike to opening a barrow. The feeling is very strong, and those who own property do not care to go against it. It is believed that certain misfortune will fall on the household of anyone digging into a tumulus, and that generally a death follows the intrusion upon an ancient tomb. Possibly this idea may be an unconscious memory of prehistoric times, when sacrifices to ancestors and heroes were made in the precincts of tumuli. They were considered sacred then, and the feeling seems to have lingered on down to the present day. Places where battles have occurred, and where human bones are known to lie, must not be disturbed for the same reason.

S

"It happened that some misfortune fell upon a household without any apparent cause; but one day there was found in the house an ancient sword with a gold hilt. A younger member of the family, free from the superstitions of the elders, then confessed that he had been digging over and exploring a battle-site, or ancient burial-place, in the district, and had discovered the sword, and hidden it in the house for fear of displeasure. Here at once was the cause of the trouble that had visited them."

In his seventeenth-century *View of Devonshire* old Westcote records the following incident, which, according to tradition, took place in the parish of Challacombe, and which might well have deterred farm-hands and others from deeds of sacrilege:—

"A daily labouring man, by the work of his hand and the sweat of his brow, having gotten a little money, was desirous to have a place to rest himself in old age, and therefore bestowed it on some acres of waste land and began to build a house thereon, near, or not far from, one of these barrows named Broken Barrow, whence he fetched stones and earth to further his work. And, having pierced into the bowels of the hillock, he found therein a little place, as it had been a large oven, fairly, strongly, and closely walled up, which comforted him much, hoping that some good would befall him, that there might be some treasure there hidden, to maintain him more liberally and with less labour in his old years. Wherewith encouraged, he plies his work earnestly until he has broken a hole through this wall, in the cavity whereof he espied an earthen pot, which caused him to multiply his strokes until he might make the orifice thereof large enough to take out the pot, which his earnest desire made him not long a-doing.

"But as he thrust in his arm, and fastened his hand thereon, suddenly he heard, or seemed to hear, the noise of the treading or trampling of horses coming, as he thought, towards him, which caused him to forbear and arise from the place, fearing the comers would take his purchase from him (for he assured himself it was treasure). But, looking about every way to see what company this was, he saw neither horse nor man in view. To the pot again he goes, and had the like success a second time; and yet, looking all about, could ken nothing. At the third time he brings it away, and finds therein only a few ashes and bones, as if they had been of children or the like. But the man, whether by the fear, which yet he denied, or other causes, which I cannot comprehend, in a very short time after lost senses both of sight and hearing, and in less than three months consuming, died. He was in all his lifetime accounted an honest man, and he constantly reported this, divers times, to men of good quality, with protestations to the truth thereof, even to his death."

"It is at your choice," Westcote adds pleasantly, "to believe these stories or no. What truth soever there is in them, they are not unfit tales for winter nights when you roast crabs by the fire."

The theory that treasure lies hidden beneath the ruins of ancient buildings is, of course, far from uncommon in country districts, and for the sake of those who may wish to try their luck in excavation, we will be obliging enough to indicate a spot on the borders of Exmoor, where peradventure gold may be found. In the Holnicote Valley are certain ancient chapels, one of which is in a worse state of dilapidation than was Withypool tower, and that is saying a good deal. At a point where an old trackway, traditionally known as the "Priest's Path," branches off from the road to West Luccombe are to be found the vestiges of a tiny sanctuary, the origin and history of which are profoundly obscure. It seems evident that four or five centuries ago there existed somewhere in the parish of Luccombe a chapel dedicated to St. Saviour; "somewhere" apparently means in the court or manor-house of Geoffrey of that ilk. In 1548 no chantry is returned as existing in the parish of Luccombe, and Prebendary Hancock is of opinion that the churchwardens or others foreseeing the coming storm, sold the sacred vessels and furniture, perhaps even the material of the chapel itself in order that the property might not pass into the hands of strangers.

"It is difficult," he observes, "to see why the site of this chapel was chosen. There is no evidence of there ever having been any population in its immediate neighbourhood, and the lie of the ground forbids the supposition. The chapel, however, commands the first view, coming from Luccombe, of the sea, and lies at the foot of the moor. In the early Middle Ages our forefathers considered that wild tracts of moorland, like the hills above our valley, were the haunts of demons and dragons, and wayside chapels were sometimes built on the edge of the moor to keep these enemies of mankind at bay. When the writer was excavating the site, a very ancient person, who happened to pass, assured him that her forbears had always known that a chest of gold lay buried beneath the building. He was not fortunate enough, however, to secure this interesting treasure."

Mr. Hancock's most valuable finds were some old knives and a silver instrument, the use of which was uncertain.

The suggestion that this chapel may have been, in some sort, a citadel or outpost of Christianity on the confines of heathenesse is certainly striking, though a trifle, perhaps, far-fetched. It was once a favourite belief that demons were the gods of the pagans, who, at the Nativity, fled from their customary haunts to the fastnesses of moor and fen. Our Lord, it will be recollected, was tempted *in the desert*. In Chaucer's time the perambulations of limitours, or mendicant friars, were—or so the poet pretends—the efficient cause of the disappearance of kindly and useful elves, while the poet-prelate Dr. Corbett, writing early in the seventeenth century, would persuade us that the fairies were Roman Catholics!

> " Farewell, rewards and fairies,
>   Good housewives now may say,
> For now foul sluts in dairies
>   Do fare as well as they ;

And though they sweep their hearths no less
   Than maids were wont to do,
Yet who of late for cleanliness
   Finds sixpence in her shoe?

" Lament, lament, old abbies,
   The fairies' lost command;
They did but change priests' babies,
   But some have changed your land;
And all your children sprung from hence
   Are now grown Puritans,
Who live as changelings ever since
   For love of your domains.

" At morning and at evening both,
   You merry were and glad;
So little care of sleep and sloth
   Those pretty ladies had.
When Tom came home from labour,
   Or Cis to milking rose,
Then merrily, merrily went their tabor,
   And merrily went their toes.

" Witness those rings and roundelays
   Of theirs, which yet remain,
Were footed in Queen Mary's days
   On many a grassy plain;
But since of late Elisabeth,
   And later James came in,
They never danced on any heath
   As when the time hath bin.

" By which we note, the fairies
   Were of the old profession,
Their songs were Ave Maries,
   Their dances were procession.
But now, alas! they all are dead,
   Or gone beyond the seas;
Or farther for religion fled,
   Or else they take their ease."

The dislike of the pixies (who cannot, we think, be
differentiated from the fairies as a race) for consecrated
places, at all events under the present régime, has been
already pointed out; neither have we failed to observe
in the eccentric little beings an element of caprice, and
even malice. Still we were loath to call them devils.
Demons, perhaps; but not devils. But the Devil him-

self has been abroad on Exmoor and around ; the very names of certain places tell you that. Thus we have the Devil's Bridge, the Devil's Punch-bowl, the Devil's Cheese-ring, etc. ; nor does the evidence of his going to and fro end here, for, over and above the names, there are legends.

One of the most interesting objects in the Exmoor country is a structure probably coeval with the castles and barrows, and, according to the usual terminology, Belgic-British. This structure, known as Torr, or Tarr, Steps, is a primitive kind of bridge which spans the Barle six miles above Dulverton, and it may be doubted whether in the British Isles there is anything of the same character so perfect and delightful. Post Bridge on Dartmoor resembles it, and a friend of ours informs us that in Brittany, near Carhaix, he came across a replica of Torr Steps in a little river, the Lochriste, singularly enough in close proximity to a genuine Roman bridge. The length of the Exmoor bridge, including the paved approaches, is a hundred and eighty feet. It is five feet wide, and piers extend beyond the pathway five feet on either side. Of the seventeen openings through which the water flows, the widest is in the middle. The covering-stones are both longer and wider in the middle than at the ends, where, instead of being laid singly, they are placed side by side. The longest is eight feet six inches, the average length being seven feet, and they are about six inches thick. When the stream is at its ordinary level, the height of the bridge above the water is about three feet, but in flood-time it is submerged. The average depth of the stream is two feet two inches.

There is a curious legend concerning Torr Steps, another name for which is the "Devil's Bridge." The Devil, it is said, built the bridge for his own delight, and being, of course, spiteful, resolved that it should not be used by mortals. He raised it in a single night, but towards morning, as he arrived with a finishing load of stones, his apron broke and the stones fell to the ground. One of them is to be seen at Mouncey Castle, another in the wood hard by. Taking his seat at a picturesque spot near the bridge, the Devil denounced destruction on the first creature that should venture across. A cat was cunningly sent over, and as soon as she touched the other side was unmercifully torn to pieces. The spell being thus broken, the parson was the next to cross, when some uncomplimentary expressions of the pot and kettle order passed between the two. The Devil called the parson a black crow, to which the parson replied that he was no blacker than the Devil. The latter seems to have retired from the contest, leaving the bridge open ; and here it is still. As it is believed to be not quite finished—there are signs that it was intended to go further—perhaps this may be accounted for by the accident to the apron-strings. According to another version, one of the Samson masons of old, engaged in building Hawkridge Church, was carrying across the ford a load of stones, when the Devil maliciously cut his apron-strings, so that his burden dropped into the stream.

Within easy distance of Torr Steps, is an enormous hollow in the side of a hill. This hollow is called the Devil's Punch-bowl. The size and configuration of the place are enough to account for the name, which does not appear to have suggested, or to have been suggested by, any really ancient tradition. Indeed, the only explanation that has come to our ears is quite modern. It is as follows: In the "teens" of the last century Colonel Thornton, who lived at The Green in Dulverton and kept harriers, ran a hare across Bradley bog into the huge dip. He was accompanied on the occasion by his friend and guest, Admiral Moresby, and as the veterans, seated on the brink, watched the hounds running their hare below, the colonel exclaimed—

" I say, Moresby, supposing that the hollow under us were balked up at the other end like this, and filled with water, how many men-of-war could ride comfortably there ? "

" I should think," answered the admiral, " three first-class ships of war might manœuvre."

" Then," rejoined the colonel, " then, egad ! Colonel Thornton has drunk as much port as could float three of His Majesty's seventy-fours."

This incident is claimed as having given rise to the name of the cavity, which is usually referred to as " the Punch-bowl" simply. It is worthy of mention that near Aberystwith there is a Devil's Punch-bowl, as well as a Devil's Bridge ; but each is of a totally different character from its West Somerset namesake.

In the neighbourhood of Porlock, on the heath adjoining the Exford road before it ascends Lucott Hill, are two huge stones about four feet in height. Although dark of hue, these are called the Whitestones, and the legend is that they were thrown from Hurlstone Point, four miles away, by the Devil. According to one account, they were used in a match between the Devil and a giant.

At Lynton, again, we have the pile at the entrance to the Valley of Rocks known as Ragged Dick, who, it is said, was seized with his companions by the Evil One and converted into slate for merry-making on the Sabbath. Hard by is the Devil's Cheese-ring, which in days of yore was the abode of Mabel Durham, the Mother Melldrum of *Lorna Doone.*

" Facing this from the inland side and the elbow of the valley, a queer old pile of rock arises, bold behind one another, and quite enough to affright a man, if it only were ten times larger. This is called the 'Devil's Cheese-ring,' or the 'Devil's Cheese-Knife,' which means the same thing, as our fathers were used to eat their cheese from a scoop; and perhaps in old times the upmost rock (which has fallen away since I knew it) was like to such an implement, if Satan eat cheese untoasted."

From the instances adduced it will be seen that the term "Devil's" is often used in a sense nearly approaching Cyclopean, but it has occurred to us that in some cases the habits and appearance of the stag might lead to his being confounded with Auld Hornie. Not long ago the Rev. Donald M. Owen told us of an incident which occurred when he was a young man, and which might well have been magnified into a supernatural visitation. His brother George and himself had gone on a hunting expedition to Dulverton, leaving directions to their groom to bring up their horses from Tiverton in time for the meet. Two miles below Bampton, just under Cove Cliff, there is a turn of the road sometimes called the Devil's Corner. The light was still dim when, on reaching this spot, the man was startled by a sudden apparition. Out of the river Exe, which here runs close beside the road at a regular fording-place, emerged a fine specimen of a stag, who planted himself full in the path. At every attempt to pass him, he "made meanings with his horns," and it was only after a considerable delay that he saw fit to retire. When he reached Dulverton, the man was asked the reason of his being late, and this was his story, which his masters, both sportsmen, were quite disposed to accept. Under similar circumstances it is certain that some people would have reported that they had seen the Devil.

Dr. Collyns supplies yet more convincing evidence. A fat old stag, found in 1839, after baffling his pursuers all day, ran down to water at Perry Farm, above Exebridge.

"Here in a deep hole, under cover of the roots of an overhanging elder tree, he sank himself in the river, leaving only his nose above water. His place of concealment was artfully chosen. The pack must have been frequently round and close to him, but he held on, and night coming on, the chase was abandoned. Very shortly after the hounds had left, a labouring man went down with a net to fish the river, and at his first catch poked the stag from his hiding-place. The man was dragged across the river, the deer having no doubt entangled one of his hind legs in the net. The poor fisher-man was so frightened that he forthwith started for his cottage and arrived there, as his wife said, 'quite wisht.' My pro-fessional services were called in aid, and I elicited from him that his state was caused by fright. He stated to me how he had been dragged across the river, and then, with a fearful sigh, said, 'It was the Devil, zur, I do know it; I seed his *cloven foot.*' I tried to persuade him that he was in error, but in vain, and it was not until the next morning, when I went to the spot with my patient, and showed him the tracks of the deer at the place where he had left the river, that I convinced him that it was not the original 'Old Hornie' who had served him the scurvy trick which had so completely unmanned him."

PART V

WORTHIES

CHAPTER I

SIR THOMAS ACLAND

A FRIEND of ours, chatting with a moorman, remarked that in winter Exmoor was no place for delicate people, and inquired what became of the weakly children that must from time to time be born there.

"Well, zur," replied the rustic, scratching his head, "them as can't live, dies."

A region like this, where the cold is intense and rain and fog are constantly experienced, is just the country for strong characters, for only persons that are remarkably tough and hardy would endure, or could enjoy, its rigours. In the present chapter it is proposed to sketch some typical careers in more or less detail, and thus complete our account of this most interesting district. If it be objected that our heroes are, with one exception, sportsmen—Nimrods, if you like the term— we answer that the staghunter is *par excellence* the denizen of Exmoor, more particularly of modern Exmoor which sees far more of him than formerly.

Our first hero shall be Sir Thomas Dyke Acland [b. 1752, d. 1794], eighth baronet, and Ranger of Exmoor. His love of staghunting was hereditary, since it is recorded of his father that down to the year 1770 he kept hounds and hunted the country in princely fashion. The first account of a run over Exmoor dates from the year 1759; and the circumstances of its preservation are sufficiently curious. The writer was a park-keeper, and the person to whom it was sent a barber, of whom it is averred that "he was as well known for his skill in the field as in the shop." The letter was found at the bottom of a box of wigs by an Exeter lawyer, and consigned to his common-place book, where, not many years ago, it was discovered. It reads as follows:—

"DULVERTON, SOMERSET,

"*Sept.* 4, 1759.

"SIR,—I am ordered by my master, Courtenay Walrond, Esq., to trouble you with this letter, that you may have the pleasure of hearing of one of the finest staghunts that ever happened in this country. About one o'clock Monday morning, my master with his brother and his steward, Mr. Brutton, set out from Bradfield, bravely mounted, attended by several servants, which had horses. About ten o'clock they got to the woods, and soon after roused a stag at the head of Ironmill Water (in the parish of Oakford), where he took to Stuckeridge Wood, and crossed the River Exe, from thence to Exe Cleeve, and after running over Exmoor Forest, on the whole more than seventy miles, he was killed near Lowry Gate [Lousy, *i.e.* Louisa Gate, Baron's Down?], when he appeared to be about ten years old, his brow, bay, and tree angles [antlers?] having all his rights, and seven on one top and five on the other, and was to one inch fourteen hands high. This noble chase being ended, my master, his brother, and Mr. Brutton, with about twenty gentlemen more, waited on Sir Thomas Acland at Pixton, where each of them drank the health of the stag in a full quart glass of claret placed in the stag's mouth, and after drinking several proper healths, they went in good order to their beds at two o'clock, and dined with Sir Thomas next day on a haunch of this noble creature and about fifty dishes of the greatest rarities, among which were, with several others, black grouse. Master, his brother, and Mr. Brutton rode extremely bold, and were in at the death of the stag. They set out for Bradfield to-morrow evening, and as Sir Thomas has given master one haunch, which weighs thirty-six pounds and a quarter, he desires you will dine with him on Thursday at Bradfield. I must now conclude, Sir Thomas having given notice of another stag, equally good as this I have described, in Brockeridge Wood, for which place the gentlemen are now setting out, and

"I am, Sir, your most obedient, humble servant,

"J. RICH,

"Park-keeper to Courtenay Walrond, Esquire.

"P.S.—You are desired to bring with you Mr. Brutton, the hatter, and Mr. Drake, a doctor of Exeter. You may invite likewise, if you please, any other friend of yours.

"There were at the chase more than five hundred horse and one thousand foot."

The period during which these excellent baronets kept the hounds may be fitly described as the golden age of Exmoor sport. Their hospitality was boundless, and extended to all comers, rich and poor, peer and peasant. Besides their seat at Holnicote in the beautiful Porlock Valley, they had inherited from the Dykes Pixton Park, between the Exe and the Barle, near Dulverton; and Highercombe, a hunting and shooting box in the same parish, was also theirs. At all these places the Aclands literally kept open house, and guests repaired to them unbidden, and assured of a kindly welcome from the genial and, of course, enormously wealthy owner, who could, it is said, ride from Holnicote to Killerton, a distance of more than thirty miles, on his own land.

The profuse liberality which distinguished the father descended in even greater abundance to the son, and won for him the name of Prince of the West, where, it is safe to affirm, has never been seen such a *grand seigneur*. When a run had ended in the death of a stag, he waited till the straggling field, always exceeding a hundred, had assembled, and then courteously raised his hunting-cap. The meaning of this action was well understood: it was a signal to all the gentlemen present,

friends or not, inviting them to dinner.   The polite hint
having been acknowledged, Sir Thomas replaced his
hunting-cap, and, in military fashion, touched the peak
with the back of his hand.   This gesture was an intima-
tion to the yeomen—which class was more numerous
then than now—his own tenants, and others of the same
rank that, should they wish to partake of refreshment,
they were heartily welcome.

The hunting community testified their appreciation of
the baronet's good fellowship by presenting him with a
great punch-bowl and twelve glasses.   On the bowl was
represented a hunting-scene, while each glass bore the
figure of a stag, with the inscription, " Prosperity to Staghunting."   The bowl was brought from China by Mr.
Acland, of Little Bray, who, according to tradition, had
taken out the clay of which it was to be fashioned,
together with a rough draft of the subject, in order that
the bowl might be wrought by the deft craftsmen of the
Flowery Land.   For a long while it was kept at slate-
faced Highercombe, where the hounds used to be kennelled.   It is now, we believe, at Killerton, the family
seat in Devonshire.

Sir Thomas' style of hunting had something in
common with the methods that obtained at the time of
the perambulations (see p. 31), and Mr. Hancock well
observes that " the stories that have come down of his
hunting parties sound more like extracts from the pages
of a mediæval chronicler than records of ordinary West
Country expeditions."   When, on hunting bent, " his
Honour " started for Highercombe, he was regularly
attended by a cavalcade of his Holnicote tenants, who,
on the morning following, escorted him with due
solemnity to the wood where a deer had been harboured.   Some members of the party, it is averred, were
provided with French horns, and when a warrantable
stag had been viewed away, gave notice of the fact by

HOLNICOTE

T

playing a particular tune. The length of this hunting-piece determined the extent of the "law" granted to the deer.

In the stables at Holnicote are preserved thirty stags' heads obtained between the years 1785 and 1793. This number, it would seem, does not represent the full tale as it existed before the disastrous fire which, in 1794, destroyed the old manor-house. It is stated that on this occasion forty thousand ounces of magnificent family plate were melted by the flames, and when an intimate friend condoled with Sir Thomas on the loss of so much valuable property, referring especially to the silver, the baronet replied, " I care little for the house or the plate; the one can be rebuilt, the other repurchased. But I am indeed grieved at the loss of my splendid collection of antlers, which I have preserved from stags killed by my own hounds, and which I shall never live to form again."

It is recorded that Sir Thomas sometimes, when staying at an inn, would share his bed with one of his friends, the person usually preferred being a Mr. Henry Karslake, who much appreciated the compliment. The merit which led to his selection—his qualification, as it were—was his immunity from the unpleasant, though very common, habit of snoring.

This grand sportsman did not hold office uninterruptedly as master of the hounds. From 1775 to 1784 the pack was kept by Major (afterwards Colonel) Bassett, of Watermouth, who seems to have been the first person, not being a grantee of Exmoor or Ranger of the Forest, to occupy that position. In 1784 Sir Thomas again took the reins, which he retained to the time of his death. His record for the nine seasons was one hundred and fifty deer, of which seventy-three were stags and seventy-seven hinds. This appears small compared with the totals attained in these days, but greatly exceeds the poor results achieved in the middle of the last century, when staghunting sank to its nadir.

At the end of the Selworthy parish register may be found this curious entry: "Sir Thomas Dyke Acland went to London the 4th of May, 1794; was taken ill in the way thither; and on the 17th day of the same month, ab^t 6 o'clock in the evening, died; he was brought down to Broadclist to be buried in the vault of his family.

" Hic finis fatorum Priami, hic exitus illum
    Sorte tulit!—Vale.   Vale.   Vale.
  Nec meridies nec Aurora unquam vident ejus ora
  Reliquit nobis cornu, canes; tandem quiescant ejus manes."

The last two lines, it will be noticed, make no attempt at scansion, in which the first is by no means brilliantly successful. As some sort of compensation, however, they are garnished with rhymes—" Aurora," " ora "; " canes," " manes "—which Milton describes as " the invention of a barbarous age, to set off wretched matter and lame metre." Concerning the matter, inasmuch as the poor baronet had left them his horn and his hounds, the poet probably thought it of no use to wish him good luck in happy hunting-grounds, and therefore expresses the hope that his spirit may " at last " rest in peace.

HIGHERCOMBE

CHAPTER II

THE REV. JOHN FROUDE

FROM baronets to clergymen.—It is quite certain that no parson on the borders of Exmoor ever gave occasion to so many good stories as Froude of Knowstone, who kept a pack of hounds there at the time "Jack" Russell, his younger and more respectable contemporary, obtained his first curacy, at George Nympton. Alluding to that period, 1819 and onwards, Russell says :—

"My headquarters at that time were at South Molton; and I hunted as many days in every week as my duties would permit with John Froude, the well-known vicar of Knowstone, with whom I was then on very intimate terms.

"His hounds were something out of the common; bred from the old staghounds—light in their colour and sharp as needles—plenty of tongue, but would drive like furies. I have never seen a better or more killing pack in all my long life. He couldn't bear to see a hound put his nose on the ground and 'twiddle his tail.' 'Hang the brute,' he would say to the owner of the hounds, 'and get those that can wind their game when they are thrown off.'

"Froude was himself a first-rate sportsman, but always acted on the principle, 'Kill un if you can; you'll never see un again.'

"I saw him once shoot a hare sitting near a farm-house, where his hounds met on the following day, and where, of course, they did not find. He hunted three days of the week, and shot on the others, when he would walk most men off their legs. I never saw him with a rod and line in his hand, but he was very expert with nets on land or in water. He was the most original man I ever met with. He had an old liver-coloured spaniel called Crack, a wide ranger, but under perfect command. He used to say he could hunt the parish with that dog from the top of the church tower. You could hear his view-halloo for miles; and his hounds absolutely flew to him when they heard it. Let me add that his hospitality knew no bounds."

Anecdotes of Froude are legion, and many have found their way into print. Some stories however remain, so far as we know, unrecorded, and, as they are eminently characteristic of the man, may well be told here.

An old labourer now living in Dulverton — Dick Gathercole—was the hero of the following adventure. As master of an establishment, Froude was bound to keep maidservants, and the good-looking girls naturally attracted "followers." Being very human himself, Froude did not object to "followers" as such; he only stipulated that they should go about the business in a straightforward manner, and not sneak into the house at uncanonical hours, and without his knowledge and consent. It appears, however, that certain swains, probably from shamefacedness and dread of Froude's banter, did their courting surreptitiously, and slipped into the kitchen by the back door, when, as advised by the young women, the master was not likely to get wind of the occurrence. By some means Froude came to know what was going on, and resolved to put a stop to the game.

One evening the said Gatherccle was basking in the smiles of his inamorata when suddenly Froude's footsteps were heard approaching. A hasty consultation between the alarmed females, and the intruder was quickly stowed away in the large furnace in which, as was customary in those days, the family brewed their own beer.

Froude now strode into the room, and turning to one of the girls, observed—

"I say, Mary, look sharp and light the fire in the furnace, or the puppies'll die. It's bitter cold."

"All right, sir," answered Mary, in a fright. "I'll do it directly."

"No, do it at once," and as she still hesitated, he repeated, "at once."

The maid dared not disobey, and fetching some faggots, soon made a roaring fire. Meanwhile, Froude stood with his hands in his pockets, watching the proceedings and unconcernedly humming an air. Inwardly, he was much diverted at the girl's perturbation and blushes, but gave not the slightest sign that he knew of any occasion for them. The poor suitor stayed in his lurking-place as long as flesh and blood could endure the ordeal, but at length the heat became overpowering, and out he plumped.

"Ah!" said Froude, chuckling, "I thought you were there."

According to Gathercole, however, he did the plucky thing and knocked the parson down.

As may be inferred from this instance, Froude was uncommonly fond of a practical joke,* and occasionally he tried to victimise his huntsman, Jack Babbage. Babbage afterwards acted in a similar capacity to the Devon and Somerset Staghounds, and was rated a great success. It may perhaps be observed that the well-known engraving in which he appears riding behind the master, Mr. M. Fenwick Bisset, does anything but justice to Babbage, who, though a little man, was not

---

* As Froude has not left behind a particularly fragrant memory in the West Country, the following remarks of Macaulay will be appreciated :— "He [Frederick the Great] had one taste which may be pardoned in a boy, but which, when habitually and immediately indulged by a man of mature age and strong understanding, is almost invariably the sign of a bad heart, a taste for severe practical jokes."

quite a man-monkey. Very popular with all classes, he was the subject of a rattling hunting-song, which began—

"The honourable Jack laid on the pack."

To return to those early days, the relations between Froude and his huntsman were most comical. When the man had the misfortune to offend the master, he was always addressed as "Mr. Babbage," and if he waited on Froude for instructions with regard to meets, would be answered shortly—

"Go where you please, Mr. Babbage."

The huntsman accordingly would arrange the fixtures, send round the notices, and at the proper time take the pack to the trysting-place. In these circumstances it was not often that Froude could resist the temptation of turning out, but he would ride at a great distance behind, or follow the sport from the opposite ridge. All this that Babbage might be impressed with the enormity of his offence and his master's deep displeasure.

One day Froude conceived the idea of punishing his dependant still further. Babbage had returned home after a day's hunting, and, putting the little mare in the stable, went indoors to change his clothes. Froude, seizing the opportunity, stole out and locked the stable door, after which, taking the key, he sauntered down to the village and regaled himself with Messrs. Fisher and Folland, farmers of the neighbourhood, at the "Froude Arms." By-and-by he suggested to his companions that they should stroll up to his house, as he thought he could show them something worth seeing. Suspecting some jest, they laughingly consented, and the party adjourned to the Vicarage.

Meanwhile Babbage, having changed his clothes, had betaken himself to the stables, intending to make the mare comfortable, but found to his dismay the door locked. This he at once perceived to be a trick ; his master was

up to some game with him. However, not to be outdone, he planted a ladder, mounted to the stable tallet,
and, removing two planks from the floor, let himself
down into the stable, where he rubbed down the mare,
fed her, and bedded her. Having finished his task, he
climbed up again into the tallet, replaced the planks,
descended the ladder, and returning to his cottage, sat
down to tea with his wife Jane. It was not long before
he heard a stentorian voice calling to him, "Mr. Babbage!
Mr. Babbage!"

HIND LEGS

Jack put on his hat and went out.
"I have summoned you, Mr. Babbage," said Froude
in his severest tone, "in order that you may show these
gentlemen what excellent care you take of your mare
after riding her all day. Open the stable door."
Jack advanced to do so, but, having shammed an
attempt, turned back with the report—
"If you please, sir, the door's locked."
"Oh, here's the key," replied the parson, producing it.
"Do as I say, and open the door." At the near prospect
of Babbage's humiliation, Froude began to exchange

nods and winks with his associates ; but the tables were turned when, a moment later, the three entered the stable and found everything in order.

"Sold, by G——!" exclaimed Froude, quite staggered and crestfallen. He soon recovered, however, and respectfully addressing the man whom he had thought to outwit, but who, instead, had outwitted him, invited him to partake of his hospitality.

"Come in, Jack, and have a glass of grog."

Another story is to the effect that Froude invited a brother sportsman, generally known as "little Roach," to dine with him one Saturday, made him drunk, and, having put him to bed, "mopped up" the curtains so as to exclude every ray of light. Roach woke up at intervals, thought the night long, but, seeing that it was still dark, turned over and went to sleep again. After his protracted slumbers "little Roach" was called and presented himself at the breakfast-table. No remark was passed until, breakfast over, he announced his intention of preparing for church, when he was politely informed that he had slept all through Sunday, and that it was now Monday morning.

As anecdote, however, nothing can beat Russell's story of plot and counterplot between Jack Froude and the redoubtable "Henry of Exeter" (Bishop Phillpotts). In the *Memoir of the Rev. John Russell* the narrative is thus given :—

"The bishop at length was determined to have an interview with Froude, and as his lordship was staying at the time with, I believe, that pattern of a country gentleman, Tom Carew, of Collipriest, he ordered a pair of horses from Cannon, and started for Knowstone with that object in view.

"By some intuition, however, peculiar to himself, Froude suspected that such an event might occur, and at once set to work to frustrate his lordship's design. He stationed a signalman within hail of his house, on the only road leading to it from Tiverton, giving him orders if he saw a chaise and pair travelling towards the vicarage, to hasten thither and sound the alarm.

"Accordingly, when the bishop did appear, Froude and his household were not only apprised of his approach, but duly prepared for his reception.

"'Can I see Mr. Froude?' inquired his lordship in that mild, measured tone which he habitually adopted when he meant to carry his point. 'Be good enough to say the Bishop of Exeter wishes to have a few words with him.'

"'Please walk in, my lord,' replied the old housekeeper Jane, who had gone to the door, and would have gone to the stake to serve her master. 'Mr. Froude is at home, but is up abed wi' some ailment or other.'

"'Nothing serious, I hope?' said his lordship, taking a seat in the state apartment; 'and, if so, I dare say he would not object to see *me* at his bedside.'

"Jane paused for a moment, and then, with some hesitation, replied, 'Perhaps not, my lord: leastwise, if you bean't afeered o' going there. 'Tis a faver o' some soart, but I can't mind what the doctor call'th it.'

"The bishop cocked his ear, and looked uneasy. 'A fever, did you say? Rheumatic, perhaps, from exposure to wet?'

"'No, no; I've got that myself, bad enough. 'Tis something a deal worse, I reckon.'

"'Not scarlet fever, I hope?'

"The housekeeper shook her head despondingly. 'Worse than that, my lord.'

"'Typhus?' inquired his lordship, no longer able to hide his look of alarm.

"'Iss, that's it; seem'th to me that's what the doctor ca'd it. 'Tis a whisht job, fai!'

"The bishop clutched his hat, and with little ceremony took his departure; and, although he announced his intention of repeating his visit at a more convenient season, he never again set foot in the parish of Knowstone. When, adds Russell, the bishop had fairly disappeared, Froude put on his long gaiters and went out hunting for the rest of the day."

On one occasion his lordship met Froude when the latter was accompanied by a greyhound, which in Devonshire is commonly styled a "long dog."

" And pray, Mr. Froude," inquired the bishop, " what sort of dog may you call that ? "

" That ?   Oh, a lang dog, my lord ; and if you was to shak yeur appern to un, he'd go like a dart."

The bishop's reply is not recorded, but it is safe to conjecture that, being sensible of his position and all that went with it, he did not take the hint.

CHAPTER III

THE REV. JOHN RUSSELL

AND now for Russell himself. John, better known as "Jack," Russell was born in 1795, and was the son of the Rector of Iddesleigh, in North Devon, who, however, resided at Dartmouth. Russell's father kept hounds, and the son followed in his footsteps. He began early, keeping hounds at Tiverton School, where he was being educated, and by reason of his untimely indulgence narrowly escaping expulsion. But whatever his master might think, his father was not sorry to observe the budding instinct, which, on proper occasions, he was quite disposed to encourage. It was on the thirtieth of September, 1814, that Russell first made the acquaintance of the staghounds. The meet was at Baron's Down, near Dulverton, the seat of Mr. Stucley Lucas, who afterwards became master of the pack; and to that gentleman Russell attached himself, assured that he would thus see the cream of the sport. It so happened that Mr. Lucas was riding a racehorse called "Erebus," apparently a vicious animal, for, on Russell coming within range, he let out with his heels, kicked him under the stirrup-iron, and landed him on the heather. After that Jack deserted Erebus, and steered his nag to the high ground at Hawkridge, whence the hounds could be viewed in close pursuit of their quarry, and the field following. Russell was meditating a move in the same direction, when he was joined by a young gentleman, who advised him to remain.

"They'll be sure to come this way," he said, "and you can see the sport from this point better than if you were with them."

This sage counsel proceeded from one who, though only two years Russell's senior, was already a skilful staghunter—none other, in fact, than Mr. Charles Palk Collyns, of whom more will be said presently. The result was that Russell kept his post, and he had his reward. In a few moments the hounds were seen heading towards Torr Steps, where they crossed the Barle, and pointed directly for Hawkridge. Jack was soon speeding along with them, and for three hours there was never a check until the deer soiled under Slade Bridge, with hardly his nose visible above the deep pool in which he fondly hoped to evade his pursuers. Woodcraft, however, was equal to the occasion, and though five or six couples overshot the mark, John Tout, the huntsman, turned them back, and the stag was winded in his last refuge. Russell, it is said, was so carried away with excitement at this his first taste of stag-hunting, that he plunged waist-deep into the water, in order to hearten the hounds ; and, later, he was subjected to the rite to which all young hunters must submit at the death of their first stag, being duly "blooded."

On leaving Oxford Russell was admitted to Holy Orders, and became curate of George Nympton, whence he afterwards migrated to his father's old living at Iddesleigh, and thence to Swymbridge, both North Devon parishes. Meanwhile he had married Miss Penelope Bury, a lady who rode to hounds almost as gamely as her husband. Notwithstanding his devotion to sport, it was never brought home to Russell that he ever neglected his duties as a clergyman, and though stories are circulated to the effect that he sometimes confounded the parts of parson and hunting-man, it is extremely doubtful whether all or any of them were founded on fact. One thing is quite certain, that tales have been told of Russell which properly relate to men of an older generation—Froude, for instance, and Radford; whilst in other cases imagination has gone a long way.

On this point his biographer observes :—

"Much has been said of the active service which Russell expected from his curates in the hunting-field, when parochial duties did not absolutely require their attendance at home; but, of course, some of the stories told in that respect were utterly untrue. One, for instance, describes him as testing the voices of rival applicants aspiring to become his curate, by making them give 'view-holloas,' and then accepting the one whose voice sounded the most penetrating and most sonorous —a capital story, no doubt, for those who cultivate charity by believing and circulating such tales, but, as a matter of fact, it is one which rests on as baseless a fabric as the fleecy clouds that float through the sky."

It would appear, however, that, if a clergyman undertook to be his curate in the hunting-field *as well as* in the parish, Russell exacted a high standard of duty. The memoir, from which so much has been taken, is understood to have been written by a gentleman known to his friends as " Otter " Davies. Seemingly, therefore, the following anecdote, though inserted as a contribution, refers to the author himself :—

"Once and once only did a slight skirmish take place between us, and that was on the wild open moor near Lanacre Bridge. It was a cold, biting day in February. We had found in Twitchen Town Wood, and the hounds with a grand scent having brought their fox up to the bridge, had there come to a check. A hound called Castor, however, hitting the fox under the archway of the bridge, through which the flood had carried him, dashed into the angry river, and by some means became unable either to pass under the arch or land on the opposite bank.

U

"'The hound will be drowned! Jump in and save him!' shouted Russell to me, in a state of the wildest panic. 'Jump in, I say!'

"But, in truth, I saw no danger for the hound, whereas a plunge into the roaring Barle, forbiddingly keen as the wind blew, was likely to be one for me. I hesitated for an instant, and, as I did so, Castor struggled out, and, like a brave dog, threw his tongue manfully on the opposite side of the river. Directly afterwards, on my rating a hound for some fault he had committed, Russell turned sharply round and said, 'That's a puppy; let him alone; don't rate him, or you'll ruin him.'

"'Don't speak to me in that way,' I said, fairly roused this time by his peremptory manner, 'or I'll never turn a hound for you again.'

"It remains to be added that we killed our fox soon afterwards; and no two men could have jogged home together on better terms than Russell and I after that event. My act of rebellion, however, was not forgotten; for to this day, when the hounds pass Lanacre Bridge, he is wont to tell the tale with infinite zest and humour, pointing out to those around him 'where Davies mutinied—threatening, if I dared to rate him, that he'd never turn a hound for me again.'"

The foregoing recital may be safely received as gospel; the following will probably be classed as apocryphal, though, we are bound to confess, our authority is distinctly good. Russell, then, it is said, was preaching in the parish church of Dulverton, when a thunderstorm came on and so darkened the stained-glass window that the preacher had no longer light enough to read his manuscript. He made a vain attempt to preach the rest of the sermon extempore, and then, addressing the clerk, desired him to fetch candles. The clerk could not find any in the vestry, so he had to repair to his cottage, and it was some time before he returned with them. How did Russell employ the rather embarrassing interval? Well, the story goes, by a disquisition on staghunting. And our informant avers that he was there and heard him.

In a few pages—all that we can give—it is impossible
to do justice to Russell's marvellous aptitudes as a
follower of hounds, and the many amusing experiences
that came to him by way of sport. Space, however,
must be found for a remarkable story—almost unex-
ampled, one would think, in the annals of the chase. In
November, 1845, a club was formed at Southmolton
for the promotion of foxhunting, the three leading spirits
being Russell, Sir Walter Carew, of Haccombe, and
Mr. Trelawny, of Coldrenick. A month before the first
meeting of the club, Russell is said to have received
the following missive from a farmer near Exford :—

"HONOR'D SIR,
        "Do ee plaise bring up the dogs first chance; us
a got a fine litter, sure enough, up to Hollacombe brake.
They'm up full-growed a month agone; and last night was a
week, what must em do but kill Mistiss' old gander and seven
more wi' un—her's most gone mazed owing to't; so do ee
plaise come up, Sir, and gi' 'em a rattle. They'm rale beauties,
they be, as ever you clapped your eyes upon."

This is an excellent specimen of the way they talked
at Exford, where, as Savage observes, the dialect is very
broad ; but somehow we cannot bring ourselves to fancy
that a farmer would ever write in that style, unless he
were a wag, and did it on purpose. Be that as it may,
Russell was not slow in complying with the request.
Setting off alone, he slept and kennelled his hounds for
the night at Hawkridge Rectory, then the home of a
great friend of his, the Rev. Joseph Jekyll, whom he
pronounced "one of the finest and hardest riders in that
or any other country."

The next morning Russell crossed the Barle at Torr
Steps, and traversing the moorland roads over Winsford
Hill, arrived at Exford, where he threw his hounds into
the covert pointed out by his correspondent. The
brushes of two of the litter were soon handed to the

farmer, who carried them home, with vast delight, to his wife. Russell now cast his hounds round the outside of the covert, and forth came the old dog, who led them a merry chase twelve straight miles across the wildest tracts of Exmoor. At Bray coverts they were close upon him, but here Russell, fearing a change, stopped the pack, and Reynard was respited. But not for long. At the first meet of the new club, in November, Mr. Trelawny's hounds drew Sherracombe Brake, close by Yard Down, whilst Russell studied the proceedings from the opposite side of the combe. The gorse, which grew thick and strong, presented an almost impenetrable obstacle, and Limpetty, the huntsman, after doing his best to encourage the hounds, passed on to another covert.

Seeing this, Russell shouted—

"You've left that fox behind you, Limpetty!"

The huntsman doggedly denied the impeachment, but a moment later a hound spoke, and away flew a fox over the moor and the dogs after him. Russell at once recognised him as the same grey fox he had brought away from Exford, twelve miles off, a month earlier, and communicated the fact to Mr. Houlditch, who, however, was decidedly sceptical. There was no time to argue, and the " field," which included Mrs. Russell, raced at a tremendous pace over the hill to Sittaborough, and from there, guided by Reynard, to Simonsbath, the Warren, Badgeworthy, and up to Gallon House, where he managed—Heaven knows how—to scale the boundary fence, high enough to stop a forest deer! Mrs. Russell followed, and for some distance was the only member of the " field" with the leading hounds. They were now less than half a mile from the very covert which Russell had drawn on the previous occasion, and for which the fox was evidently heading. At this juncture a heavy downpour of hail and rain intervened

TWO "PASSUNS"

to spoil the sport. The scent disappeared, and for the second time the fortunate animal escaped the fate prepared for him. The identity of the fox was no longer questioned, even Houlditch admitting that Russell was right ; and, after two such gallant fights, no wonder that Reynard was honoured that evening at the " George."

Such was the fame of the Southmolton Club that it drew sportsmen from all parts of the West Country, with the result that a great deal of partisanship was displayed by people attached to different Hunts. One of Russell's followers was so infatuated that he would charge impossible fences with the cry, "*L'un ou l'autre !*" meaning, apparently, that he and his horse would get over or perish in the attempt. The worst sinner, perhaps, was the before-mentioned Limpetty. Once upon a time Trelawny's hounds met at Cuzzicombe Post, and, drawing an acre of gorse close by, found, as Russell had predicted, a flyer.

"The fox was in view, the hounds running into him, and Limpetty 'home to their sterns,' when a barrier interposed, which no man with a heart less intrepid than his own would have cared to encounter. It was a flood hatch—broad, deep, and dangerous ; and a thrilling sight it was to see him on Jack Sheppard flying over it, like a dragon on wings, looking back as he did so, and singing out to Jack Cumming, 'Where be they Knights to now, I should like to knaw?' alluding to Messrs. Frederick and Lewis Knight, of Simonsbath, two well-known, brilliant performers over any country, but especially hard to catch over Exmoor."

Russell kept up his foxhunting and staghunting to a period far beyond that at which most men, whether they will or no, are forced to consider themselves on the retired list. In 1877 he received a visit from Frank Goodall, the Queen's huntsman, who came to see what sport on Exmoor was like and was accompanied by Mrs. Goodall. On this occasion Russell found it convenient to drive to the opening meet at

Cloutsham in a gig, and, although he was then in his eighty-second year, the sight of the fine old man out of the saddle struck all beholders, and gave rise to many speculations and prophecies. One old staghunting farmer remarked : " Zee, there he go'th ; Passen Russell in a chaise ; never zeed un avore off a horse's back, never. But there, us must all come to't ; you can't have ten forenoons to one day." Russell, however, was able to demonstrate then, as well as on the following Friday, that he was almost as good as ever, and could still ride to hounds with the best.

Towards the end of his life Russell appears to have seen a good deal of the Prince of Wales (the present King Edward), at any rate far more than would be thought likely from his position as parson of a small parish in a remote part of the country. Their first interview took place in 1865, at Plymouth, on the occasion of the visit of the Royal Agricultural Society. By command of the Prince, Russell was invited by Admiral Sir Henry Keppel to dinner, and among the guests was Lord Charles Beresford, Sir Henry's flag-lieutenant. In the autumn of 1873, Russell was asked by his friend, Mr. Harry Villebois, to spend a week at Marham Hall, to meet the Prince and a party of friends ; and during his visit attended a ball at Sandringham. Shortly before his departure, Colonel Ellis appeared with a message from the Prince, inviting him to Sandringham for the approaching Christmas week. " And as we hope to hear him preach, tell him to put a sermon in his pocket before he leaves home," the Prince had added. This command was obeyed. At Sandringham Church on the Sunday Russell preached before their Royal Highnesses, and was afterwards thanked for his discourse by the Rev. W. Lake Onslow, the rector.

At a tenants' ball, held during his stay, the venerable

clergyman danced the old year (1873) out and the
new year (1874) in with the Princess of Wales—a fact
of which he was very proud. "Now," he remarked,
"I can say what no man else can ever say again." In
1876 he paid another visit to Sandringham, which, however, appears to have been less enjoyable. "The Prince's
time is so occupied," he wrote, "by a houseful of foreign
grandees and magnates that I wonder he can find time
to pay, as he does, the most minute attention to all."
Nevertheless, the old man came away highly delighted,
for he bore with him the Prince's promise to go down
for a day's hunting with the Devon and Somerset Staghounds. The illness of one of his sons delayed the
fulfilment of the promise, but it was redeemed, much
to Russell's satisfaction, in 1879 (see p. 87). In his last
and fatal sickness the doyen of the Hunt was consoled
by a kind message from the Prince. Russell died on
the 28th of April, 1883, aged 87, and was buried a few
days later, amidst a large concourse of sorrowful friends,
in his old parish of Swymbridge.

CHAPTER IV

THE REV. JOSEPH JEKYLL

ALLUSION has been made to the Rev. Joseph Jekyll, in his time one of the best all-round sportsmen on Exmoor. He was at Blundell's School, Tiverton, not long after his old and life-long friend Russell, *i.e.* about 1816 ; and in 1833 he came to Hawkridge, which in those days was indeed a wild spot. Knowstone and Hawkridge are not many miles apart; and, as was inevitable, Jekyll knew Froude very well and could tell many stories about him. However, that particular worthy has received, perhaps, his due meed of attention, so that we had better select other anecdotes from Jekyll's ample répertoire.

About forty-five years ago the game of "Aunt Sally" was the rage, and the late Duke of Beaufort, then a young man, got into some scrape—at Brighton, we believe—in connection with the pastime. The papers were full of the story. Soon after this little affair the Duke, by invitation, brought down his hounds for a fortnight or so to try conclusions with the Exmoor foxes. One day the hounds were running a fox in the parish of Hawkridge, and the Duke, a rather bumptious young fellow, shouted in an offensive manner to Jekyll, who was riding well with the hounds—

" You black-coated parson, why don't you go home to your parish ? "

Whereunto Jekyll replied, "I am in my parish, and I suggest that you should go and play with your 'Aunt Sally.'"

The Duke said no more.

On one occasion a Hawkridge farmer came to see the rector about some business in which he had to employ his pen. He did his best, and Jekyll jokingly remarked—

"I am afraid I can't compliment you on your scholarship, James."

"Lor', sir," the farmer replied, "I know I bain't much of a scholar. I only went to school four days a week. The fifth day father wanted me home to dig tatties" (potatoes).

Once, in the depth of winter, he invited the Rev. John Carwithen, of Challacombe, to dine and stay the night with him at Hawkridge. The day came, but there was no sign of Mr. Carwithen, and at eleven o'clock some of the guests departed, whilst others retired to rest. At seven the next morning his little rough servant-maid knocked at Jekyll's door, announcing—

"Please, maister, the gentleman's a-come to dinner."

"Tell him," was the reply, "we shall breakfast at nine, and light the dining-room fire at once."

The girl, however, dissatisfied with these instructions, persisted, "Oh, sir, do 'ee please come down. The gentleman has gone a masquet; his beard and his hair be full of conkerbells and he's most ago." She meant that he had lost his way, was covered with icicles, and nearly dead. Mr. Carwithen had not only lost his way, but, in trying to lead him over a fence, had lost his horse. When he recovered the animal—which was after a lapse of several days—bridle and saddle had vanished, and a circlet round the ears was the only thing left to testify that they had ever existed.

Mr. Thornton, from whom by the way we stole the

foregoing story, has another equally good about Jekyll.
It is as follows :—

"One day in the spring of 1848, mounted on the long-
suffering Polly, I was at the meet of Mr. Stoate's hounds
at Luccombe.   A young farmer also was there, who said there
was queer goings-on at Hawkridge.   Parson Jekyll was writing
his sermon, and he heard hounds a giving of it down in his
wood; then they stopped, and he, mistrusting something,
took his hat, and went out, and sure enough there was old
Mr. Chowne a digging out of a fox.   They two had not been
chummy like for some time, and so Jekyll he goes up to
the other, and says he, 'Mr. Chowne, I should have thought
you knew better than to dig out a breeding earth in another
man's country in the month of March.   Now you call your
man away, or I will prosecute you for breaking bounds.'

"'I have brought my fox from Anstey,' said the other; 'and
I mean to have him out; and as for you —— !'

"'You dare quarrel with me, do you?   Don't you know
that I have only to say "Bones, bones!" at Hawkridge, and
name no names, and there are those about me as will take
good care that your carcass is lying under a hedgerow before
the week is out?'

"'And with that,' said the farmer, 'he (Chowne) got on his
horse and rode down to Dr. Mitchell, at Winsford, and swore
information against Jekyll for stealing his dog.   So Mitchell
gave him a warrant and sent the constable to search the
rectory, and then was not Parson Jekyll in a rage?   Besides,'
added the farmer, 'there was no terrier, after all.'"

Jekyll, who died in 1881, was descended from a celebrated anti-Jacobite judge, and, as a near neighbour,
was probably one of those to whom Collyns refers in
saying—

"For myself I will say that, without wishing to see the
dignitaries of the Church again maintaining their kennels
of hounds, I should feel regret if I were to miss from the field
the familiar faces of some of the members of the clergy who
now join in the sport of the country, and whose presence is
always welcomed at the covert side."

CHAPTER V

MR. CHARLES PALK COLLYNS

OF Charles Palk Collyns the Hon. John Fortescue, in his *Records of Staghunting*, speaks as follows:—

"Dr. Collyns had been a keen staghunter for more than forty-seven years. A friend to all sport, he had ever since his migration to Dulverton at the beginning of the century made the chase of the deer and the habits of the animal his favourite study outside his profession. He had seen the sport in its palmiest and in its most desperate days, had cherished it (to quote Mr. Bisset) in prosperity and shielded it in adversity. In the course of his long experience he had gathered an immense mass of materials on his favourite subject, which, after long delay, were worked up into his book on *The Chase of the Wild Red Deer*. His last public work was to attend a meeting of the Devon and Somerset Hunt Committee on the 1st of April, 1864; and less than a fortnight later he was carried to his grave, followed by a great concourse of people from every rank of life, who knew him, not only as a good sportsman, but as a kind, genial, and generous friend."

Kingsley also, in his *Water Babies*, makes a happy allusion to Dr. Collyns, whose professional services were generally available in case of mishaps. When the present work was first contemplated, the writer made up his mind that, whatever else might be omitted, it should at least include some account of this remarkable man, of whom no biography has yet appeared. He communicated his idea to Mr. John Barrett Collyns, who, in consequence, pencilled the following sketch of his father's life. The public will doubtless be interested to know that most of it was written by Mr. Collyns in his eightieth year, during a month's confinement to bed caused by a little accident on Whit Sunday, 1901. *The Chase of the Wild Red Deer*, which was long out of print, has been lately republished by Messrs. Lawrence and Bullen.

Against the eastern wall of Dulverton Church, over the family vault, stands a simple tombstone of granite, bearing the following inscription :—

" Here rest
The Mortal Remains of
Charles Palk Collyns,
Surgeon,
Born at Kenton, in September, 1793 :
Died at Dulverton 7 April, 1864.
He resided for fifty years
in this parish,
Relieving pain,
Succouring the poor,
Promoting local improvements ;
Upholding manly pursuits,
And actively performing
The duties of a loyal Englishman.
While we have time,
Let us do good unto all men,
Gal. vi. 10."

This memorial of a notable man was drafted by a notable friend, Mr. John Kent, whose birth dates in the first decade of the last century, between those of two other notable men, the late Right Honourable Sir T. D. Acland, Baronet, and W. E. Gladstone. Mr. Kent practised as a lawyer at Dulverton in the early thirties, and became, on the recommendation of Mr. Collyns, the first tutor of the late Earl of Carnarvon, the statesman, who held consecutively the seals of the Colonial Office and the Vice-royalty of Ireland. He still survives at the age of ninety-one, spending a few months in summer at Wellington College, Ottery St. Mary, and retiring for the winter months to sunny Madeira, intolerant of the leaden English skies.

Mr. Collyns came to Dulverton in the year 1814, the winter of the deep snow, and by his indomitable energy managed to bring up a large family on (almost exclusively) his professional income, carrying on his large country practice on horseback, ignoring wheels, which indeed were uncommon in his day. He married on the 31st October, 1816 (her birthday), Anne, the eldest daughter of Aaron Moore, Esq., of Spreydon House, Broadclyst, now the property of Sir T. D. Acland, and renamed Sprydoncote.

The younger son of a medical man at Kenton, who attended the family at Powderham Castle, Mr. Collyns brought with him an introduction from Lord Devon to Lord Carnarvon at Pixton. Not long after Lady Emily Pusey was taken in labour at Pixton, and Mr. Collyns was sent for as a sort of stop-gap pending the arrival of Dr. Sully, of Wiveliscombe, some fourteen miles distant, who had been retained to attend the case. After a while, recognising his responsibility, he sought an interview with Lady Carnarvon, and requested that he might see the patient. Whereupon the Countess, presenting him with a pair of white kid gloves, preceded him to her daughter's room, where, disdaining artificial skin for his fingers, he pocketed the gloves, and soon had the satisfaction of ascertaining that Lady Emily Pusey was doing well.

What, however, probably brought the young doctor quickly into general practice was the advent of an epidemic of "low fever" (the term "influenza" had not then been coined), when the old doctors bled their patients according to custom, with the usual results, whereas Mr. Collyns, eschewing the lancet, did not lose a single case.

Curiously enough, Mr. Collyns had on his books about the same time the Lord Bishop of Bath and Wells, Lord Auckland, whose carriage, whilst leaving the town after a confirmation, ran over a little girl and broke her thigh; the Lord Chief Justice Cockburn, on a visit in the neighbourhood; Isaac Newton Fellowes (afterwards fifth Earl of Portsmouth), at Churchtower; and the Earl of Carnarvon.

Mr. Collyns was a contemporary of the Rev. John Froude, the notorious Vicar of Knowstone, who, his brother parson Jack Russell averred, had been guilty of every crime under the sun save actual murder! He innocently incurred the vicar's revengeful ire in the following way: As the doctor of Mr. John Hill, of Moortown, one of Mr. Froude's parishioners, whom he had assaulted, Mr. Collyns attended under subpœna the assizes at Exeter, and gave evidence of the injuries inflicted, and the vicar had to pay heavy damages. Not long after the doctor during one of his rounds came across Mr. Froude's harriers, and whilst, seated on his horse, he was watching them over a gate, the master rode up and sneeringly exclaimed—

"Thee'st been feeding lately upon my fat, hasn't?"

"No, it stank so I couldn't abide it," was the caustic reply.

Mr. Collyns took his due share of contract work, and on the formation of the Union was appointed the medical officer of No. 1 District. He was also the first local registrar of births, deaths, and marriages under the Act, and both these appointments he held till his death.

Among his riding feats he delighted to tell of his having been in the saddle on an early day of October, 1816, and done a good day's professional work before breakfast, and then joining the staghounds, which met at ten o'clock in those days, and following them from

Burridge Wood, where they found their stag and ran him across Exmoor to the Bristol Channel above Lynmouth. Hence, after seeing him killed, he returned home, a distance of twenty-six miles, to dinner, after which he started on his third horse for a further twenty-six miles' ride, and was in the Exeter ball-room at ten o'clock, fulfilling an appointment to meet his fiancée there, having carried his pumps and silks in his pocket.

Another memorable ride occurred in the thirties, when Mr. Collyns, who was an ardent politician, rode down to Exeter on a nomination day to support his friend Sir T. D. Acland, tenth baronet, the Conservative candidate, to whom he subsequently dedicated by permission his book on staghunting. The day was a typical wet Friday, for it "rained cats and dogs" the whole time. Whence he started clad in his stag-skin suit.

This dress consisted of a pair of overalls reaching up to the waist, buttoned on the outside, and a large overhanging cape, all of tanned stag-skin, with the hair outstanding. It was improvised before the inauguration of mackintosh, when it gave way to the lighter fabric. A special face protector obtained in a sort of loose cap or short tube of drab cloth held over the head by a cross-bar of narrow ribbon, with eye-holes and a larger orifice for breathing.

On entering the Castle Yard Mr. Collyns was jokingly received with the exclamations, " Robinson Crusoe," " Man of the Woods," etc.; but ere the long-winded speeches were over, the Dulverton doctor laughingly turned the tables upon his drenched friends by assuring them that he was perfectly dry.

A curious and somewhat puzzling incident occurred during the forties, when the Rev. W. Comins was Rector of Rackenford after having held for nearly twenty-five years the curacy of Dulverton. Mr. Comins naturally

x

maintained the intimacy of his old friends, and among other hospitality was wont to entertain his former parishioners at an annual dinner on Trinity Monday, Rackenford Revel, when the old-fashioned wrestling-ring was the chief attraction, which the parson and his guests duly honoured with their presence.

Returning home from one of these carousals, Mr. Collyns on his well-bred galloway spurted off at a canter in the van of his party, and was soon out of sight. Mr. Warren, following, about a mile on the narrow road at the foot of a hill, came upon a saddle, which he picked up and carried on, having been joined in the meantime by the rest of the party. Further up the hill they found the doctor, who had just caught the mare. He told them she had fallen with him coming down the incline, and run off. Mr. Warren placed the saddle on the mare's back, and passing his hand under her belly for the girths, failed to find them. Then he felt under the right flap of the saddle to ascertain if the buckle-straps were right. To these he found the girths attached, and on examining the other side found a similar state of things, the girths extending across the animal's back under the saddle.

In the darkness the girths had not been thought of or looked for till wanted to fix the saddle. How the saddle with girths fully attached could have come off the animal is a puzzle. The general opinion was that she must have shaken or kicked it off, after displacement in the fall, over her hips, which were somewhat narrow.

Mr. Collyns used to parody this story with the following: Mr. Mead was the medical apprentice of Dr. Peppin, one of the old practitioners, and they had accepted an invitation to dine with a patient, Mr. Lyddon, of Withiel, after enjoying some coursing with his greyhounds. They were returning home somewhat late, and going up a steep hill, Mr. Peppin, a heavy-weight, rolled off his horse. Mr. Mead, following, came to his assistance, the horse quietly standing by, and found the near stirrup gone. Looking round he soon discovered it, and was astonished to find the leather unbroken and buckled up. He at once unbuckled it, and passing the end up under the bar, readjusted it to the saddle.

Mr. Peppin, having been helped up, made a fresh start, but repeated the fall ere he quite reached the top of the hill. Mr. Mead found the conditions much as after the first fall, renewed his kindly services, and his chief started off again. Getting safely over the brow, they journeyed a further mile, when breasting the next hill, Mr. Peppin sustained his third fall. This was too much for Mr. Mead, who rushed past him and galloped off home, crying out, " Witch, begad ! Witch, begad ! "

Rationale : Mr. Mead had never seen or heard of the new spring-bar with which Mr. Peppin's new saddle was furnished, and did not notice that the bar was fully *horizontal* when he readjusted the stirrup-leather.

Mr. Pearse, the other old doctor, gave scope for another anecdote. In drawing out one of his bills for a patient, after enumerating and separately charging for sundry journeys, batches of powder, draughts, etc., as was the custom, he concluded with the item : " To the great perturbation and anxiety of mind experienced during your long and painful illness, 10*s.* 6*d.*"

Tradition says that the old doctors, who lived on opposite sides of Fore Street, used to display on Sunday mornings in the running water of the surface gutters before their doors the several basins of blood they had just drawn to cool. They served also to indicate to the people walking up to church the relative practice of the rivals. It was customary then for the labourers and young farmers to come and be bled at springtime for the benefit of their health and complexion, bleeding being considered effectual for the removal of pimples, blotches, etc.   The writer during his apprenticeship has frequently bled three or four men of a morning and drawn as many teeth on the simple mandate, " Please, sir, I want to be blooded " ; or, " I want a tooth tooked out."   The unasked payment for either operation was a shilling, and on these perquisites he made money.

Among the old customs which the advent of the railway and its attendant monthly market annihilated were the Dulverton fairs, held on July 10th and November 5th respectively, when the doctors and better class of tradesmen gave good dinners and re- ceived their payments, the bills having been previously sent round by hand, for at that time there was no country post.

On one of these occasions the following colloquy took place.   Mr. John Collyns, who practised with his father, having given Tom Quick, a fine specimen of an old English labourer, a batch of bills to deliver, told him to go on to the Cuckoo.

" Where's that ? " quoth Tom, who failed for some time to understand his instructions.   At last, after Mr. Collyns had minutely described the road " from Farmer Hodge's of Barton towards Southmolton, down the hill and across the water, and a little way up on your right," Tom scratched his head and exclaimed—

" Why, 'tis the Gewkew you do mean.   Christ a massy, Measter Jan, why ever don't a kall things by their proper names, then vokes 'ud understand 'ee."

Another cuckoo story obtained about the same time. Mr. John Collyns was professionally attending a bed- lying nonagenarian at Cloggs, Hawkridge, and during a visit on a Sunday afternoon in April asked Farmer Bawden if he had heard the cuckoo yet.   He replied, " Noa, but he's come."

" You've seen him then ? " queried the doctor.

" No, I han't. Our vokes coming home from market [Southmolton] yesterday heard en spake!" was the quaint rejoinder.

An older cuckoo story may be told. In the early thirties Mr. Collyns obtained the family's milk from Perry Farm, a mile and a half down the Barle, whence the groom fetched it every morning on horseback. Galloway used to give the boys "in rotation" a treat on fine mornings by taking them up for a ride behind him. Returning one day in April up the ham below New Bridge, he suddenly stuck his heels against the horse, which started off at a gallop, giving Master Willie a flier, and injuring the boy's arm. On his master subsequently scolding him, the groom excused himself by saying—

" We must always bustley, sir, when we first hear the cuckoo."

Mr. Collyns was very fond of whist—what good man isn't?—and used in company with his friend at The Green, Mr. Arthur Bassett, who afterwards lived and died at Watermouth Castle, to champion the Dulvertonians against combined Dunster and Minehead, whence friends occasionally met them at the " Rest and Be Thankful," a convenient half-way hostel at Cutcombe. They always returned by daylight.

For some years Mr. Collyns was the local Conservative agent, and during one of the unsuccessful contests after the 1832 Reform Act, when party spirit ran high, some Radical miscreant discharged a gun one night at his surgery door, the perforated shutter of which is still to be seen. Strange to say, many of the shot, after passing through it and the glass within, became embedded in the edges of the shelves opposite without breaking a single bottle.

Admittedly a many-sided man, Mr. Collyns was a

good all-round sportsman.   In one of the early forties
he shot under Combe a bittern, which was stuffed and
preserved in the old manor-house.   He used to join
the heron-shooting parties, which took place about mid-
June in the heronry in Steart Wood below Pixton Park
(and a feature of which was strawberries and cream),
up to 1831, when the herons shifted their quarters across
the river to the thick firs at the upper-northern end of
Ellers Wood, where they have never been molested.
They have decreased, however.   Query: Is it because
(as they used to say of the rooks) they haven't been
shot?   At the last heron-shooting Mr. Charles Clarke,
who lived in Dulverton and kept harriers, caused a sensa-
tion by shooting perchers with a rifle and ball.   It was the
custom to give a bird to each of the shooters.   Skinned
and roasted, the young heron much resembles the leveret
in flavour, and similarly stuffed is equally good.

Mr. Collyns' chief delight was in staghunting.   He
was mainly instrumental, after the sale of the old
hounds in 1825 by their last master, Mr. Stucley Lucas,
of Baron's Down, in preserving the few remaining deer
from the hand of the poacher, and most active in
inducing neighbouring masters of hounds to hunt them
(at one time he improvised a scratch pack himself) until
1855, when the late Mr. Mordaunt Fenwick (afterwards
Bisset), whilst tenanting Pixton, established the present
Devon and Somerset Hounds.

Mr. Collyns published, after much labour, in 1862,
with the help of Messrs. Longman, his well-known book,
The Chase of the Wild Red Deer.   So long, indeed, was
its publication delayed by pressure of ordinary work,
that his son one day exclaimed, to the great amazement of Mr. Bisset, that he feared it would be a post-
humous work.   It may be worth recording that the
paragraph near the end of the preface—

"I have also to acknowledge gratefully the assistance which

has been rendered to me by a dear lover of the sport, in revising my manuscript and preparing these pages for publication"—

refers to Sir John B. Karslake, who afterwards became Solicitor- and Attorney-General, and whose younger brother, Mr. Preston Karslake, a London solicitor, furnished the spirited illustrations, also appreciatively acknowledged.

An anecdote of the late Attorney-General may be mentioned. Whilst staying in Dulverton, on one of his hunting visits, Mr. J. B. Karslake consulted Mr. John B. Collyns for a little throat ailment, from which he speedily recovered. On leaving, he asked his doctor what he was indebted, and having been told by Mr. Collyns that he made no charge on good staghunters for trivial help, he asked and, after repeated pressure, obtained the date of his birthday, which he noted in his pocket-book. On the doctor's next birthday he received a barrel of native oysters, which was renewed on each successive birthday up to Sir John's death, many years afterwards. Upon one occasion, when his elder brother, Mr. Edward Karslake, was parliamentary candidate for Colchester, Mr. Collyns received a double barrel.

The few remaining copies of his father's book were purchased from the publishers about the year 1870 by Mr. John B. Collyns, and mostly given by him to the landlords of the inns in the staghunting country, for the amusement of their visitors. The last copy, however, awaited a unique and unlooked-for fate. In 1879 it pleased H.R.H. the Prince of Wales to join, on the only fine hunting day in that wettest of seasons, the Devon and Somerset Staghounds. He came from Dunster Castle with his host in Mr. Luttrell's carriage, accompanied by Prince Louis of Battenberg and the Rev. John Russell, to the meet at Hawkcombe Head. After a capital run across Exmoor, ending in a death, Mr.

Collyns was introduced by Lord Fortescue to the Prince, and, thinking that His Royal Highness might like to possess it, offered him the last uncut copy of his father's book, then long out of print, which the Prince graciously accepted.   In due course the volume reached Marlborough House, and was suitably acknowledged.

It may be interesting to chronicle this royal hunt. The covers near the meet proving blank as regards a warrantable stag, a move was made after lunch to Mr. Snow's deer-park, where a young stag was soon found, which, crossing the Badgeworthy Water, gallantly led the chase through the Doone Valley to the head of Longcombe, thence, turning to the right, across the wet North Forest to the Brendon Common fence, up which he turned and kept along it for a while above Two Gates. Breaking under Cheriton ridge, he crossed it to Hoar Oak, and ran down the water to Farleigh.   Then, turning to the right, he came up to Brendon Common, and crossed it to Badgeworthy Wood, where, taking to the water, he beat it up and down for a quarter of an hour before he was taken, giving the large field time to come up and witness a unique finish—unique, for Arthur the huntsman having offered the Prince his knife, His Royal Highness gave the *coup de grâce* by dexterously stabbing the animal to the heart instead of cutting the throat, which mode had, up to that time, obtained, but has since been abandoned in favour of the royal and more excellent way.

The subjoined stanzas introduce some noted characters of Mr. Bisset's Hunt in the closing fifties, among which Mr. Collyns appears, though not at his best.

"AUGUST, 1858.

"Scene : A Cloutsham Fixture, with Mr. Mordaunt
Fenwick Bisset's Staghounds.

I.

"Come, awake from your feathers, jump out of your corner ;
  Kiss your wife, spur your horse, and away to Pyke's Horner,
  For who'd miss the scurry or wish to be late,
  When F. Bisset's crack pack at Cloutsham's green wait?

II.

"There's 'Sportsman' and 'Banker,' oft cheer'd by Jack Bab-
    bage,*
  So fast o'er the moor and of dare-devil courage.
  If with these staghounds you would play a good part,
  Both rider and horse must be quick at a start.

III.

"Hark, hark ! they have found him. Who would not quick rally
  To the hounds-bringing scream of young Bestlers's tally?
  He's away, I can swear ; don't you hear Blackmore's † holloa?
  And now let us see who's the best man to follow.

IV.

"There's scarcely a light-weight and ne'er an old stager
  For the first forty minutes can live with our Master ;‡
  Tho' supposing this run down to Barum should last,
  I hope he'll not find he has started too fast.

V.

"Who's mounted on Wild Buck ? His horse seems to fly,
  'Tis the Rhyll-ruling squire,§ who's worth a Jew's eye.
  In this run, I can wager, he'll keep a front seat,
  For unless his horse stops he will never be beat.

VI.

"With a seat that's so graceful and hand that's so light,
  Now racing beside him comes Worcestershire's Knight,‖
  His heart ever with us. I really don't brag
  When I say no one better can ride a good nag.

VII.

"But who's that in the Black Pits ?—Do tell me, I pray !
  Crying, 'Help a poor fellow !' and cursing his grey,
  Mahommed's own son, whose sides are so flat,
  With the head of a buffalo, tail of a rat.

---

* Jack Babbage, the huntsman.   † Jem Blackmore, the harbourer.
‡ The Master, Mr. Bisset.   § Mr. J. Froude Bellew.
‖ Mr. (afterwards Sir Frederick) Knight, M.P.

VIII.

"'Tis the sporting George Toms, a rum one to follow,
  Who dearly loves lifting the hounds to a holloa ;
A straightforward man, who no misdealing knows,
  And forgets all his pain when a-hunting he goes.

IX.

"And next, snug and quiet, without noise or bother,
  Comes Locke of Northmoor, or, I should say, our brother.
But, mind ! the first flight he will keep in his eye,
  And be thereabout, should the stag mean to die.

X.

"Then there's Baron's Down's Squire, he'll never say no,
  For I've seen him ride well when he chooses to go,
Staunch preserver of red deer, staunch friend to the sport,
  Though he proves no preserver of claret or port.

XI.

"But who's that, may I ask, who in grey hue is clad,
  Riding wide of the pack, and tight holding his prad?
'Tis a rare sort of parson, and if there's a run
  The Rector of Swymbridge *will see all the fun.

XII.

"His phiz I can't see—by his figure I twigs
  It can be no other than Russell on Figs.
If hunting's salvation, he's nothing to fear ;
  His soul has been hunting for many a year.

XIII.

"Now hunting, and hustling, and beating about,
  And pushing his way in the midst of the rout,
Little Gardner comes up ; for a front place he strives,
  Through rough and through smooth he the 'Tom pony' drives.

XIV.

"Now casting a head over Badgery's hill-top,
  Sit Snow† upon ' Nora ' and Palk‡ upon ' Gallipot.'
But, alas ! as no staghunt's without its alloys,
  'Tis decreed he shan't reach there, ye cunning old boys !

XV.

"Going straight to the hounds, never known to cast wider,
  There comes Master Chorley, the chestnut mare's rider,
Whip Heal and Sam Warren§ on Brendon so steady,
  And Tom Roach,‖ who always for ' poor Puss' is ready.

* The Rev. John Russell.   † Mr. Snow, of Oare.
‡ Mr. Collyns.   § " Mr. Sam " Warren, Secretary of the Hunt.
‖ Mr. " Tom " Roach, Master of Harriers.

XVI.

"'He's to water!' cries Tom,* whom I'd almost forgot
To bring into this run, the best 'slot' of the lot,
Who's always in place, and no check ever fears,
He's so clever on pathways, roads, rivers, and weirs.

XVII.

"And now, having sung the most of our field,
All staghunting men, to no others we'll yield.
While the whisky and punch is going its rounds,
Let us drink to F. Bisset, wild deer, and the hounds."

The fourteenth stanza is apparently a plagiarism on the lines :—

"When lo ! far away upon Oare Common top
Sit Snow upon 'Nora' and Palk upon 'Gallipot.'
Now hunting's a pleasure that has its alloys,
For the stag never goes there, you cunning old boys."

These lines appeared about the year 1843, in a somewhat similar record of an opening meet of a former pack at Brendon. Penned by the moor poet, Mr. Parminter, who lived on the southern side, the description took in the three sons of the owner of Exmoor, Messrs. Frederick, Charles, and Lewis Knight, the Hon. Newton Fellowes and his son, heirs of the Earl of Portsmouth, Mr. Willoughby Stawell, a former owner of Rhyll, the Rev. Silas Brown, Rector of Porlock, Tom Snooks, the huntsman, and other well-known characters.

Mr. Collyns was an active manager of the Dulverton School, of which the new buildings were erected in 1861-2, on a site purchased and given by his son, Mr. Bayly Moore Collyns. The following receipted account, which still exists, is interesting from the comparison it affords with the yearly salary of the present school staff—£264 6s. 6d. :—

"The Trustees of Dulverton Free School.
"Dr. to Samuel Palmer.

"To instructing the Charity Children Half a year from Midsummer the 24th June to Christmas the 25th December, 1861, £6 10s. 0d."

* Mr. "Tom" Webber, of King's Brompton.

It is only fair to say that the master received in addition the children's pence—they paid a penny a week—and a third of the Government grant.

For many years Mr. Collyns was first parson's (1839–41) and afterwards parish churchwarden(1847–63). In 1860 his position was challenged by Mr. J. A. Locke, of Northmoor, who was defeated at the poll by eight votes ; and again in 1861 Mr. Collyns was assailed by a farmer nominee, but was re-elected by eighty-three votes against his opponent's thirty-six. His first signature at vestry meeting was affixed on March 25th, 1816, and his last on March 28th, 1864, just ten days before his death. In 1854–5, during his term of office as churchwarden, the church was rebuilt.

Mr. Collyns was instrumental as churchwarden in preserving the old belfry tree, a fine sycamore, which during a hurricane in 1845 was struck by lightning and so mutilated that its preservation was despaired of. The central large limbs were split and decapitated. After consultation Mr. Collyns' conservatism prevailed, and the attempt at restoration was entrusted to Tom Serle, an able local mechanic, who braced up the severed limbs with iron chains and girders so effectually that the stumps soon began to throw out new vertical shoots, which have grown into branches filling up the lost centre and now overtopping the battlemented tower. The iron chains and bars are still visible to the scrutineer, and the new central growth clearly discernible.

Though never an extremist, Mr. Collyns was abstemious, especially in his earlier days. He drank toast and water with his dinner out of a polished buffalo horn, which he was very particular in having daily cleansed. Smoking was prohibited in the house, as the smell of tobacco made his wife faint. In his latest days, however, he enjoyed his pipe, Mrs. Collyns having

learnt to tolerate it. In the spring of 1863 he gave
up his house, which he had rebuilt in the thirties, to
his son on his marriage, and retired to Belmont, a
smaller house at the head of the town. He maintained
his activity to the last. On Easter Day, the 25th March,
1864, he went to church, and partook of Holy Com-
munion ; and the following day, after attending the
vestry meeting, dined with the farmers at the Lamb Inn.
On the 30th he obtained an order at the magistrates'
meeting for the repair of a road on Blagdon Common,
and, on April 1st, attended a committee meeting of
the Staghunt. On Saturday, the 2nd, he rode to call
on Lady Carnarvon at Pixton, and on Mrs. Sydenham,
at Brushford Rectory ; and the Dowager Countess
afterwards spoke of having watched him cantering down
the park. On Low Sunday, April 3, his diary closes
thus : "Prevented by medicine from going to church."
Having taken cold during the cold Easter, he developed
acute pneumonia, and sank after four days' illness.

Few men have been more deservedly mourned. His
daughter-in-law, who was very fond of him, collected
together his prayer-book, his walking-stick, hunting-
horn, drinking-horn, and lantern, and fixed them around
his impromptu full-length portrait (cut out of black
paper by an itinerant artist and stuck on a white ground
—a capital likeness) in her husband's dressing-room,
where they still remain as a loving memorial of both.

CHAPTER VI

MR. MORDAUNT FENWICK BISSET

IF the name of Charles Palk Collyns must be for ever associated with the revival of staghunting after the sale of the grand old pack in 1825, that of Mordaunt Fenwick Bisset will always be linked with the glories of the Devon and Somerset Staghounds during the brilliant era which he inaugurated. Mr. Fenwick, as he was then, was a Berkshire gentleman, who came to Pixton as tenant of Lord Carnarvon for the sake of the shooting. At that time, as he afterwards confessed, he had never heard of a "forester" in the sense of a wild deer, but once initiated in the chase he became warmly interested in its fortunes. The position of affairs on his first arrival is best described in his own words :—

"The sporting community in the neighbourhood having long felt that their country was not sufficiently hunted, and being possessed with an itching desire to have a pack of foxhounds which they could call *their own*, in the spring of 1855 Mr. Froude Bellew (a nephew of the celebrated Parson Froude) consented to start a pack for their edification. Mr. Bellew had inherited from his uncle a beautiful and unequalled pack of harriers, which up to this time he had himself hunted, aided by the faithful Jack Babbage. The well-known yellow-pied pack, however, being rather on the small side for fox-hunting, Mr. Bellew, in the month of May, purchased the pack belonging to Mr. Horlock, a well-known M.F.H. of that day, who was just then giving up a subscription pack in Cornwall.

318

"This pack having arrived at Rhyll, Mr. Bellew on the 13th of that month announced in the most liberal and sportsmanlike way that, if the country thought it desirable ever again to have a pack of staghounds to hunt the wild deer, and anyone would undertake the management, he would present them with his large draft.

"A start having been made towards raising a pack, the next question was how that pack was to be kept up. A meeting was held on the 23rd to consider the subject, and finally it was agreed by Mr. Fenwick that he would undertake to hunt the country for one season, trusting entirely to the liberality of the country to supply him with requisite funds, without making any conditions as to the amount of support, etc., and that, should the subscriptions fall short of the required sum, it should be entirely at his discretion to give up the hounds at once. In fact, though there was great plausible support and confident assurances that there would be ample support from those who had been staunch supporters in former years, there were evidently great misgivings as to what support the staghounds of the day might find; and, as it proved, those misgivings were not without foundation. Thus Mr. Bisset, though but a novice, and with much reluctance, undertook the mastership, and thus were established the Devon and Somerset Staghounds."

In his youth Mr. Fenwick Bisset had been a subaltern in the Dragoon Guards, in which regiment he had been known as "The General." Singularly enough, his rather brusque speech and upright attitude, as he stood watching the hounds through an opera-glass, again led to this nickname being imposed, when, in the later days of his mastership, he could no longer ride as of yore.

When Mr. Bisset undertook the command, the deer were extremely few—probably not a hundred in all. By the year 1870 they had become so numerous that there was no longer any question of their extinction, and the master, who had always disliked taking hinds, found as the consequence the country swarming with their progeny. "The cry," he writes, "is legion."

Meanwhile no blame attached to Mr. Bisset's general-ship, which won the highest admiration, and in this same year 1870 it was proposed to present him with a testimonial. As soon as Mr. Bisset heard of the intention, he expressed himself as entirely opposed to it. On being told, however, that it had originated with the yeomen and farmers, he relented, and the sum of £757 having been subscribed, Mr. Samuel Carter was commissioned to paint a picture. The subject of the picture was a stag at bay in Badgeworthy Water, and it contained portraits of Mr. Bisset on his favourite grey horse, Jack Babbage the huntsman (whose career was just ending), and Arthur Heal the whip, together with a few hounds, the most prominent being " Nelson," " Finisher," and " Nemesis."   When finished, the work was first hung in the Royal Academy and afterwards presented to the master at a banquet in Dunster on September 14, 1871.   Various opinions have been expressed as to the merits of the painting, but Mr. Bisset, at any rate, was well pleased.   "You may criticise," he said ; " I am delighted."

In person Mr. Bisset was decidedly a heavy-weight. Considerably over six feet in height, he was broad and large of limb. This was naturally of some disadvantage to him in hunting, and only the best of mounts could have carried his twenty stone at such a pace over a country like Exmoor. His knowledge of the district, however, and thorough comprehension of the sport more than made up for his unpractical proportions, and enabled him to be in at the finish, sometimes alone.   At the time of Mr. Bisset's death a correspondent of the *Field* gave the following illustration of his remarkable equestrianship :—

"About the year 1873 the hounds drove a stag from Withy-pool, in the south-eastern corner of the district, far westward from the Forest of Exmoor. The pace was tremendous. On

they went from one end to the other, and finally bearing
right-handed, lost their deer in the sea by Porlock Weir. For
over twenty miles the pack had raced without a check, and
had at last disappeared from all.   One who had struggled to a
standstill finally found himself in Porlock village, and there
heard that an hour before hounds had passed close by towards
the sea.   He jumped on a pony to find out the end, reflecting
with no little satisfaction that he would get to the finish—
never mind when—and that after all there would be no
one but himself to determine the time.   On he went as long
as he could kick his pony along, scrambled to the top of the

"ARE YOU LOST TOO?"

rough beach, and there a few yards below by the incoming
tide stood the stalwart form of Mr. Bisset, surrounded by his
hounds, and watching through his glasses the deer swimming
safely away in the far distance."

The truth is, Mr. Bisset was a very fine and accomplished horseman, with plenty of decision and nerve.
He would send his horse—at a good pace, too—down
the steepest and most rugged of Exmoor's sides, where
many a young man would have been glad to get off and
lead his mount.   In his time he rode over thousands

Y

of miles of heather, and no man delighted more in a grand moor run. It is estimated that during his mastership he killed over a thousand deer, and he maintained the Hunt and the hunting establishment in a most princely manner. Probably he spent quite £50,000 in the interest of staghunting. The kennels and the hunstman's lodge, erected and endowed by him, will long remain as monuments of his generosity and of his keen interest in the sport to which he devoted so many of his best years. In 1880, when he resigned the mastership, there appeared a singularly ill-informed article in which his merits were decried and he was censured as a silent, exclusive sort of man—anything rather than genial. In this connection it is well to remember that Mr. Bisset's reign covered a period of transition, during which the Hunt, from being a purely local and businesslike institution, passed into a kind of national picnic, to which crowds of persons were attracted by motives perfectly harmless perhaps, but foreign to the traditions of the sport.

That Mr. Bisset may have been occasionally hard on these strangers is not improbable—indeed, we know that he disliked them—but against this we must place his cordial regard for sportsmen in a humbler sphere than his own, as attested by entries in his diary. There has been quite a succession of Nicholas Snows, of Oare, one of whom is still in the flesh, and till lately was Master of the Exmoor Foxhounds. Of his father, who died in 1868 in his eightieth year, Mr. Bisset writes :—

"Up to the very last season he had been a constant attendant on the staghounds on his favourite mare 'Norah Creina.' Few went harder, and none knew better how to go, and where to go, than he and the old mare."

And of Tom Webber he writes :—

"He was at once a pattern yeoman, husband, father, neighbour, friend. As a stag-hunter, he was the best of all patterns.

Passionately fond of it, to the exclusion of all other hunting, strictly careful and ever jealous of its ancient and time-honoured laws, always in the field and ever at his post and ready to assist, a thorough master of the art, cool and collected, modest and unassuming, he was, in short, as he has been truthfully described, the best and truest stag-hunter that ever cheered hound."

We may add that Tom Webber died in 1863, and lies buried in King's Brompton churchyard, a few miles from Haddon, the scene of many of his hunting adventures.

In 1875 Mr. Bisset met with a serious accident. As he was trotting out of a dealer's yard his horse reared and fell on him. This unlucky occurrence not only prevented his hunting much during that season, but had a bad effect on his general health, which from that time began to fail. However, in 1880 he was well enough to contest West Somerset in the Conservative interest, and actually beat the heir of the Acland family, the most influential in the division. Politics and political life, however, did not suit Mr. Bisset. Writing in June, 1883, he observed :—

"I cannot attribute my illness to anything else than the confinement of the House of Commons, for, though a silent member, I am not by any means an uninterested or unobservant one, and, in my own peculiar way, worked hard."

And referring to the worst bog-tract on Exmoor, he told the farmers at a Hunt dinner that he would far sooner be anywhere on Exmoor than in the House of Commons, always excepting the Chains in a thick fog. Mr. Fortescue records a characteristic anecdote respecting Mr. Bisset's initial experience of the House, which shows how much he felt out of place :—

"On his first visit to the House, he met Sir John Amory, then member for Tiverton, an old supporter and subscriber to the staghounds. 'Come here,' said Mr. Bisset in his slow, deep tone, 'come here and show me the way; I don't know the country. Now,' he continued, when the inspection was over, 'I know where I am. What's going on now? Do you think there is any occasion for me to stop here?' Sir John who, being a Liberal, was politically opposed to Mr. Bisset, replied that he didn't know. 'Oh!' was the answer; 'are you going to stop here?' 'No, I am not.' 'Then *I* shan't; I shall go to the Rag.' And, having thus tacitly paired, to the Rag he went."

Mr. Bisset died at Bagborough on the Quantocks on the 7th of July, 1884.

We cannot more fitly conclude this portion of our subject than with a fine, spirited hunting lyric written by Edward Capern and printed in his *Sungleams and Shadows* (p. 212). Capern was probably not much of a hunter, but he had evidently caught the enthusiasm of the chase, which has never perhaps been more adequately expressed than in the ensuing stanzas :—

"Song of the Exmoor Hunt.

THE CHASE OF THE WILD RED DEER.

Written for that grand old veteran of the field, the Rev. John Russell.

" Hark ! hark to the horn ! how it rings in the ear,
  Of the Exe and the Barle and the bonny red deer,
  The harbourer's pride with his branches and tines,
  A forest-king bearing his 'rights' for the 'signs'—
  And Bisset afield on his stout trusty grey,
  The Parson's black nag and the Dulverton bay :
  For the tufters are hard on their quest in the wood,
  With snuffle and traverse and thirsting for blood,
  When Challenger raises his head, giving tongue,
  As the hazels go crash to the jolly old song,
' Hark back ! give him play, let him get well away,
  Then off all together at Forrard ! Hooray !'

" There's a northerly breeze blowing in from the sea,
  And the hunters are merry as merry can be—
  For the sun has popp'd out from his bed in the cloud
  As the pack is laid on, while bold Arthur, aloud,
  Cries, 'Tighten your girths, they are hard on the spoor,
  It's O for a jolly good run on the moor.'

Hark together ! Away ! We are off with a bound,
As the horn its tantivy, tantivy doth sound,
For a warranted stag, with its brow, bay, and tray,
Is making for Dunkery Beacon to-day.
'Hark together ! Away ! Hark together ! Away !
Hark ! Forrard together ! Hark ! Forrard ! Away ! ! '

"Just hear how they chirrup ! The running is hot.
No fear of a fault, they are right on the slot,
While Russell, the lusty old chief o' the Chase,
Shouts, 'Swift as a brocket, too, look at his pace.
A six-year-old beauty, let's follow the spoor,
It's O for a jolly good run on the moor ! '
See, see ; how they swarm ! We are off with a bound,
And 'Bird on the Wing' runs as true as a hound,
As our right royal hart, with his brow, bay, and tray,
Makes straight for Black Barrow at Hark ! Hark away !
'Hark together ! Away ! Hark together ! Away !
Hark ! Forrard together ! Hark ! Forrard ! Away ! ! '

"O'er hills red with heather, combe, forest, and bluff,
We follow the line, and the riding is rough,
For the 'cry' has been chiming its merriest tunes
From Dunkery Hill to the Vale o' the Doones ;
So 'Ware Bog' the 'Bay' makes amends for the toil—
In Badgeworthy Water he's certain to soil,
Where Russell is sure in the pink o' the sport
To honour Jack Babbage when sounding the mort—
And bearing off slot and broad antlers, hooray,
With, 'Now then, my lads, for the next Hark Away ! '
'Hark together ! Away ! Hark together ! Away !
Hark ! Forrard together ! Hark ! Forrard ! Away ! '"

CHAPTER VII

MISS ALICE KING

IN the foregoing pages we have often had occasion to mention, and to quote, Miss Alice King. This lady, who was born in 1839 and died in 1895, was the authoress of the following novels : *Hearts and Coronets, Twice Loved, Queen of Herself, The Woman with a Secret, Spellbound, Eveline, The Lady of Winburne, Sir Tristram's Will, Forest Keep, A Tangled Skein,* and *The Strange Story of Lee,* several of which achieved considerable popularity. Miss King was also an accomplished writer of verse, as well as a frequent contributor to the *Argosy* and other periodicals. She was totally blind—a fact which lends pathetic interest to the story of her brave life, which was not exempt from the struggles and disappointments incidental to almost every career in letters.

The following autobiography, which appeared in the *Argosy* shortly after her death, is reprinted by the kind permission of the proprietors of that magazine, and, it is hoped, will serve to keep alive the memory of a worthy lady—worthy in the highest and best sense of the word—in the West Country she loved so well.

" In West Somerset there is a beautiful tract of country, bordered on one side by the Bristol Channel and on the other by the sister-county of Devonshire. It is a land of heather-clad hills and sheltered valleys, the smaller of which are called, in the language of the West Country, 'combes'; a land of petulant, sparkling streams, where the wild red deer browse and wander at will—now over the wilds of Exmoor, now in the thick woods ; a land, the inhabitants of which, in their character, superstitions, and manners, and even their language, are in some respects a peculiar people, distinctly different from the rest of the peasantry of England.

"Fifty years ago the characteristics of this corner of the West Country and its people were more strongly marked than they are now, when the steam whistle and the printing-press and the schoolmaster had not yet found their way ; and it was about this time when my scholarly father, who had been a

CUTCOMBE

private pupil of Dr. Arnold, and my beautiful mother came to live at Cutcombe, a hill-country village, situated in the very heart of the West Country I have described.

"Cutcombe is placed about one thousand feet above the sea-level, and Dunkery, the highest point in the West of England, is in the parish. There I was born, the youngest of four children, two sons and two daughters.

"The Kings are a Yorkshire family, descended from John of Gaunt, from whom came the strawberry leaves in the ducal coronet seen in their crest. They have always been on the side of civil and religious liberty ; one of them garrisoned the church of Kirby Malham for the Parliament. My parents

were cousins, and were both Kings.   My paternal grandfather
was the Vice-Chancellor of the County of Lancaster; my
maternal grandfather was the Bishop of Rochester, one of the
two bishops—the other being Bathurst, Bishop of Norwich—
who laboured so nobly against overwhelming odds in the cause
of Roman Catholic emancipation.   His wife, whose maiden
name was Dawson, was a woman of much wit and great
personal attractions, and was the intimate friend of Burke.

"My great-uncle, Captain James King, sailed with Captain
Cook in his famous voyage round the world, and shared with
him the glory of the discovery of the Sandwich Islands.
When Cook was murdered, Captain King took command of
the expedition, and brought his vessels successfully back again
into English waters.   He was one of the most fascinating of
men.   Even Fanny Burney, accustomed as she was to the
conversation of that age of brilliant talkers, owned and bowed
to his spell, as she has recorded in the pages of her diary.

"I mention these circumstances connected with my family
because they were an incentive to spur me on to get the better
of the disadvantages of my blindness.

"My sight was from the first extremely weak and imperfect;
all the objects around me appeared to my childish eyes as
objects in a mist.   Gradually this faint gleam of sight faded
away. and when I was seven years old I became entirely blind.
This, however, did not in the least terrify or grieve me.
Throughout my whole life my blindness has had this remarkable feature in it: I have always before my eyes a brilliant
light, so that the whole world around me seems. as it were,
incandescent; I appear to be walking in light.   In this light
I can call up at will all sorts of beautiful colours, which I see
mingled with the radiance and forming part of it.   Thus my
blindness has always been for me in a certain sense brightness.

"As I grew older there came to me other abnormal peculiarities, which have been mercifully sent as compensations.
I can always tell when others are looking at me, and I can
generally tell whether they are looking at me in kindness or
the reverse.   My sense of hearing is extremely sensitive, and
through it I can read character in the tones of men and
women round me.   I can also discern character pretty accurately in the touch of the hand.   I have certain instincts for
which I have no exact name, which sometimes make me
foresee future events.   My senses of touch and smell are

excessively delicate ; the former gives me the keenest pleasure in flowers and in their different scents, the latter is of much practical use to me. I can knit the finest silk in the most intricate stitches, and I have invented for myself a watch, by which I can, by feeling, tell the time to a minute.

"In childhood I did not have any special education, on account of my blindness. I was instructed by my mother, who was a woman of much culture and of great natural ability. She taught me chiefly by heart and by my memory, which is very retentive and clear. I learned geography so thoroughly under her instruction, that when I was a child I could describe with precision the position of any province in China or Tartary, or any country the most remote.

"I was very fond of foreign languages from my earliest years, and I understand, with more or less correctness, seven languages besides my own—French, German, Italian, Spanish, Latin, Greek, and Hebrew. Some were taught me by my mother whilst I was a child, some I have learned with my sister since I was grown up. My father read aloud a good deal to my mother, and I was generally in the room, and took in part of what he read ; thus as a child I picked up in this way much miscellaneous knowledge. My youngest brother also read to me a great deal, chiefly poetry, and talked to me about what he read. I owe much of my education to the pains my father and he took in directing my reading and talking to me about various subjects. I always think that girls should be in part taught by men ; it gives breadth and solidity to their character.

"Our life in our retired West Country vicarage was more like a fragment of the old-world life of the last century than anything of to-day. We had few neighbours of our own rank, and our intercourse was chiefly among our village people— going in and out among them, and trying to uplift and help them. It was thus that I gained that thorough knowledge of the West Country people—their characters, their manners and dialect, their superstitions and legends—which I have portrayed in so many of my stories and papers.

"I spent much time out of doors in the free, bracing hill-country air, well used to Exmoor rain and mist, for both came sweeping down pretty frequently upon us from the moor. In winter the roads were often, in a long frost, like glass for weeks at a time, so that we lived as in an enchanted palace, cut off from the rest of the world. At night the wind from the moor would moan and sigh with a voice peculiar to itself, and would wake up all sorts of vague, weird fancies in an imaginative girl.

" My parents accustomed me to the saddle from my earliest days, and I became a fearless horsewoman, and used to scamper over the hills dressed in their regal mantle of purple heather and golden gorse, and would ride merrily up and down paths that would be little less than a nightmare dream to ladies and gentlemen who sail over the fields of the mid-land counties. I generally rode an Exmoor pony; there were two of them to which I was especially attached, beautiful, spirited animals, called Hebe and Colly—the West Country word for a blackbird. They were both most inveterate shyers, and retained the habits contracted on Exmoor throughout their lives. Their tricksy ways, and capricious starts and bounds, would have unseated many an experienced horse-woman, but my ponies and I knew each other thoroughly, and I seldom, if ever, parted company with my saddle. The intelligent eyes of my favourites used to change their ex-pression in a moment when I came to their side to mount. I have always had a great love for all animals; my dogs have been my most constant and truest companions. My special pets have been black and tan toy terriers; two lie now in the vicarage garden, Sylph and Mimie; and two are now frisking in my present home on the shore of the Bristol Channel, Chica and Jack, the latter a Bedlington terrier.

"I began to write poetry about as soon as I could speak, and I cannot remember the time when some of my thoughts and fancies did not run in rhyme. My father was engaged when I was a child in translating the Eneid of Virgil into English verse; I used to sit on his knee while he was at work, and he would tell me the classic story, and all the personages in it would be as real to me as the people round me in my daily life. Then he would translate the Latin words into simple every-day English, and I would try to put them into rhyme, an exercise which helped to give me facility in language. My first appearance in print was when I was about ten; I then wrote two hymns in a volume of religious poetry published by my father.

"When I was just gliding from childhood into girlhood my parents took all their children to Italy for some months, thinking it would be a finishing chapter in their education. It was a wonderful opening of my mind, in spite of my blindness, and seemed to waken up all my imagination.

"My first novel, *Forest Keep*, was written when I was still a girl in my teens, and was published by Messrs. Hurst and Blackett; other novels followed at various periods, the most popular of which was *Queen of Herself.*

" I have all my life owed a debt of gratitude to many literary men for the helping hands which they have stretched out to me. Foremost among these I must mention Professor

A LITTLE GIRL SPORTSMAN

Henry Morley. I became acquainted with him when I was a young girl, and he took the greatest pains in forming my literary style, in reading over what I wrote, and criticising it carefully. He would often make me rewrite several chapters at a time, and would never suffer me to be content with mediocrity. He used to tell me that every word must fit into its place like the bits in a mosaic pavement. Charles Dickens also gave me much advice and encouragement, and did his best to bring me before the public. Mrs. Henry Wood put her kind strong hand into the hand of the young unknown authoress, and led her into her own literary path. The guild of literature is generally said to be jealous and

slow with regard to the admission of new members, but I
can personally testify to the reverse ; there are names in
literature that I can never mention without affection and
gratitude.   I have found literary men to be the most true,
most loyal, most generous friends that ever trod; chivalrous,
and reverent, and tender, alive to my infirmity and to my
womanhood.

"My literary work is all done by an American typewriter;
I can write my MSS. as easily and quickly with it as a person
with sight writes ordinarily with a pen, and my MSS. are,
of course, much more legible than written MSS. usually are.
I have made in my typewriter one or two improvements,
which would, I think, be found a useful addition in all type-
writers for the blind.   My sister, who is my constant companion, and most emphatically my second self, looks over all
my MSS., and corrects them with her pen ; she has always
read to me so much and so constantly in different languages,
and in books of all sorts, that I have never taken the trouble
to learn the Braille character, which is now so much in use
in all blind schools for both reading and writing.

"All my time which was not filled up with literature was,
during many years of my life, even when I was but a girl,
occupied in teaching and influencing the working men and
lads in my father's parish.   I held every Sunday a large Bible-
class for them ; there were upwards of seventy members in
it of all ages, from men of sixty down to boys of twelve.
There were many married men, fathers of families, and father
and son would often sit on the same bench side by side.
I was accustomed to use verbal instruction only in my class,
and I always went into the room without having prepared
a subject beforehand.   I talked to all my men and boys in
private separately, and thoroughly looked into the characters
of each.   I established for them by my own efforts a reading-
room, a cricket club, a brass band, etc.   I had great influence
over them, even over the roughest and wildest.   My blindness
seemed to rouse their chivalrous instincts, and to make them
peculiarly susceptible to be upraised and ruled by me ; they
appeared often to have an almost superstitious reverence for
me, and I could frequently impress and subdue them by a
touch of the hand.   Every Christmas I gave a large party
for them and some of the members of their families, in which
a large brilliant Christmas-tree was one of the chief features,

and in which were often danced those picturesque West Country dances of strange names and graceful, antiquated figures, which no doubt were popular in the West Country in the days of Queen Bess and before them.

"From speaking to my men's class, I learned to speak in public. I used to address large meetings, and always spoke with facility and confidence. I never troubled myself much to elaborate my speech; what I said appeared to come naturally, and somehow I always had incidents and illustrations at hand.

"At my father's death, some five years ago, all my work in his parish was unavoidably given up. I had also then a nervous illness, from which I have never quite recovered; my health does not allow me now to engage in work amongst working men and boys, and I am not able to speak in public

"I have always been very fond of music, and listening to good music has ever been one of my chief pleasures; but for many years of my life I found no time to learn any instrument, and I did not acquire even the most rudimentary musical knowledge. During my illness, however, when I was not allowed to engage in any literary work, I resolved to fill up my time by learning some musical instrument; so, with my sister's help, who is a good musician, I mastered the first elements and then learnt the guitar. My beautiful guitar is now my constant companion, and I can learn and retain by memory air after air, and piece after piece; it makes a charming accompaniment to the piano. I also acquired in that period of enforced literary idleness the art of making macramé lace, and that of working with the needle on large canvas.

"I have written this slight sketch of my life and work, in the hope that it may help and rouse others to battle with similar disadvantages, and successfully overcome them."

INDEX

INDEX

Warren, Mr. Herbert, 64
Warren, Mr. S. H., 87, 306, 314
Wassailing, 244–247
Watchet, 8, 16, 17, 18, 21, 22
Water Babies, 301
Webber, Tom, 322
Welsh, 16, 72
Wessex, 15, 169
West, Captain, 85, 86
West Somerset Free Press, The, 56
West Somerset Word Book, The, 165
Westcote's *View of Devonshire*, 258
Whitestones, 264
Whyte-Melville, Major, 122, 123
Williton, 18, 28

Wilson, Mr., 161
Winsford, 28, 69, 100
Winsford Hill, 6, 25, 26, 32, 126, 129, 151
Witches, 213–221
Witches, White, 214, 216
Withypool, 25, 28, 45, 112, 151, 252, 254
Worth, Mr., 78
Wyndham, Francis, 47

Yonge, Walter, 204
Youatt, 146
Young, Arthur, 149, 159